Mexico-Path to a Failed State?

Michael Lauderdale

To: Camille, Gregory and Marisa

Mexico- Path to a Failed State?

Introduction-A Dying Elephant

Mexico is the second most populous nation in North America and with the United States and Brazil represents the economic engine of the Americas. Such economies are like elephants on the plains and jungles of Africa where others must take into account where the elephants are and what they are doing. If one should die, it will have far-reaching consequences for other elephants and non-elephants alike. Small nation states of ten or twenty million could fail but likely without severe consequences for its neighbors. But if a large state, a nation fails, large impacts will likely come. Mexico's violence during the last decade has begun to raise questions about the long term future of the nation. I seek to examine some of these questions and make some estimates of what the outcomes might be.

From the 1960's until the last decade, I was often in Mexico monthly on research activities and personal travel. Since 2006 I reluctantly have avoided traveling to Mexico's border cities carefully planning when I do, first to Juarez and then by 2008 to Nuevo Laredo and other nearby cities. For a few years, trips into the interior were advisable if you avoided some locations such as the states of Guerrero, Sinaloa, Michoacán or areas south of Matamoros in Tamaulipas, but today much of Mexico can be unpredictable.

In 2007 I began again writing about Mexico in my effort to reconcile some of my notions about that country and its future. I was spurred by the violence I saw growing in Mexico and the increased migration of Mexicans, poor and wealthy, to the U.S. I inventoried what I saw in Mexico and compared it to influences I saw in my work especially with public schools and the city police in Austin. Since 1990 I have worked with the Austin Police on a number of initiatives particularly to improve the Police's ability to relate to changes in the neighborhoods of Austin, enhance leadership abilities within the Police Department, and to forecast changes and challenges to their goals. Here in this capital city of the State of Texas, police officers face rapidly growing and changing neighborhoods often with limited parental and family participation in children's lives as well as with the public schools.

One of the nation's most rapidly growing cities, Austin adds over 60,000 new people each year. This phenomenon of growth with low connection with civic institutions is greater in the neighborhoods where many newly migrated people live especially those from Mexico and Central America. The new residents reflect a pattern from Mexico and Central America where governments are often imposed on the residents and not trusted. In the case of those without official immigration status, there is the additional fear of them being reported to Immigration and Customs Enforcement and facing deportation.

The Austin Police joined the Greater Austin Crime Commission and me in 2003 to create a college class to bring high profile University of Texas at Austin students to Austin middle schools to create positive reference groups for youth in Austin to improve schools success, lessen gang activity and drug use. Fred Ligarde, one of the founders of the Commission, approached me to see if I could find a means to create a positive reference group for youth. Working with the Austin Schools, the Police and colleagues in the University, we field every regular semester high profile college youth in a leadership class to serve as a positive reference group for young adolescents. Brian Davis, in charge of academics for football, says the experience of college athletes in the class both reminds many of challenges in childhood themselves and helps them be strong leaders in class and in athletics. Part of the intent of the class is to address the marginalization and alienation that is common among many of these youth. The class has served as a regular laboratory to examine how well children become part of the larger community. Increasingly I see in that class as I teach it in the fall and the spring, increased numbers of students who with and without parents somehow make it to Texas from Mexico, Honduras, Guatemala, and El Salvador as well as other countries in Latin America.

Through these efforts at individual and community level change, I see the growing influence of travel and trade with Mexico, and Mexico's problems as well, in the City of Austin. These issues in Austin are reflective of similar phenomena appearing across Texas and now in much of the United States. This reality merits a close examination of what is occurring in Mexico as well as those countries south of Mexico and some forecasting of what may come to pass there and in American communities. This book is an attempt to do that.

In these pages I address popular concerns that exist in the United States about Mexico. The concerns are most strongly felt in the American states of Arizona, California, New Mexico and Texas, the Border States. Since 2006 the most visible news about Mexico has been the brutal battles between and among Mexican organized crime groups including attacks on law enforcement, the media, citizens, and tourists. Ciudad Juarez across from El Paso, Texas seemed to come first but now this violence has spread across Mexico. This has led to official warnings from the State Department for Americans to be cautious of travel to some areas of Mexico, the curtailment of joint research and educational programs between American and Mexican universities (including my own), and an end to casual and holiday trips for shopping and visiting friends and family. This is a tradition that generations of Texans have done in Mexican border communities.

Mexicans still come in large numbers to shop in cities like San Antonio and Houston and for skilled medical care. Yet for them auto travel in Mexico is far more unpredictable than before. Such events are sharply dissonant in a neighboring nation of 115 million that with Canada and the United States significantly defines North America. Wide-scale violence in a more distant country like Ecuador or Syria is like crime in another city or on the far side of town: it has little immediate consequence. But this violence in Mexico is like a disturbance on the front lawn of the house next door.

It is violence that has likely killed nearly 100,000 in the last decade with very few arrested and brought to trial. Mexico's dismal record with its law enforcement and courts systems makes it impossible to secure accurate figures. The violence features street warfare with groups armed with military weapons, brutal executions including the beheading and dismemberment of bodies. American government personnel have been targeted and killed in Mexico and Federal agencies such as the Bureau of Alcohol, Tobacco and Firearms found as dupes or bunglers in trying to control arms trafficking. A long and formerly peaceful waterway, the Rio Grande, is now patrolled by gunboats of the Texas Department of Public Safety with 50 caliber weapons mounted to face heavily armed traffickers and the airspace increasingly patrolled by armed helicopters and camera-carrying drones. Violence occurs in border communities in the United States and governmental corruption cases abound from district attorneys, candidates for the U. S. Congress, police officers, sheriff's deputies, county judges, mayors, city council members, school superintendents and criminal court judges in American communities near the border.

The violence has spurred a small publishing industry and Internet community among academics, journalists and citizens, even as Mexican journalists have been killed to suppress reporting, about the organized crime entities that have been labeled "cartels." Their structure and methods are not unique to Mexico.

Their development was clearly influenced by cartels in Columbia in the 1980s and they have properties similar to organized crime as it appears and has appeared in Italy, especially Sicily, the south of France, Russia, Poland, Turkey, China, Japan and the United States. The Wild West nature of the crime reminds one of the South and the West in the United States after the Civil War, Mexico in the years leading up to and during the 1910 Revolution, and the United States during Prohibition and the Great Depression.

Beyond the violence, which is visible and widespread, my concern is whether it suggests a significant threat to the integrity of Mexico as a nation-state. I think it could, and I examine that question in these pages. If Mexico's integrity fails, then it will have vast implications not only for the border, but also for the entire United States. It would mean millions of refugees coming into the United States from Mexico and even greater criminal activities by the well-established drug trafficking organizations that fought the Mexican government to a standoff during the last decade.

This writing does not attempt a re-telling of the history of Mexico but rather seeks to identify key events that reflect themselves in current Mexican culture and the psychology of individual Mexicans. The major focus of this effort is upon current factors in Mexico, consequences for the United States, actions that will become necessary in the United States and attempts to forecast the future.

As I seek to understand some of the reasons for changes in Mexico, I use the concept of cultural beliefs. Belief is used in the sense of a cultural fact that is often rooted in some specific event but becomes a generalized orientation in the culture. As an example, a child's history of George Washington will relate a story of him chopping down a cherry tree and then admitting it when chastised by his father, declaring, "I cannot tell a lie." The story is a creed and an expectation that George Washington did not lie and sets the standard of honesty and fidelity for national political leaders as well as folklore in American culture.

Beliefs often reflect aspects of historical facts and may in some cases represent a distant past but not the present. Boundless optimism and the expectation of an open frontier was a belief of Americans in the 19th century. Politicians in the 20th century like John Kennedy, Lyndon Johnson and Ronald Reagan sought to continue aspects of those principles with concepts like the New Frontier, the Great Society and Morning in America. Beliefs are important as they can call a people to greatness, but beliefs may be destructive if they encourage a reach beyond reason and resources.

The beliefs must be examined today in terms of global economies and the rapidly changing ways, in which energy is developed, foods are grown and things manufactured. For the world, and for Mexico and the United States, demography is as critical as the changes in science and technology that drive economies. What solutions to a failed state scenario exist derive from history, modern life and demography today.

I will start this broad examination of Mexico with a story from a friend who was a career employee in the State Department. He had his office in the U. S. Embassy in Mexico City and would often provide his advice on working in Mexico as I would find that I needed his office as an occasional base of operations in the 80s and 90s. In Mexico, no one is assured full knowledge of the official world. Kin and informal networks are critical to success. Rumor is often the surest source of coming disruptions, and sometimes-civic life can appear to hang in the balance. I would check in at the Embassy to exchange stories and rumors, much as I did with my Mexican friends.

One afternoon I finished some meetings with Mexican government officials and at the national university (UNAM) and headed to the American embassy to chat with the friend that had worked in the State Department for many years, including several assignments in Mexico. I had mentioned to him that I would leave in two days with pressing meetings in Austin and then to Washington. He said, "Well, I have heard that tomorrow the airline or airport employees are planning a strike so you might move your plans up to this evening or in the morning by the latest." He said that they were anticipating a strike that might last a week or more!

That disturbed me as I had much to do back home promising my wife that I would be there, had finished all I had planned for Mexico City, and was more than ready to leave. I asked to use his phone and hurriedly made new reservations to leave in the late afternoon that day.

When I got off the phone, I shook my head and said, "Perry, you wonder each day, what will happen next!" His agreement was not reassuring as he commented about how unpredictable life was in Mexico and especially Mexico City. Electrical brownouts, taxi strikes, subway failures, medical shortages, street protests, irregular phone service all lent a sense of fragility to life in the City. I asked him if he ever worried that he might be stranded in Mexico City and how he would get out if there were general labor strikes, food shortages and civic turmoil. Recurrent problems with the Mexican peso made people, especially in the cities, concerned about the use of credit cards, the latest dollar-peso exchange rate, and the availability of imported items. Technology and health items, including some prescriptive medicines, were things one sought to keep in a well-stocked supply in case of interruptions.

Wealthy Mexicans would have a bank account in the United States and often a house or apartment in Texas, California or New Mexico. My friend's wife and children lived in Mexico City with him and getting back to the States might be a challenge.

He smiled at my voiced concerns about them and said, "All you need is a late model Mercury Monterrey, dark green is the color. You smoke the windows and pull the license plates." We both laughed, as that was the vehicle then favored by the high-ranking drug traffickers in cities like Mexico City, Tijuana, Matamoros, or Guadalajara. It was presumed that such persons would own the local police and maybe even the *Federales* (the Mexican Federal Police). If you were with them, you were beyond the law.

As I pulled my papers together, I said to him, "Why do we continue to try to understand Mexico. Perhaps it is best left alone. The United States has many other concerns and maybe we can ignore Mexico." He said, *"Mike, the great fear for 50 years is what we do with a **dead elephant on our doorstep?"***

The title of this introduction, "The Dying Elephant," comes from conversations held over the years by Americans that work with Mexico, as well as Mexican friends. When relations with Mexico would reach a frustrating extreme, a seasoned employee, "an old hand," would caution walking away and would note that the alternative is a "dying elephant" left on the American doorstep. That is the consequence of a failed state in Mexico for the United States.

Michael Lauderdale
Austin, Texas
September 1, 2013

Table of Contents

Intent and Plan of the Book

The intent of the book is to examine the culture, economy and social structures of Mexico to uncover likely probabilities of the direction of Mexico as a state and culture. It is written from the perspective of my experience working in Mexico in demographic research and community assessment and in the Southwest with communities, and particularly with two primary civic institutions: the police and public schools. I use research concepts drawn from social work, social psychology, sociology and anthropology to provide some answers of why Mexico is prone to authoritarian governments, poverty, violence and distrust of government.

These are some of my crucial questions. Why are the members of Mexican and Mexican American communities less likely to volunteer at schools, be in attendance "at back to school nights', vote and be involved in civic groups in Mexico and the United States? Why are school completion levels among the lowest for this ethnic group? What are the consequences of these social psychological patterns? How does one work in such communities to increase social trust and participation?

Mexico is one of the most significant factors in the future of the United States and the most prominent for the states of the

American Southwest, Texas, New Mexico, Arizona and California. Changes are occurring in Mexico that will determine in the next decade the patterns for Mexico and the American Southwest for much of the rest of the 21st Century.

While cartels are frequent topics about Mexico, I view them as indicators of more fundamental issues in that culture and society. The development and visibility of the Mexican drug cartels are best understood as similar to rumblings of a great volcano. The tremors and rising plumes of smoke foretell what might be coming.

The book is divided into three sections. The first, Prelude, covers the history of Mexico and critical events in the culture and social psychology of the Mexican that provides a normative structure for the people that persists over generations. Examining the norms and principles of the culture developed through history provides a basis for explaining the Mexico of today and potential alternatives for the future.

The second section, A Modern State, provides an overview of contemporary Mexico with a focus upon economic and demographic features. It examines a Mexico very different from the country during the 1910 Revolution yet with the visibility of cultural norms from the past. It details some of the economic achievements, the great population growth and urbanization and the shortcomings.

The third section, The Road Ahead, starts with an examination of how the cartels came into existence and their likely future pattern. It stresses the impact of Mexico's changes on two critical American social institutions, the police and the public schools. It concludes with a comparison of cultural norms in each society and the sobering economic and demographic challenges that exist and will come. The writing task began as an effort to understand the increase in violence in Mexico. It ends with an assessment that global changes make it improbable that Mexico will survive in a form that would be recognizable from the start of the 21st century.

PART I-PRELUDE

Chapter 1: Mexico, Past, Present and Future

An Early Breakfast

One morning in the winter of 1986 I drove from my hotel in the Zona Rosa in Mexico City to the offices of the Deputy Secretary of Health, Dr. Jose Laguna, for a 7:00 a.m. breakfast. Already the city had begun to hum, though the daily toxic brew of auto exhausts and open home heating fires had not yet filled the air, and one was invigorated by the high altitude crispness. I looped down the Paseo de la Reforma and by the Angel of Independence and turned down a quieter street for my friend's offices. I noticed in the distance the Zocalo[1] and remembered being there in 1968 shortly after abortive student protests against the Mexican government that led to the "Tlatelolco Massacre" as part of the harsh reprisals of then President Diaz Ordaz. Mexican troops and police had opened fire upon the protestors and many were killed, but no full accounting of those events was ever concluded. For years stories persisted of the unaccounted dead and rumors from 200 to several thousand killed. I thought about how long suffering the Mexican people could be, and how there was always the sense of something

---

[1] Plaza de la Constitución in the traditional heart of Mexico City. It is a large open, paved area where important Federal addresses are often made.

brewing beneath the calm surface. I remembered the contradictions of those days following the massacre, and how they remained today.

I slowed my car and found parking near my destination secluded from the cacophony of awakening Mexican traffic. The health offices were in stately governmental buildings well over a hundred years old with large interior patios framed by bougainvillea and jacaranda. There were papaya trees with early fruit. The cool air required a jacket, but if you put your chair in the sun you would be comfortable.

The Deputy Secretary was an early riser and liked to get ahead of the day by having working breakfasts. He was a delightful and generous host who always provided some history lesson about culture, medicine and health in Mexico when we would meet. I had called him from Austin, as I planned this trip specifically to meet with him. Unclear about differences in some of the population data I was gathering from Mexican states and cities, I wanted to go over the figures obtained from the Mexican health ministry (*Salud*), the Mexican census (*INEGI*) and the interior department (*Gobernacion*). I was looking at Ciudad Juarez, the largest Mexican city on the Mexico-U. S. Border and just across from El Paso, Texas. The three estimates I had obtained varied by more than 30 percent in the years I was using.

Dr. Laguna, who was the director of health planning for the Mexican Department of Health (*Salud*), as well as an academic and physician, had taught for many years at the Mexican National University (*Universidad Nacional Autónoma de México*). He had been dean of the medical school during the student activism days of the 60s and 70s and was known as refusing to yield to a student sit-in and being carried in his chair from his office by student protestors. Dr. Laguna was an old school academic who felt that science and teaching were a calling, not a vocation. He was revered as representing an institutional quality of a dedicated scientist and educator-physician. A generation or more beyond many of the faculty and staff of the Health Ministry and the University, he had the patience of a man who had seen many changes in his country.

With modern-day Mexico City and the surrounding communities totaling around 30 million people densely squeezed into one of the most populous settings in the world, he would recount the beauty of Mexico City in 1939 when he was a student and the population was only a million in the city. He recalled the clear air, the open streets, and the perpetually spring-like climate of a city with an elevation of a mile and a half above sea level. This was all set against the backdrop of the visible twin volcanoes of Popocatépetl and Iztaccíhuatl to the south, and very unlike the crowded, dirty and noisy city of today. In those days of his youth, he said, most of the city's residents had been born there while today there was a sense that thousands of rural people descended upon the capital city daily. He lamented the crowding and felt it would worsen for years ahead as people from the poverty-stricken villages throughout Mexico headed for the comparative advantages of the nation's capital.

As we sat down to rich, dark Chiapas coffee, fresh mango, eggs, chilies, and tortillas, I immediately pressed my host with my questions about how to resolve the alternative population figures I had secured from the Mexican government offices. Moving quickly to my business, I said, "Dr. Laguna, I need these data to be able to make comparisons we have planned with all of the twin cities on the border. To accurately map social forces we need the hard data"(Lauderdale; 1986). I explained I was frustrated with my discussions with each of the separate Mexican Federal authorities, as none could account for the three sets of very different official estimates of the population. Dr. Laguna sighed, as he often felt I took too little time for social niceties before pressing work objectives, and said to me, "Miguel, you will never find the real population of any Mexican city by looking at the official statistics. There is plenty of time. Let's enjoy the morning."

I shook my head and responded that that could not be! I asked, "How can you run a modern country if you cannot trust the official statistics? It's like flying an airplane without instruments." Dr. Laguna replied, "No it is not hopeless. This is just Mexico. We do it differently here." He paused taking a long sip of the coffee and finally said, "You have to ask your cousin." By now my frustration was evident. I shook my head and said, "How can I do that? I have no family in Mexico!" It was Dr. Laguna's time to shake his head and said, "You Americans are too influenced by the English and the Germans; too much raw empiricism! Truth does not always reside in physical facts and you can spend far too much time in compiling such."

He paused for several moments and then said, "In Mexico we look to our family for truths." I said, "Then where does that leave me? Where does it leave anyone not from Mexico trying to understand or work with Mexico?" Dr. Laguna replied, "Mexico is different. We are realistic about our official government rules. There are ways. Mexicans are generous and will make you part of a family, a *compadrazgo. Confianza*[2] is Mexico. We bargain with data but to find the truth you have to find a cousin there and ask the cousin. That is how Mexico works."

My exchange with my Mexican colleague and friend early that winter morning has been repeated many times in many similar ways in meetings with Mexican associates over the years. The

---

[2] Compadre is the parent to godparent relationship of a child. Compadrazgo refers to the co-parent relationship and is a strong social bond in most of Latin America and comes from medieval European Catholicism. Confianza is a relation between persons built on mutual trust.

most frank discussions were at early morning meetings or late in the day, especially in the homes of colleagues in Mexico City, Juarez or Guadalajara. It seems to mean that even the highest authorities in Mexico do not fully trust aspects of the government. Or perhaps Mexican authorities may be more candid about bureaucratic reality than Americans. In any event, in the homes of Mexican friends you always found generous hosts and a directness, a candor that never appeared in the formal offices.

For the Mexican, the Mexican government is external and to be reckoned, but never trusted. The family is the place of trust.

How did this very different perception between Mexicans and Americans come into being? What role do history and culture play? Mexicans do not view the world as Americans do. Every culture creates to its own extent a worldview. For Mexicans their worldview is one that finds constancy, security and the truth in the context of the family, including the extension of family ties to close friends (Kemper, 1982). This separation of the external world from kin is relatively less true for most Americans.

Summary: The Fundamental World View Differences of Mexicans and Americans

One aspect of the Mexican worldview is the world of the family, where there is support and familiarity. The Mexicans use the term *confianza* to refer to the well-knit kin and friendship system that protects the individual. The other part is the external world, where one must venture but be wary. You must navigate the external world of business, government and other organizations carefully, but you only know truth through those close to you (Diaz-Guerrero, 1986; Diaz-Guerrero & Szalay, 1991; Holtzman, Diaz-Guerrero, & Swartz, 1975; Krauze, 1990; Lewis, 1959, 1963; Madsen, 1964; Riding, 1988).

This is an important cultural and psychological concept and one that causes much misunderstanding between Mexicans and Americans.[3] Part of understanding this caution by Mexicans about the non-family part of one's world and the challenges it poses for Mexico and the United States can be understood through an examination of Mexican as well as American history.

Official agreements and casual meetings with the people of Mexico always carry some part of the thread of this dualism, most eloquently presented by their Nobel Laureate, Octavio Paz (Paz, 1950; 1994; Paz, 1985). The straightforward and matter-of-fact practicality of the Anglo may miss the critical nuance of the Mexican. Paz expressed the dualism in the *Labyrinth of Solitude*, portraying Mexicans as though wearing masks of solitude hiding unresolved indigenous pre-Columbian and Spanish identities. This enduring dualism requires an examination of many years of history much in the same way to understand the positivism and practicality of the American.

In contrast to Mexicans, Americans have more of a sense of pragmatism and work toward an immediate future they feel they can control. The American culture was rooted in the 18th and 19th century experiences of English, Irish, German, and Scottish colonists many of whom came to North America seeking a world with fewer class and clan restrictions, resulting in a violent revolution against British colonialism.

---

[3] It is important to make a distinction between the cultural worlds of Mexicans in contrast to Mexican-Americans. Mexican-Americans share a cultural and linguistic system of all Americans while coming from a distinct culture in Mexico much as all Americans do from cultures in Europe, Asia and Africa. Unlike other cultures in the United States, the Mexican-American has the nearby culture of Mexico. However the closeness of that culture to the Mexican-American and the way the Mexican-American views the Mexican and vice versa is complex and has changed over the years. Those reciprocal views and expectations may be in flux today more rapidly than seen for many decades. This is perhaps nowhere more evident than in the expectations of young Hispanic females around topics of career, education and having children.

Americans are optimistic, quickly engage in business trades, and form civic organizations such as clubs and committees with gusto. This is a fairly singular cultural attribute, noted at least as early as 1826 by French writer and statesman Alexis de Tocqueville in his travelogue through the new world's first democratic nation (Tocqueville, A., 1835 and 2000). These principles and practices extended as *manifest destiny* to support westward expansion by the Jacksonian Democrats, and were extolled a generation later as *American Exceptionalism* by many including Frederick W. Turner (Appleby, 2010; Ferguson, 2011; Goetzmann, 2009; Turner, 1984).

The Enlightenment, especially the thinking of Condorcet, Voltaire, Montesquieu, Locke, Rousseau, and Hume influenced Americans of the Revolution especially American thinkers including Franklin, Jefferson, Washington, Mason, Madison, Paine, and other philosophers and activists. They framed the founding documents and beliefs of the new nation and shaped the initial culture. By the start of the 19th century American thought and practice had centered upon the popular vote as the mechanism to determine leadership and solve problems, a form of limited government that stressed local control, the use of a balance of power among branches of government, and a practical and optimistic tone.

This outlook gave rise to American Exceptionalism that viewed the development of the popular vote, freedom of religion, and cutting of ties to class, property and royalty as the dawn of a new order, not just of government but of civic relationships among people. It presumed that status, *the worth of the man*, was earned (achieved) not given (ascribed) as a birth status. Americans sought to extend this view to much of the Americas, and coupled with mid-19th century concepts of *manifest destiny*, sought to distribute the concepts to all of the Americas. In contrast with Mexicans, Americans have a more complete and new culture significantly created from ideas of French, Scottish and English thinkers and little influenced by existing indigenous people of the New World. We treat this history as the source of unique American beliefs in Chapter 15.

Mexicans, in contrast to Americans, are mindful of their own longer, conflicted history, which is often remembered with pain. Significant European contact with Mexico began one hundred years or earlier than that in eastern North America along the Atlantic. That conflict is remembered among Mexicans as violent, not like the shared Thanksgiving between colonists at Plymouth Rock and Indians that is part of the American dogma of its founding.

The psychology of the American is present-time oriented and positive about the future. The psychology of the Mexican is deeply influenced by the past and cautious about the future. Paz and others following him reflect on the role of the past in configuring the Mexican's view of the present. These chroniclers of the culture of Mexico emphasized the unresolved tension between the Indian and Spanish worldviews.

These two significantly different worldviews of the United States and Mexico explain much of what each country is today, some of the prospects for the future, and the complexity in crafting agreements between the two countries and cultures. Persons concerned with trade in Mexico, law enforcement authorities' efforts to work with Mexican counterparts, and even travel in Mexico need some understanding of the very different worldviews of Americans and Mexicans.

For the Mexican, the past is always prologue to the present and the future. For the American, the focus is upon the present and the positive promise of the future. There is less attention to the past. To understand Mexico today, the border with Mexico and the orientations of people in the United States from Mexico, Mexican history provides unique clues (Díaz del Castillo &

Cohen, 1963; Fehrenbach, 1979; Meyer, Sherman, & Deeds, 2003; New Cambridge Modern History, 1962).

Chapter 2: Pre-Columbian Mexico and the Conquest of the Aztec

When European explorers reached North and South America in the 1500s, they encountered not empty lands but substantially populated villages surrounding agricultural fields and highly varied, complex cultures occurring irregularly across both continents (Berler & Prescott, 1988; Fehrenbach, 1979; Johansen, 2006-11; Joseph & Henderson, 2002; Middleton, 2011; Thornton, 1990).

Mexico, A Far More Ancient Land

While earliest man populated Alaska, Canada and the United States on through Mexico and to the tip of South America, the groups and cultures were far from uniform. Some of the grandest cultures of the Americas flourished in Mexico from the central highlands of Mexico City into the tropical regions of the south and east to the Gulf more than a thousand years before Columbus arrived in the Gulf near Veracruz. The greatest architectural achievements of antiquity in the Americas occurred in Mexico in the Yucatán and in the most populated urban areas in the valley of Mexico City.

Mexico has many historical similarities to the United States and is twined with both of its North American neighbors, Canada and the United States; yet is very separate (Díaz del Castillo & Cohen, 1963; Fehrenbach, 1973; Fuentes, 1997). Unlike Canada and the United States, the Native Indian cultures, populations and blood are far more evident in the peoples of Mexico today, and in many areas remain dominant in numbers and local language. Thus, Mexico is more ancient than the United States or Canada in the extent to which these cultures of Mesoamerican antiquity still play a significant role in Mexican society and culture.

The geography of Mexico and the United States influences both the historical and the contemporary cultures and economies. The geography of Mexico was more difficult to traverse in the 1500s to 1900s with vast deserts, tropical forests and high mountains. This helped to assure more isolated and independent cultures that resisted assimilation. The United States does not have significant mountain ranges or impassible deserts for the eastern two-thirds of the country and is favored by rivers and rich alluvial soils, which can be readily farmed. The Mississippi, Ohio and Missouri Rivers provide ready north-south transits and, with the waterways of the Great Lakes, very early the economies and cultures of farms and villages in the United States were knit by travel and commerce. In contrast, Mexico has no north-south navigable rivers and no forests or prairies readily adaptable to farming, but rather has small valleys with limited arable land. Much of the region north of Mexico City has high mountains and formidable deserts that limited travel by men on foot and even on horse when the Spanish came. This geographical separation and identity in Mexico served to preserve local cultures across the land and weakened the national homogenization of identity that occurred more fully in the United States.

The Indian Continuity

Mexico, like the United States, was populated with complex cultures thousands of years prior to the arrival of Europeans in the 15th century. From the first contact in the 15th century and through the next two centuries, war and disease eliminated large percentages of the indigenous populations in both the United States and in Mexico and elsewhere in the Americas (Farb, 1968; Thornton, April 1997). Disease, even more than war, destroyed the existing Indian cultures and populations in many areas, reducing native populations by 90 percent. These waves of cultural and population collapse, however, were far more extensive in the United States and Canada than in Mexico. Additionally, through mechanisms like the 1830 Indian Removal Act, the United States forcibly marched many of the American Indians from eastern states, including the Carolinas, Georgia, Ohio, Indiana, and Illinois, and placed them on reservations in Oklahoma, New Mexico and the Dakotas. This left small indigenous populations isolated and carefully hidden from the swelling ranks of immigrants from Europe, Africa and Asia. Thus the Native Indian population had less significant impact on the development of culture in the United States. Language, culture, commerce, media, compulsory education, and government entitlements were implicitly directed to building a nation state with a common culture, a "melting pot," to produce a national culture. Through the way communities were populated, through public schools, the unions and the military, a unique American identity was forged. There was a far different process in Mexico.

There are additional detailed and important reasons for the greater continuity of the indigenous populations and cultures in Mexico, and they are critical to understanding the contemporary Mexican personality. One was the fact that most of the European immigration to Mexico consisted of men, alone, from Spain and Portugal that were soldiers of fortune rather than families coming to establish farms, businesses and communities. These men saw the New World as a source of mineral riches, especially gold, and intended to return to Spain and Portugal after discovering wealth and lead lives of prominence and leisure. This reality, and the fact in the Aztec conquest Spanish soldiers responded to far superior numbers of Aztecs by building alliances with other Indian tribes that were suppressed by the Aztecs, made the participation of the existing population and cultures with the European conquerors more significant in Mexico than in the United States.

This set a path for Mexico where its population and cultures had a considerable degree of collaboration with the conquerors and maintained significantly more of the Indian population and cultures in the surviving peoples, in contrast to events in the United States. The Conquistador alliances meant greater communication with the Indians and this resulted in both marriages and alliances with Indian women that began the creation of mixed families of European males and Indian females.

Such relationships were symbolized in cultural fact and norms by the sexual and political alliance between the Spanish Conquistador, Cortez, and one of the favored young women of the Aztec emperor, Moctezuma II. This woman, Malinque, was said to be involved as Cortez's concubine and assisted Cortez through her knowledge of Moctezuma in the overthrow of her emperor. She may also have been from one of the tribes conquered by the Aztecs, increasing the complexity of intrigue and oppression in the founding beliefs of Mexico. Thus, in one of the founding beliefs of the Mexican state, there is the issue of the exploitation by the state, first by the Aztec and then Spanish, of the indigenous populations and the willingness of one woman to be a traitor to her people and collaborate with the conqueror. (Diaz, 2001; Paz, 1950; 1994; Thomas, 1995; Beezley, 2010)

Norms and Indian population numbers in Mexico are significantly different from American founding beliefs and original indigenous populations. To a far greater degree, the indigenous populations of the United States were eliminated through war, starvation, removal, and disease. Indian names of places and rivers, such as Mississippi (Ojibwa-*Great River)*, Chicago (Algonquian or Potawatomi-*stinking onion field*), Oklahoma (Choctaw-*Red People*) are many, but few of their descendants are left in the American population. The American experience, far more than Mexico's, is one of immigrants from many lands coming to the nation and being enculturated into a new American culture.

The Mexican State and the Mexican Family

The Mexican experience is one of conquerors, fewer in number coming and gaining control, but being absorbed by the existing population and cultures. For the Mexican, the state is imposed from the outside and remains alien, but the family is near and trusted.

This reality underlies the tenuous hold that the state has on the Mexican. The civic space where one meets and works with non-family, and builds trust and reciprocity, is attenuated for the Mexican. The bargaining with representatives of the state such as the "mordida" one pays when stopped by a law officer, the need to have a "cousin" to find the real story (as Jose Laguna so artfully explained to me that winter's day in Mexico City) and, lastly and critically, the vulnerability the state has during times of economic crisis are deeply important in understanding Mexico today.

The Aztecs

In the Central Highlands of Mexico they found the Aztec culture, then about 300 years old and existing as the region's most powerful colonial entity. They subjugated other Indian tribes hundreds of miles to the north, south and east from the Gulf of Mexico to the western mountains of Mexico. However, they were blocked from the Pacific by the Tarascans, perhaps the only Indian culture in Mexico not controlled or colonialized by the Aztecs.

In time it was discovered that the Aztecs had been preceded by three or four other older cultures dating back probably 2,000 years. The Aztecs appeared to have migrated around 1200 AD during a great drought from the Four Corners area (where Arizona, Utah, Colorado and New Mexico meet) of the American Southwest, arriving in the Valley of Mexico initially as a poor, small tribe of hunters and gathers. In about three centuries they achieved colonial domination in the Valley of Mexico using aquaculture in the great lake at the center of the Valley. They established the Aztec capital city of *Tenochtitlan*, which grew to a population of 40,000.

Aztec Antecedents

Yet, the Aztecs were only the latest immigrants to these lands. They were influenced by existing cultures, most likely the Toltecs. Even then, far older cultures had come and gone in Mexico including the Olmecs, the Mixtecs, and the Mayas. Toltecs and Mixtecs had populated the central highlands of Mexico City for hundreds of years prior to the Aztecs, while the Maya homeland was along the Gulf including what today are the Mexican state of the Yucatan, and the countries of Belize and Guatemala. Maya civilization apparently reached its peak 500 years before the arrival of the Aztec. Throughout Mexico, then and even today, there were and are dozens of cultures varying in populations from a few hundred to several thousand and reaching back in time hundreds and hundreds of years.

This complex cultural mosaic of Mexico probably began with a people that have only left stone artifacts to mark their presence. Somewhere around 1000 BC, the first of Mexico's ancient civilizations, the Olmecs, (1500 BC to 400 BC) established themselves in what are now the states of Veracruz and Tabasco along the Gulf of Mexico, though pre-Olmec evidence extends back to 2500 BC (Coe, 1980; Fisher, 1988). The Olmecs worshipped a jaguar God, built cities, constructed massive stone head carvings, and spread throughout central and southern Mexico until their civilization mysteriously vanished around 400 BC. The anthropological record is not clear on whether they left the region or were absorbed or defeated by other civilizations. Though the Olmecs left behind relatively few artifacts, their influence on later cultures was profound.

In their wake came the Maya of Yucatan (300 BC to today) in the most southerly regions of Mexico, including communities on the Pacific, followed by the Teotihuacan in the Valley of Mexico (100 BC to 700 AD). The Teotihuacan were perhaps the first pyramid builders and built among the largest and most elaborate in Mesoamerica, which are still evident today in one site 30 miles northeast of Mexico City. Evidence of human presence in the Valley is recorded as early as 12000 BC, but it is the Teotihuacan pyramids that both influenced later cultures and remain in and near Mexico City, today.

The Zapotecs (400 BC to 1000 AD) predecessors of the Toltec developed in a mountainous region of Mexico, south of Mexico City, Oaxaca and featured conflicts between perhaps three city-states of this single culture. The Toltec (800 AD to 1000 AD) were viewed by the Aztecs as their immediate cultural predecessors and had their center in the city of Tula in the state of Hidalgo, northeast of Mexico City.

Mixtecs of the states of Oaxaca, Guerro and Publa were in many ways the successors to the Zapotecs. These cultures devoted energies, resources and lives to balancing the spiritual and earthly realms. To appease their pantheons of gods, many of these civilizations practiced human sacrifice, a fact that often overshadows their great achievements in the realms of mathematics, astronomy, architecture, farming, textile weaving, art, and pottery (Fisher, 1988). The Maya, for example, were so advanced in mathematics and astronomy that their calendar was the world's most accurate until this century. They could predict solar and lunar eclipses, had complex writings and farmed extensive areas from today's Yucatan into Belize and Guatemala.

The Empire At First European Contact

But none of Mexico's pre-Columbian civilizations is more storied or more central to much of modern Mexico than the Aztecs. Though other civilizations in Mexico achieved equal artistic and greater scientific feats, none advanced as quickly or ruled as much territory. Prior to the 15th century, the Aztecs were a marginal tribe living on the edge of Lake Texcoco, the site of present day Mexico City in the great Valley of Mexico. By 1473, after subjugating neighboring tribes, they ruled the largest empire Mexico had ever seen. Their capital of Tenochtitlan, set on man-made islands in the lake of Mexico City, was a picturesque city of pyramids, mile-long floating roads, aqueducts, vibrant marketplaces and one hundred thousand residents. Aztec military and trade routes dominated from the tropics several hundred miles to the south in Central America to city-like dwellings north to the Rio Grande in today's Texas and New Mexico. Mexico City was the hub of a wheel with spokes radiating out as trade routes, which were established and controlled by the military east to the Gulf through Maya territories, west to the Pacific through several subjugated cultures, south into modern day Guatemala, El Salvador, Honduras, Costa Rica and Nicaragua, and north into the American Southwest. In many instances the existing cultures were required to pay tributes to the Aztecs including slaves as well as agricultural produce, precious metals, shells, and stones. Slaves from the subjugated tribes were also sacrificed in religious rituals.

Among the rituals of the Aztecs was the belief that tribute must be paid to the Sun to ensure its rising each morning. At intervals priests of the Aztecs would conduct human sacrifices at the great pyramid in Mexico City by using a stone (obsidian) knife to open the chests of slaves and pull the bleeding and beating heart to offer it to the Sun God. These rituals were known and feared by the subjugated tribes and were used by the Spaniards as part of the effort to secure support from these tribes to overthrow the Aztecs and destroy the warriors and priesthood.

The lake was central to the city as a source of foods including reed islands that were built to support farming. It also served as a moat to protect the city. Leading a highly codified government was an all-powerful emperor who exacted taxes from the conquered and distributed land to his people, especially the warriors.

Conquest of the Aztecs

The Aztecs were at the height of their empire and about three centuries old when European contact occurred(Berler & Prescott, 1988; Fehrenbach, 1979; Prescott, 2000). Europeans learned of the Aztecs through the reports of Hernan Cortez, the Spanish conquistador who invaded the Aztec empire in 1519. When the Spanish adventurer Hernan Cortez arrived in 1519, the rich city met his expectations for conquest and wealth (Cortés, 1986; de Sahagœn, 1950-1981; Díaz del Castillo, 1986; Díaz del Castillo & Cohen, 1963; Fehrenbach, 1979), but that Indian empire was, simply, the latest in an ancient world of migration, conquest, and conquered peoples in the Americas. The war against the Aztecs by Spain lasted about 50 years, imposing a new colonial power from Europe, the complete destruction of much of the Aztec culture and a population reduction from approximately 10,000,000 in Mexico to 1,000,000 by the 1700s (Banks & Prescott, 1916; Berler & Prescott, 1988; Bonfil Batalla & Dennis, 1996; Krauze, 1990; Octavior Paz, 1950; 1994).

The conquest of the Aztecs and the creation of New Spain, a great and tragic history, begins in April of 1519 when Cortez lands in Veracruz on the Gulf Coast, about 200 miles east of the Aztec capital in the central highlands. Only about 30 years earlier, the Spanish adventurer, Columbus, had discovered the New World and many Spanish soldiers of fortune began to sail to this new world to seek riches. Stories of a civilization of gold had reached the Caribbean years before and entranced the newly arrived Spaniards. Spain spawned many young men of limited means that set sail to secure riches and return to Spain to have a life as wealthy "grandees". Cortez was but one adventurer coming from there. Others like Coronado and Ponce de Leon prowled the upper Gulf Coast in search of the riches of one of the fabled seven cities of gold, Cibolo, and Pizarro scorched a path to Peru destroying everything in his path for treasures of gold and silver.

Cortez on the eastern Mexican coast had a singular mission: defeat the Aztecs and take their gold. To do so, he had less than 400 soldiers, 16 horses, 14 pieces of artillery, 11 ships, guns, and ammunition. His first act upon landing was to burn all but one of his ships, so there could be no retreat. His goal and that of his men was to conquer for gold and then return to Spain to enjoy lives of privilege and leisure. That he was able to defeat an empire of many thousands with just a few hundred men seems nothing short of miraculous, but some of his success can be attributed simply to luck and exploitation of existing religious dogma, and some to the readiness of subjugated groups to participate in the overthrow of the Aztecs.

The first lucky break came from an Aztec principle of Quetzalcoatl, a light-skinned man – their most important god – who had long ago traveled to the east, but was expected to one day return. When the Aztec ruler, Moctezuma II, heard stories of the white men landing great ships on the east coast, and then when he saw Cortez and his light-skinned men upon their arrival in Tenochtitlan, he believed them to be emissaries of the great Quetzalcoatl himself. Wearing armor that glistened in the sunlight and riding horses that were unknown to the Indians, they did, indeed, seem some sort of gods. The opportunistic Cortez did not attempt to correct Moctezuma, and this is where the Belief of Malinche appears. She was thought to have been one of the favored of Moctezuma and knew the Aztec court and Moctezuma well. She was said to have been from one of the subjugated tribes to the east of the Aztec capital. She advised Cortez that Moctezuma thought Cortez came from this most powerful god, and he could use that advantage by playing on Moctezuma's desire to seek favor from Quetzacuatl. Cortez seized on the information and subsequently returned the emperor's hospitality on meeting the Spaniard by taking Moctezuma hostage.

The next stroke of luck came when the compliant Moctezuma ordered his people to stand down against Cortez' men and their Indian allies. By the time the Aztecs began to resist, Cortez had already brought in reinforcements from the coast. The Aztecs finally disowned their cowed, captive emperor, who died a prisoner in his own palace. When the Aztecs laid siege to the palace that Cortez had seized, Cortez and his men slipped away in the middle of the night and ran for the coast. On the way, over half his force was killed by the pursuing army, but Cortez's luck held and he with the survivors returned with thousands of Indian allies to conquer the city a year later.

Summary: *The Destruction of the Aztecs*
The reign of the Aztecs was about three hundred years. They were preceded by four other empires and Spain sought to build a sixth. Spain unlike earlier conquerors sent only men and intended that the wealth taken from the Aztecs and other Indians be sent back to Spain as trophies of war. When the gold and silver were gone, Spain then sought to create agricultural plantations worked by native Indians. That was put in place in the 1500s and continued for three hundred years.

Chapter 3: Conversion to a Colony

After a hundred years of war and conquest beginning in the 1500s, the Aztec empire collapsed and Spain then turned to efforts to convert the indigenous people to Roman Catholicism and settle them into farming communities. By then most of the Aztec temples had been razed, writings and cultural artifacts destroyed, their warriors and priests killed, and the very stones from their greatest temple then used to build Mexico City's first great Roman Catholic cathedral. What gold and other precious metals and gems existed had been shipped to Spain and Portugal. Now the Spanish Crown and the Church sought other means of bringing riches back to Europe. Their goal was to change the Indians into peon farmers, providing the Spanish with agricultural surplus from their colony to support Spain's imperial aims.

The Aztec empire was gone but the Indians, though in greatly diminished numbers, remained. Colonial lands were seen as agricultural areas that could be either populated by Europeans or developed through conversion of the locals to farmers, which would help build national mercantilist empires in Europe. France, the Netherlands and England soon followed Spain's model of exploiting riches from the New World.

Spain continued then the tradition of dominating and subjugating cultures long patterned in Mesoamerica. The dominant culture demands tributes from the conquered and rules the subjugated people as gods. This repeating pattern through hundreds of years and across many cultures is important to help understand modern Mexico and the psychology of the modern-day Mexican.

Tools for Cultural Conversion

For Spain, the State and the Church became the vehicles to convert the indigenous people into workers to contribute agricultural produce, mining output and taxes to the Spanish empire. With State protection the Church established missions across Mexico and into what is today Texas, New Mexico and California. Missions reached as far north as San Antonio in Texas, Santa Fe in New Mexico and San Francisco in California. Yet conversion to Catholicism was a slow process.

The slowness was partly and perhaps mostly due to the fact that the Church was faced with cultures that had already powerful religious traditions that were integrated into the societies. Each of the hundreds of Indian cultures had strong dogmas, often a pantheon of gods, and incorporation of the religious beliefs into the social organization, thereby influencing tribal and city political leadership and roles for women and men.

Often women, in contrast to Catholic dogma, played more significant roles than men in the continuity of the religious beliefs through their responsibilities of raising the children and maintaining the home. Roman Catholicism, brought from a region of very different history and environment, was a difficult transplant. The new religion, proffered by the conquering Spanish with its male priests, was unfamiliar and not compelling to the Indians.

Appearance of the Virgin of Guadalupe

Indian conversion was significantly accelerated with the reports in 1531 of a Nahautl-speaking young woman appearing in a vision to an Indian man and urging for a mission to be built. The Church explained this as a heavenly sign calling Indians to the Church. The appearance of this woman known as the Virgin of Guadalupe is a second fundamental Belief of the modern Mexican state. It served to announce that God had sent a message through the image of an Indian woman to call all Indians to the Holy Church.

The message would be used to counter the racialism that has always existed in the emerging society between those of European bloodlines and the Indian. It additionally served to make the Roman Catholic Church a special institution for any people of Mexico with Indian blood. A form of the Church developed that was both the Catholicism brought from Spain and many of the norms and practices of the various Indian cultures.

Mission Culture in Promoting Trade and Banking

Part of the mission role in the culture was to establish trade and banking. Other traditions from Spain were brought to Mexico. Portuguese settlers provided the banking through purchased franchises from the Church and would provide loans to the Indians and the mixed Indian and Spanish population. Interestingly, some of these settlers were Sephardic Jews skilled in trade and banking but beginning to flee the Spanish Catholic Church's cruel and ruinous Inquisition. In the 16th century the Church forbade the collection of interest on loaned money, and the franchise arrangement with these settlers provided that economic function and revenue to the Church. In the New World the Church created a relationship with European Jews that profited both groups as they collectively exploited the Indians.

This arrangement of the Church, merchants and the Crown explains much of the wariness and even the deep antipathy of today's Mexican toward the Roman Catholic Church. This feeling is vividly expressed in the murals of Orosco and Riveria, in violent protests against the Church, and in seizures of church lands especially in the 1910 Revolution as well as the Cristero Revolt of the 1920s. It was not until 1992, during the presidential administration of Carlos Salinas, that many of the strictures in Mexico against wearing clerical garb and Church ownership of land were eased.

The Years Under the Spanish Crown

By the eighteenth century Mexico was firmly established as a colony of Spain with a far-flung missionary structure, a complex population of pre-existing Indian cultures and a rapidly growing population of mixed bloods, who later would be referred to as *mestizos* (the mixed ones). Mexico, with its fertile valleys and great mineral wealth, became the crown jewel of Spain's colonies (Frye, 1996). It was heavily taxed, ruled directly from Spain, and permitted no autonomy. The Spanish monarchs distributed land to Spanish settlers in the form of *encomiendas*. These were the predecessors to the hacienda, known as Spanish land grants, which included the Indian residents as part of the property. Slavery of the Indians was part of the new culture brought from Spain, but was also a continuation of thousands of years of colonialism and oppression in the lands of Mexico.

The Caste System

Indian slaves who the settlers were charged to protect and convert to Christianity worked the farms and the mines. A caste system developed: *Espanoles* (Spaniards born in Spain), *criollos* (born in Mexico- but Spanish blood), *mestizos* (Spanish and Indian), and finally the *indigenes* (the Indians). It was the Indian that worked the fields and did the heavy stoop agricultural labor, road building and land clearing chores. Because of their forced dependence on the hacienda owners, and without resistance to European ailments, the Indians were riddled with disease, malnutrition and debt long after Spain abolished slavery in 1548.

Indian Remnants

Like the United States, the deaths of the indigenous Indians due to war, disease and starvation were stark. For both countries some estimates are that in a hundred years the original populations were <u>reduced to a tenth</u>. But in Mexico, unlike in the United States, the remaining Indian populations served to create the basis of the modern Mexican population.

In the United States most of the population today originated via immigrants from other countries. However, the Mexican population traces the bulk of its history and blood to the original indigenous peoples. Indeed Mexico is unique to Canada and the United States with a high percentage of the total population having Indian blood, including the wealthiest and most powerful of the society.

In Canada and the United States the indigenous populations were almost completely eliminated. In some countries of the Americas the remnant indigenous populations continue to live in remote areas with dominant control by highly European-oriented elites. Mexico holds something of a distinctive role with Indian blood common in most socioeconomic levels of the population.

Summary: The First Two Fundamental Beliefs

One of the two fundamental beliefs of the Mexican nation in its first two centuries was the betrayal of Montezuma's concubine, Malinche, and her collaboration with Cortez and his Indian allies to overthrow the Aztecs. The belief takes many forms in Mexican culture. One is an idealized and contradictory role for the woman, both as a temptress and as a conspirator. The temptress is not unlike the view of Eve in the Garden of Eden where the serpent gives the fruit to Eve to tempt Adam to commit the original sin and lose his immortality. Mexican culture assigns to the woman a status of distrust and women are thus less visible than might be seen in the cultures of France, England or the United States, where persons like Joan of Arc or Queen Victoria are seen as playing heroic roles not simply as an adjunct to men.

The second belief was the appearance of an Indian-speaking vision, the Virgin of Guadalupe, to a young Indian man calling the Indians to the Roman Catholic Church. The vision was a woman in a role of messenger of salvation and a powerful tool used to convert Indians from their traditional cultures to an institution of Spanish conquest.

Chapter 4: Patterns of Oppression and Revolt as the Mexican Republic Appears

For 450 years after the first European contact, Mexico saw oppression of the native populations and successive revolts of the oppressed against Spain, France, large Mexican landholders and the Roman Catholic Church. As late as the 1930's there were efforts to expel foreign interests, particularly American and British oil companies. Thus the history of Mexico is one of repeated invasions, wars and the imposition of one political power violently over existing societies. Much of the culture and political discourse of Mexico, even today, reflects concerns of domination by foreign interests, colonial exploitation of natural resources and people, and efforts by the Mexican population to secure independence.

This history also illustrates, using a geological metaphor, that change in Mexico comes not smoothly and progressively but rather through sharp discontinuities, like earthquakes. Cultural and institutional mechanisms for gradual, smooth change and adaptation are scare. Indeed, Mexico sustains a revolution about every hundred years as it betrays a brittle response to changing pressures.

Revolution

After its initial conquest, Spain spent nearly 200 years consolidating the colony of Mexico, seeking to extend its control into South America and northward from Louisiana to the Pacific Northwest. It sent armies accompanied by traders to secure wealth for Spain and Catholic priests to convert the residents to loyal subjects of Spain, as well as providing vast agricultural and mining resources to Spaniards choosing to come to the New World (Frye, 1996). The years were filled with bloody though limited conflict and prepared the stage for successive large revolts in the conquered territories.

For most of the 18th and 19th centuries Mexico was beset by revolutions attempting to reconcile the colonial ambitions of Spain and France and the tensions in regions of Mexico, as the colonial powers sought to subdue existing cultures and convert them to plantation-type agriculture. The conflicts included the efforts of the Roman Catholic Church to convert the Indians, competing loyalties to Europe, and the growing young population born in Mexico but of Spanish and *mestizo* origins. While the country's southern border was relatively quiet with no large powerful nation, the north faced first predatory activity of indigenous Indian tribes and then, in the 19th Century, the intentions of Anglo populations for local self-governance separation from Mexico and ultimately wars with Texas and then the United States.

The First Two Attempts at Mexican Independence

The most significant event in Mexican independence came about 30 years after the American Revolution. On September 16, 1810, Catholic priest Miguel Hidalgo, angered by the exploitation of the *criollo, mestizo* and *indigenes* populations, agitated for independence. He joined with friends and rang a church bell in the small village of Dolores calling for all Mexicans to rise up and fight for their independence from Spain. Hidalgo, a *criollo* raised in Queretaro about 150 miles northwest of Mexico City, was a member of a group of educated *criollos* that met in a salon society that railed against European domination, were influenced by the success of the American Revolution to the north (including the same European writers such as *Rousseau, Montesquieu,* and *Voltaire),* and seized upon the relative weaknesses of a Spain that was embroiled in wars on the European Continent. Outraged at the treatment he saw of the Indians and *mestizos* (the offspring of Spanish men and Indian women), he urged them along with Spaniards born in Mexico (*criollos*) to rise up against the European colonial power.

Mexico, like Bolivia and Venezuela in South America, was moved by the forces of the Enlightenment and Reformation beginning in Europe that had stripped the British colonial powers of the American Colony to their north. That American Revolution created the first full expression of those movements of a society freed of the world of the *ancien regime* where power was vested in hereditary royalty, landed gentry and the Roman Catholic Church. Central to the appearance of American Exceptionalism in the 1700s is the sense of the authority of government rooted in the consent of the governed expressed through voting and other mechanisms of social participation, including free assembly, a free press and government structures representative of the will of the populace.

Much of Latin America sought similar freedoms like those achieved in the United States, yet lands like Mexico saw much of their revolutions' promises stalled or reversed. Father Hidalgo was executed by government forces, which set a pattern in many successive revolts with the tragic deaths of revolution heroes. Too often Mexican heroes are killed often in betrayal and American heroes live to a ripe old age!

Hidalgo was a controversial figure as a priest because of his participation in the salon society, his drinking, gambling and his fathering of children. He is remembered for his cry for independence, the "Grito de Delores" and through recognition of Dieciséis de Septiembre as the day of Mexican independence. This cry from the small town of Dolores, near Guanajuato, on September 16, 1810 began the Mexican War for Independence. However, the war did not succeed until ten years later in 1821 when Spain granted independence after having reacquired Mexico from France during the Napoleonic wars. And like many of the great beliefs of Mexico, it began with the hero, Father Hidalgo, as he marched across Mexico and gathered an army of nearly 90,000 poor farmers, only to see them defeated and destroyed by a much smaller but well-armed and trained force of Spanish troops. Hidalgo was later executed by a firing squad on July 30, 1811. But Mexicans revere the 16th of September of 1810 as the founding date of Mexico much as Americans regard the 4th of July, 1776.

Tensions in the North

Also involved were a series of wars and border conflicts with Texans, Americans and finally the United States. Of particular note are the Texas War for Independence in 1835, the Mexican and American War of 1848 and the Gadsden Purchase of 1854, which resulted in Mexico losing much of its northern area, almost half of the country. This lost area is now composed of states of the American Southwest and West and remains a controversial and painful memory for some Mexicans and a source of distrust of the United States.

Democracy Achieved and Lost

A sense of democracy grew in Mexico with Spain agreeing to its independence in 1821, and it reached its height in the late 1850s and 1860s with the election of Benito Juarez. Forty years after first securing independence from Spain, Mexico was involved in another war with a European power, as France sought to impose colonial rule after Mexico failed to pay debts on French and other European loans. France invaded and set Maximilian I on the throne with strong support from Mexican wealthy monarchists.

Benito Juarez

The attempt to create a throne was in the face of an elected Mexican President, Benito Juarez. Juarez was from Oaxaca, a Zapotec and the only President of Mexico ever that was a full-blooded Indian. He was long allied with liberal/republican forces that sought to provide legal equality for all Mexicans, lessen the control of the wealthy and the Catholic Church, and sought to create a society much like that of their neighbor to the north, the United States. In the war with Maximilian and the French forces, Juarez was forced to retreat north from Mexico City all the way to Chihuahua City. But as the United States ended its Civil War, American resources began to flow into Juarez's forces and they were able to push back to Mexico City and defeat the Maximilian forces. This May victory is widely celebrated by Americans of Mexican descent as Cinco de Mayo.

During the years from Mexican Independence until the 1850s, wars occurred with Texas and then the United States that severed the claimed territories of Mexico in much of North America. France attempted a re-conquest of Mexico with an invasion of Mexico in 1861 but was repulsed by 1864 after victories such as the one on May 5, 1862 by a Mexican Army facing an experienced and formidable French force. Then a brief period followed with democratically elected leaders.

The Porfiriato

After the repulsion of the French, traditional forces regrouped and elected Porfirio Diaz, a military hero in the war against the French. But rather than reasserting the long fought-for democratic traditions he ruled as a dictator though formally elected as President from 1876 to 1911. Mexicans term this dictatorial period as the *porfiriato*. The agricultural and banking reforms achieved under Juarez were completely reversed, and by 1910 a few land owners and once again the Catholic Church owned most of the land in Mexico, leaving 90 percent of the people landless.

During most of the years of Mexico's existence the ownership of land was crucial, as little factory or trade work existed and people secured their existence by farming and animal husbandry. In many parts of the country the land was not surveyed, registered and owned but rather held as a communal property with rights to use coming from tribal membership. European conventions, including property rights of land ownership and associated taxation, were alien to the bulk of the Mexican population. In the early 1800s and then again after the 1860's, land ownership concentrated in the hands of the few, leading to the establishment of a landless peasant class with rights even less than under a feudal system. Repeatedly in the 19th and into the 20th Century, revolutions would attempt to meld the various groups in the Mexican population into a common national vision.

The Restless Wilds of the North

The historical reality of the original northern territories of Mexico is less a part of Mexico and its national culture than many Mexicans and some scholars would argue. The Aztecs, then the Spanish and then the Mexican governments, readily brought under control the central highlands around Mexico City, the lowlands to the east to the Gulf of Mexico and west to the Pacific.

Beyond the Orb of Mexico City

Both the northern and southern realms strongly resisted Mexico City's political, religious and economic control. South of Mexico City even today Indian traditions are strong and often Spanish is a secondary language. Vast deserts, isolated populations, difficult to traverse mountain ranges, and great distances made control north of Guadalajara, Leon and San Luis Potosi problematic. The reach of Mexico City has always been a hundred to two hundred miles north but ever weaker as one travels closer to the United States. San Antonio, Texas; Santa Fe, New Mexico and San Francisco, California were each so distant from Mexico City that reaching these settlements until nearly the 20th Century required an arduous journey by horse and wagon that took between 1 to 2 years. Trails were not well-marked, water and food had to be carried for long distances as forage, supplies were not available, and there were few communications back to Mexico City along the trail. Further, hostile populations along many of the routes were ready to raid traveling parties from Mexico City.

Comancheria

The Indian populations across these lands resisted both Spanish and Mexican control, and repeated uprisings occurred in California, Arizona and New Mexico as well as in many of the Mexican states. The most complete resistance came from a tribe in the southern plains that simply stopped the advance of all central governmental control of first the Spanish and then the Mexicans from Mexico City. Mexicans, Texans and Americans found these people to likely be the equal of the Asian hordes of Genghis Khan that ruled central Asia during the 14th century, reaching from parts of China and India to Europe. These were the Comanche, the fabled horse warriors of the Southern Plains.

At the time of Columbus, the Comanche, an offshoot of the Shoshone, were migrating as a weak and poverty-stricken band of hunters and gatherers from Montana to the southern plains (Wallace, 1952). They encountered and avoided the powerful and numerous Sioux, Cheyenne, Kiowa, Wichita, and Apache (Smith, 1996; Trigger & Washburn, 1996). To the east as they crossed south on the Great Plains were the Caddo, a formidable southern agricultural culture, who the Comanche quickly learned to avoid.

The Horse

Sometime in the late 1500s the Comanche began seeing Spanish soldiers on horseback. For the peoples of all of Mesoamerica this was a puzzling and frightening new creature. Time passed before Indians began to realize that these were men riding on a creature unknown in the Americas. Only in time did Indians come to understand that the horses were domesticated animals and that a soldier or warrior on a horse was more than a match for several men on foot.

The Comanche were, perhaps, the first to understand this and far and away the first to build their entire culture around the horse. They became a fully migrating people using horses to hunt bison, which became their main source of food, clothing, equipment, and shelter. They secured stray horses and then stole horses first from the Spanish and then the Mexicans, quickly becoming the first American tribe to fully use the horse. In fact, they were the conduit of the horse to other Indian tribes on the Great Plains as well as a source of horses in trade with Mexicans and Anglos in the territories of northern Mexico and the American Southwest. By the time Anglos began to appear in the Southwest in the early 1800s, the Comanche were a powerful and wealthy people numbering in the tens of thousands.

They ranged north into Kansas where they met the Cheyenne and the Sioux, west into the mountains and deserts of New Mexico, and south as far as Saltillo about 400 miles north of Mexico City, and east into the pine forests of Texas. This vast area of grass and shrub land was a range of over a thousand miles from north to south and seven hundred miles east to west. Bison roamed this area, and there were an estimated 25 to 30 million on the Great Plains prior to the arrival of Europeans and the horse.

Comanche Empire

By the time of the American Revolution, the Comanche had blocked both Spanish and later Mexican expansion into lands north of Monterrey and west to El Paso. Though they were claimed by Mexico, these lands were owned and controlled by the Comanche. These lands, called the Comancheria, extended south of the Rio Grande 200 miles, north into Kansas where they met the Lakota-Sioux, east toward Louisiana where the Caddo Federation lay, and west to the Rockies and deserts.

Developing into brilliant horsemen able to fire from a moving horse, the Comanche became the same sort of mobile force as the Mongols in Asia six hundred years earlier, able to pin down and destroy soldiers on foot and hold Mexican ranches and Roman Catholic missions hostage. Their raids isolated Mexican villages with activity extending as far south as Saltillo, Coahuila, about 300 miles south of San Antonio, Texas. They effectively cut the Catholic missions, citizens with land grants, and military garrisons in San Antonio, Texas and Santa Fe, New Mexico from Spanish and then Mexican control.

These experiences, this reality forever haunts Mexico in that the North is not theirs. Mexico City's grasp is always tenuous after 200 miles north, and the rise of the United States deepens those fears.

The Comanche were the reason that the Spanish and then the Mexican state could never secure Texas, a state of affairs that opened the path for Anglo migration into the area. Without the Comanche, Texas would still be Mexico (Fehrenbach, 2003; Fuentes, 1996; Gwynne, 2009; Hagan, 1993; Hamalainen, 2009; Neeley, 1995; Noyes, 1999; E. Wallace & Hoebel, 1952).

Summary: The Third Fundamental Belief

Stolen lands are the third fundamental Belief of the Mexican state. For 300 years the Aztecs sought to claim people and territories hundreds of miles north of Mexico City but never secured those lands. Spain and then Mexico were mesmerized by those aspirations, but harsh lands, hostile peoples and great distances thwarted them as well. The hold of the lands from 200 miles north of Mexico City was as always difficult and tenuous.

Along the Pacific Coast to California it was perhaps the most successful, but from Arizona to Texas and particularly in the Comanche lands, it failed. Some in Mexico view its legitimate claim from Central America north to the Great Lakes and west to the Pacific. This was a vision of the 19th century and remains part of Mexican history. The wars with Texans and then Americans resulted in a deep fear in Mexicans of their lands and resources being seized by others.

Chapter 5: Mexico's Last Revolution?

The history of Mexico is a cycle of revolutions. They date back before the time of the Aztecs and have characterized human settlement and contact in Mexico for thousands of years. The cycle continued in the 16th, 17th, 18th and 19th centuries, though with less activity in the 17th and 18th.

20th Century Revolt

The most recent revolution was in the early years of the 20th century. It was not a revolution against a European colonial power as had been the conflicts since the 1500s, but rather was one against entrenched privilege and persons and institutions of Mexico that exploited people no less than those of colonial powers.

This 20th century revolution in Mexico, a long and bloody war, started in 1910 and lasted until 1920. It resulted in a single party, the Party of the Institutionalized Revolution (PRI) that emerged out of the Revolution and controlled the nation for almost the remainder of the century. The very name of the dominant political party of the 20th century signals the primacy of revolt in Mexican history and culture.

The revolution came at an enormous cost of life with between 1 and 2 million people (out of a population of 14 to 15 million) killed in combat or through starvation and disease. Additionally, nearly one million more Mexicans fled the country for the United States between 1910 and 1920. The 1910 revolution was largely a reaction to the 40-year dictatorship of Porfirio Diaz. Diaz had come to power via military coup, which overthrew the elected president, Benito Juarez, a common man and the only full-blooded Indian to be President. While initially allied with Juarez, Diaz became a total dictator. Elections were held but Diaz was the sole candidate. While Diaz's presidency was characterized by promotion of industry and the pacification of the country, it came at the expense of the working class. Farmers and peasants both complained of oppression and exploitation. His rule is known as the Porfiriato. The economy took a great leap during the Porfiriato, as he encouraged the construction of factories, roads, dams, industries, and better farms. This resulted in the rise of an urban proletariat and the influx of foreign capital (principally from the United States).

Part of his success in maintaining power came from balancing U.S. influence in Mexico by permitting European investments—primarily from Great Britain and Imperial Germany. Progress came at a price, however, as basic rights such as freedom of the press were suspended under the Porfiriato. The growing influence of the United States was a constant problem for Diaz, and his tactic to control this influence was to seek to balance it with alliances with European nations that were competitive with the United States.

Wealth, political power and access to education were concentrated among a handful of families, overwhelmingly of European descent, known as *hacendados*, who controlled vast swaths of the country by virtue of their huge estates. (One family, the Terrazas, had one estate in Sonora alone that comprised more than one million acres.) Most people in Mexico were landless, laboring on the vast estates or in the mines for little more than slave wages. Foreign companies, mostly from the United Kingdom, France and the U.S., exercised power in Mexico.

Diaz changed land reform efforts that were begun under previous leaders dating back to Hidalgo in 1810 and Hidalgo's and subsequent efforts to lessen colonialism and exploitation of Mexico's masses. Diaz undid virtually all the accomplishments by leaders of the previous half-century such as Juarez. No peasant or farmer could claim the land he occupied without formal legal title. Few of Mexico's masses were educated, and had neither the resources nor the understanding of how to secure traditional lands in a modern state that required official title to the land. Moreover, in many of the Indian villages the population held land jointly; surveying, creating title and possession were foreign European concepts. Helpless and angry, small farmers and landless peasants saw no hope for themselves and their families under a Diaz regime, and came to the conclusion that a change of leadership would be the only route that offered any hope for themselves and their country.

In the years of this dictatorship the repressive regime sold off much of Mexico to foreigners, leaving landless peasants all across Mexico. By the end of the Porfirio regime, 3,000 families owned half of the land in Mexico. More than 95% of Mexico's land was owned by less than 5% of the population! With such a great concentration of wealth there was widespread poverty among the 15 million Mexicans, with almost half being Indians. Life expectancy was 27 years, infant mortality was 25 percent, most were malnourished, and only 20 percent were literate. While Mexico was wealthy in natural resources, serving as the third largest producer of oil in the world early in the century, the wealth was owned and controlled by British and American oil companies.

The Revolution's Basis in the Peasantry

The revolution of 1910 began not in Mexico City but in the north, particularly the state of Chihuahua led by Pancho Villa and in the south by Emiliano Zapata. There were other leaders in this revolution, but these two are significant in that they were viewed as coming from the peasant class, uneducated, illiterate, and from the ranks of the Indian and Mestizo population of Mexico. Though both were killed in the recurrent pattern of betrayal and treachery, the revolution succeeded in breaking up the large land monopolies held by the Mexican wealthy, remaining European families and the Roman Catholic Church. This victory ushered in the modern Mexican State, as it exists today. The basic soldier in both the 1810 and 1910 revolution was the landless peasant. The power and revolutionary potential of the peasant became the fourth Belief of the Mexican State.

Some disturbances continued after 1920, but they were minor with one exception. A final paroxysm of the 1910 Revolution came with the Cristero War in the late 1920s. It was an effort by conservative Catholics in states northwest of Mexico City, Jalisco and Guadalajara, to reverse Federal government actions against the Catholic Church.

The Roman Catholic Church has been a controversial institution in Mexican culture since its introduction by Spanish conquerors and the subsequent forced conversion of Indians by the Church. At times, the Church was a mechanism of efforts to better the conditions of the Indians, poor, and landless, through the work of leaders like Father Hidalgo. But during much of the 19th century the Church worked hand-in-hand with the wealthy and politically powerful and, itself, became a wealthy landowner. Thus in the 19th century the Roman Catholic Church appeared in Mexico as a powerful and conservative land and wealth monopoly, much as it was viewed in the 1770s in France, Italy and Spain. Priests and the Church, itself, were among the focus of the 1910 Revolution, resulting in a sharp reduction of its wealth holdings, prominence, visibility, and power by 1920. The Cristero Revolt was an effort by Catholics to reverse those strictures that the Revolution placed on the Church. The Revolt ended in defeat with the brutal loss of 90,000 lives. The aftermath of this war saw an even sharper curtailment of the dominance and power of the Catholic Church, with the Church being forbidden to own property, run schools, and for priests and nuns to appear in public in clerical garb.

Since the founding of the Mexican state beginning with Cortez, domination and exploitation of outsiders and concentration of powers in the hands of the few have been focal concerns. Again and again people were pushed off historical lands, forced into indentured roles nearly as slaves, deprived of education and freedom of expression, and forced to stand aside as outsiders plundered the wealth of the land and the people. These concerns were expressed in the 1930s and 1940s with the expropriation of American and British Oil properties in Mexico by then-Mexican President Cárdenas. Seeing the United States and Europe absorbed by the Great Depression and then World War II, Cárdenas struck a very popular blow for Mexican street sentiment against American threats of invasion or blockades and continued flirtations during World War II with the Germans to keep the Americans cautious about any real or perceived agenda toward Mexican territory. Mexican involvement with Marxist perspectives continued to be significant throughout the 20th century. In many ways, the monopoly of the state in much of Mexican society in the 20th Century shows Marxist influences as state-controlled monopoly capitalism.

The revolutionaries came from the south and north rather than Mexico City/central Mexico, where power always resides. Mexico City is Paris, Berlin, Rome, Beijing, Tokyo, London or Washington, D.C., the seat of national power for 600 years. Part of the motives for the 1910 Revolution was to break up the large land holdings of a few families and redistribute the lands back to the peasants. This included stripping the Catholic Church of its vast land holdings and other wealth. A cry of this Mexican revolt from Emiliano Zapata was *tierra o muerte* (land or death) and expressed the desperate situation of peasants, the bulk of the Mexican population, and the fact that their historical possession of their lands had been stripped from them. The land was the basis of life for the peasant, and without land there was only death.

The Post-Revolutionary, All Powerful Centralized State

Another consequence of the 1910 revolution was to extend government involvement in many parts of the culture and economy. Mexico sought to remove foreign ownership that was seen as a vestige of the colonial domination that had plagued the country for all the years of its existence. For example, in 1938, Mexico nationalized the oil industry and created Pemex, a state-owned company that controlled all oil production, refining, distribution, and sales. Telemex controlled telephone communication, and similar government and quasigovernmental monopolies existed in many other areas of the economy. The PRI exercised power from Mexico City into every state, county and city. Roads, telephone lines and airline routes were all spokes that radiated from the hub in Mexico City to all outlying areas. While foreign colonial powers were curtailed, the pattern of central government control was enhanced.

The experiences of Mexicans across hundreds of years extending far back beyond the Spanish conquest are those of cultural contact, war and conquest. Heroism and betrayal are common themes. Revolutions succeed, heroes are assassinated and dark powers reassert their control. Social classes, racial lines and exploitation are recurrent themes. Rather than building an optimistic culture with an expectation of successful social engagements, it is a cautious culture, often fatalistic, and one where only the family exists as a true and safe harbor. Family ancestors are revered and remembered and the individual is forever anchored in the security of family when faced with the risks of the outside world. These cultural memories are part of the psychology of the individual Mexican and play a critical role in defining Mexico today and, to varying degrees, the thinking and behavior of those with Mexican heritage in the United States.

The political structure of Mexico has continued since pre-Hispanic times with central authoritarian regimes extending controls from Mexico City north to the deserts of the southwest, to the Gulf to the east, the Pacific to the west, and into the tropical lands of Guatemala and El Salvador. The centralizing pattern from Mexico City seems to exert itself even if the revolutionaries come from the northern or southern regions. The great distances, difficult travel and the enduring cultural differences in the Mexican population abridge the certainty of control.

Recurrent Fears of the North

During the years of the Spanish Crown and under early Mexican Independence, the extension of centralized control over the north was incomplete. Neither the Spanish nor the Mexicans were able to subdue the Comanche, and they had irregular success with the Apache in Chihuahua, Sonora, Arizona, and New Mexico, the pueblo-dwelling peoples, and the Yaqui. Only the scorched earth tactics of the Anglos defeated the Comanche and secured lands that were once thought to be Mexico. One enduring aspect of Mexican culture comes from its loss of its northern lands in the 19th century and the growing power of its northern neighbor in the 19th and 20th century. A constant theme in Mexican public social science education is fear of the "colossus of the north"—the United States—and that Mexico will lose more of itself to its powerful northern neighbor. Those fears resulted in many efforts to secure the north by the central government in Mexico City. Transportation and communication networks would radiate out of central Mexico and east-west patterns were discouraged. Governors and mayors of all states, and especially the north, were chosen for loyalty to Mexico City, and often lived most of their lives in Mexico City, only residing in the outlying states during their time in office.

A program of food subsidy and government encouragement of large families during much of the 20th century was created to populate the land with Mexicans and thwart perceived territorial expansionistic aims of the United States. Mexican leaders felt if the sparsely populated northern states had larger populations they would be more difficult for the United States to annex someday.

Summary: A Fourth and Fifth Fundamental Belief

In 1910 the fourth Belief appeared, and that was the power and heroic status of the peasant. The peasant population as a social class has always been both a problem and a heroic figure in Mexican literature. In Mexico the peasants are both the Indian and the Mestizo. To the wealthy and many of the highly educated they represent an embarrassment and a potential source of social disruption. Indeed this was the social class, the most marginalized that Father Hidalgo rallied to initiate the Mexican Revolution against Spain and recognition of a people that were "the Mexicans". Mexican muralists like Orozco, Siqueiros and Riveria would memorialize the peasant as the heroic basis through war and blood leading to the founding of the Mexican Republic. Mexican Marxist Thought by the 40s through the 90s would continue this heroic view of the Mexican peasant. Political figures like Benito Juarez, Pancho Villa (José Doroteo Arango) and Emiliano Zapata, the latter two heroes of the 1910 revolution and both illiterate were icons of the peasantry.

By the end of the 1970s Mexico had clearly added a fifth fundamental Belief to modern Mexico, and that is the duality of feelings about its northern neighbor. In the soul of the Mexican culture and state are concerns about foreign domination and wealth concentration. The expropriation of the oil companies' holdings by President Lazaro Cárdenas eased some of the wounds of the 1800s caused by the loss of Texas and then the region that became the American Southwest, while at the same time reaffirming the feelings on both sides of the border that mutual trust was limited. This continued during the Cold War from 1945 until the fall of the Soviet Union in 1991. Until that time, the Soviet Union maintained an outsized presence in Mexico with extraordinarily large and electronically sophisticated consulates, including one in Ciudad Juarez that kept watch on Ft. Bliss and the research programs at White Sands, New Mexico. The successful inroads of the Soviets in Cuba and the efforts of the Sandinistas in Nicaragua kept Washington on notice of the need to mend fences with Mexico.

PART II A MODERN STATE

Chapter 6: Creating A Modern Mexico

From the late 1920s until the 1980s Mexico slowly consolidated the gains of the 1910 Revolution by building many components of a modern society. National utility systems in power and telephone were developed as well as a postal system (Correos de Mexico), national airline (Aeronaves de México-Aeroméxico), train service (Ferrocarriles Nacionales de México), telephone and television systems in major cities, and highways. Most of this infrastructure was government-owned or built with significant government participation.

Oil, which had been discovered in Mexico at the turn of the 19th century, has long played an important role in the Mexican economy and Mexican concerns about foreign interests in Mexico. By the 1930s the United States and Mexico were the world's largest oil producers, with all Mexican oil production being in the hands of foreign companies. When those companies resisted efforts of employees to unionize and improve wages and working conditions, Mexican President Lazaro Cárdenas expropriated all the foreign holdings and nationalized exploration, drilling and refining of oil in 1938.

The act was strongly protested in the United States and Britain, but coming as it did with England at war and war looming for the United States, stronger responses were muted. German attention and interests were on the increase in Mexico, and Mexico City politicians played with the idea of Mexico allying with the Germans and the Axis Powers as a trump card to keep American military intervention or commercial boycotts at bay. Sensing the likelihood of American involvement is wars in Europe and the Pacific, Franklin D. Roosevelt was concerned about keeping the nation's southern flank protected.

Mexico saw this as a vulnerable moment and acted to assert its sovereignty against foreign powers. Roosevelt viewed the intentions of Germany and Japan seriously and took steps such as creating bodies like the Good Neighbor Commission to promote positive relations between Mexico and the United States.

When the United States entered World War II, manpower needs became critical and women assumed many jobs held by men in factories. But with large continuing needs for labor in factories and agriculture, the United States turned to Mexico and created a series of agreements to permit Mexican labor to come and work in the United States, and termed, the Bracero Program.

Thus Mexico continued its uneasy relationship with its larger and stronger neighbor to the north. Needing its intellectual and capital resources, partnerships were mandatory, but the long experience dating back to the days of the war with Texas made Mexicans ever wary of the true intentions of Americans.

So much of Mexico's development was spurred by the United States, and yet the States were always watched closely by Mexico. The expropriations of American investments and the flirtations with the Axis Powers and then with the Soviet Union during the Cold War fueled a like wariness of Washington, D.C. toward Mexico.

The Mexican Oil Boom

Mexico's natural resources have long been a dominant feature of the country. The rumors of gold and silver drew the Spanish soldiers of fortune to central Mexico, far south to Peru, and north into the modern day American states of Texas, New Mexico, Oklahoma and Arizona, as well as California. Silver mines about two hundred miles north of Mexico City in the Sierra Oriental have been worked for more than 500 years, and prominent fisheries on both coasts have supported great populations for more than a thousand years. Trading routes in turquoise, coral, gold, silver, seashells, birds, and animals have been traced from the Pacific Northwest, to the American Southwest, through the Valley of Mexico, and to the Highlands of Guatemala and El Salvador since 2000 B.C.

The most recent natural resource wealth was the discovery in the late 1970s of vast offshore oil deposits near Veracruz. While Mexico had been a leading oil producer all during the 20th century, this discovery catapulted Mexico into the ranks of the largest producers in the world. This oil that is owned and controlled by the state monopoly, Pemex, created the first middle class in Mexico, starting with the employees of Pemex. Oil export earnings provided better salaries for oil workers than jobs in other sectors and included retirement, health benefits, and free or low cost housing. The Pemex employees set a pattern, a goal for the middle class of Mexico.

Using Oil Wealth to Grow the Population

These oil riches caused an explosion in the wealth of many Mexicans and the Mexican nation. The foreign exchange earnings provided funds to support more schools, universities, nurses and physicians and the capital for roads, airports and utilities across Mexico. Importantly part of the state's response from the oil export earnings was to increase the subsidies on basic agricultural items such as beans, rice and corn. It used the earnings to lower the cost of food and enlarged a policy began in the 1930s to encourage population growth in Mexico as well as ensuring the support of the poor for the ruling political classes. Even today somewhere around 35 percent of all of the Federal expenditures in Mexico come from the export of oil.

Why Promote Population Growth?

A constant with Mexico is the fear of invasion and domination by an external enemy, a fear based on an event that had been repeated many times. In the 20th century this became fear of the United States and the concern that Americans would annex the largely vacant areas of northern Mexico as part of a Manifest Destiny to expand the United States of America. The evidence was there as the United States had done just that in the 1800s. Mexico's response in the late 20th century was to encourage big families with the assumption that large populations in the northern states of Mexico would be a barrier to American annexations. Mexico took great pride in its growing population and assumed that a large population would increase the security of the state especially to encroachments from the north. A large and young population has become an important feature of modern Mexico.

Mexico Becomes Urban

Modern Mexico is characterized by the changing population distribution in the country. For centuries it was a rural land with only one large population center, Mexico City, which always was less than 100,000 people. However, through the last 30 years the Mexican population has moved to urban areas, growing the Mexican Federal District to more than 25 million. Several cities along the border with the United States are home to a million or more. Mexico, always a rural nation, now has become one where only 20 to 30 percent of the population live on and are supported by the land.

The Mexican rural population since antiquity was self-sufficient in food, housing and utilities. Housing was rudimentary; water came from streams or hand-dug wells and waste disposed in dry toilets. Gardens and domestic animals provided the food supply, and maintaining all of this was the definition of work for the rural residents. These facts are no longer true.

The Search for Jobs

Urban populations participate much more fully in specialization and an exchange economy, and require jobs with food imported from the countryside. By 1980, the new urban Mexican population was desperate for jobs—so desperate, in fact, that Mexico did two things, one irresponsible and one heretical. The irresponsible was to urge Mexicans to leave Mexico but send money back to support families.

Leave they did, with more than 10 and as many as 20 million going to the United States by late 2010. The heretical was to reverse the policy of forbidding foreign interests to own properties in Mexico, as what was first a border assembly plant in Juarez became an all-out effort to get foreign manufacturers to locate plants in Mexico. These plants, called *maquilas*, did not do major manufacturing at first, but rather completed labor-intensive assembly of parts manufactured elsewhere in the world. In short order though because of the availability and quality of the Mexican labor and the proximity to the American markets, more complete manufacturing activity developed.

Cultural and Economic Fundamentals of Modern Mexico

During most of the 20th century the power from Mexico City was lubricated by profits from the control of businesses. The PRI ran the country much like the Central Committee in the Soviet Union and China. Some businesses were owned outright by the government, and others were partnered through labor unions. The government controlled Pemex, the state monopoly and cash cow through oil export earnings, and Pemex's employee union controlled labor.

Public school teachers needed to be responsive to parents and local authorities, but the national teachers union first controlled teachers. The views of students and parents were far from the concerns of the schools. In all instances the PRI was there with selected local, state and federal officials and approved candidates for union elections.

The control from the national level was enhanced sharply in the 1970s by the discovery of one of the world's greatest oil fields, the Cantarell, in the Gulf of Mexico. At the time of its discovery only the Saudi Arabian Ghawar field had larger reserves. The Arab oil embargo was increasing oil prices sharply and much of the cheap and easy to find oil in the United States had been pumped. This was Mexico's moment, and the challenge was how to make the best use of the bonanza of dollars, euros, yen, etc. coming to Mexico from the sale of its oil.

Summary: A Sixth Fundamental Belief

The Sixth Belief is that Mexico can transform its society and culture with its abundant natural resources, particularly oil, to becoming a modern, powerful urban nation on a par at least with England or France and not a second-class citizen in the Americas. With the discovery of oil and state promotion of growth, Mexico knew that it must find ways to absorb the huge population that had come from government efforts to encourage large families.

A relatively small population of about 15 million during the 1910 Revolution had grown to 70 million by 1980, and many urban areas especially in the northern border were doubling once each decade. The government had provided food subsidies to increase the size of the Mexican population, as an effort to populate the country and thwart any potential actions such as those of the United States to incorporate empty lands into the U.S. or dissuade European powers from seizing lands.

As Mexico passed mid-century it had transformed itself from a sparsely populated land to a land that was large, self-sufficient, and largely rural. But by the 1970s the population had grown beyond the resources of subsistence farming in rural Mexico, and migrations to urban areas had begun to change the nation from mostly rural to urban. With many deep in poverty, Mexico sought to transform itself from a culture of largely subsistence farmers to an industrialized and urbanized people. It had the goal of becoming much like the United States, France, Great Britain, Germany and Japan. It was a sufficiently populous nation, had great natural resources, and a large potential (if under-educated) workforce which could be mobilized to transform the country.

Chapter 7: Mexico's Third Transformation of the 20th Century

Mexico underwent three broad transformations in its population and social structures in the 20th century. The first came as a result of the far-reaching Revolution that began in 1910. During that civil war Mexico lost about one fifth of its population through violence and starvation, with hundreds of thousands fleeing north to the United States. At the end of the war, the dictatorship of Porfirio Diaz was ended, vast lands taken from a few wealthy families and the Roman Catholic Church and given as grants to the poor (peons). The Catholic Church was forbidden to own land, run schools and priests and nuns to wear clerical garb in public. Mexico severed ties with many European influences during the war, and by 1929 had created one political party that would thoroughly dominate the culture until the next century. The party was called "The Party of the Institutionalized Revolution" (PRI).

A second transformation occurred during the world wide depression of the 1930s when Mexican President Lazaro Cárdenas removed remaining significant foreign influence by nationalizing oil fields and refineries mainly owned by companies from Great Britain and the United States. Cárdenas set in motion a trend of state ownership of much of the Mexican economy including oil (Pemex), railroads, airlines, telephones and telegraph, airports, electricity generation, buses and bus manufacturing, and mining.

A third transformation began in the latter half of the 20th century, with the country moving toward privatization. In no small way, Mexico was affected by the collapse of the Soviet Union and its total control of farms, transportation and manufacturing, and the abysmal failure of this model of state planned and controlled production.

By the 1980s leaders in Mexico and many intellectuals saw the need to create a different Mexico from the one that existed in the 1800s and through the 1910 Revolution to the end of the 1970s. Mexico was now a populous land, but the population lacked education and skills as compared to that of the powerful nation-states to which Mexico aspired to be like, such as the United States, the countries of Northern Europe, and Japan. The leaders saw several steps that could be taken to transform Mexico into a nation with a strong educational and health system and a population of factory workers who had incomes high enough to move beyond a bare subsistence condition and become consumers as one would find in these comparison countries. Mexico saw that it had several advantages that could be deployed to make the transformation.

The Advantages for Mexico

One advantage was that Mexico had a large, healthy and young labor force. With prevailing daily wages on farms and ranches of perhaps $3 compared to wages of $10 for those that worked in tourism and factories, Mexico felt if they could get existing manufacturers from other countries to locate in Mexico, the country could offer an attractive labor rate of one-half to one-fifth of that in some other countries such as the United States and northern Europe.

A second advantage to manufacturers was that a factory in Mexico would be next door to the largest consumer market in the world, the United States. Transportation costs and knowledge of consumer preferences would be an important advantage to any company choosing to locate a factory in Mexico. Mexico with the United States would come to create an interesting partnership called the *maquilas* that offered to accelerate manufacturing at a far more rapid rate than was occurring elsewhere in the world.

A third advantage that Mexico held was the vast and still largely untapped natural resources in the country. While mining for silver and gold had existed since long before the Aztecs, most mines had only scratched the surface and significant ore bodies were likely undiscovered. A similar story was true for oil, and with discoveries in the 1970s and 80s Mexico was soon to return to the status of being one of the world's great oil producers. With rising world prices of oil and growing scarcity in some areas like the United States, oil promised a bonanza for Mexico. Of all the advantages that Mexico held, oil export earnings were the most attractive; as they would flow directly into government coffers to be directed to any selected areas for supporting the economy.

A fourth advantage was that Mexico's large labor force could travel and work in the United States as temporary workers and send some of the earnings back to families. This was a tradition that had begun in the Texas ranch country in the 19th century and had been accelerated during the Bracero Program during World War II. Many Mexicans knew of employers in the states and many had families there. The labor flow could be readily expanded if the United States were agreeable.

A fifth advantage was the established tourism venues of Mexican beaches, tropical forests and ruins of past cultures. Known in the United States, Canada and Western Europe,

Mexico suspected that if it could expand hotels, utilities and air and ground travel infrastructure, this would bring needed foreign currency and provide millions of jobs for citizens. Jobs in hotels and restaurants are labor intensive and could provide one of the quickest ways to expand employment opportunities. They would be low paying, but Mexico's need for millions of jobs was the critical dimension. The fact that many of the jobs would also be located in areas other than the major cities would also serve to stem the tidal wave of migration from rural villages, farms and ranches to a few cities.

The Components in the Transition

In summary, these were the existing major economic foundations that Mexico perceived it had and that could be expanded to support the transition from a rural, agricultural-based nation to a more modern one. Here were the major components of Mexico's planned transition.

Source of Capital	Jobs Created	Net Proceeds to the Mexican Economy
Export of Natural Resources (particularly oil and especially from the Cantarell Field)	In the thousands, but most would require substantial technical training and many needing college degrees	Anticipated sales of 130 billion dollars and investible profits of 13 billon. Profits would accrue to the central government to spend at will.
Maquila Workers and Other Manufacturing and Assembly Work	10 million in-line assembly workers, line managers, construction and plant maintenance workers, transport workers	15 billion in taxes and fees paid to the government, as well as improved living standards of those employed. Experience that would permit Mexican owned and controlled factories.
Export of Temporary Workers to the United States	10 to 30 million individuals working in various states in	30 billion dollars remitted to family members in Mexican

	occupations such as construction, meat processing, hotel staff as maids, waiters, cooks, etc.	communities.
Tourism	More than 40 million individuals. Maids, cooks, bartenders, drivers, clerks, managers, communication and IT employees, construction and maintenance workers	12 billion dollars through taxes and fees paid, as well as improved living standards of those employed.

Oil

A first source of wealth came from the discovery of new oil reserves in the Gulf of Mexico in 1976. It is placed first because of the amount of oil that was first thought to exist, and the expectations among Mexicans that their wealth would match that of the largest oil producers of the Middle East. Mexicans thought such wealth would place them on the fast track to becoming an equal to countries like England, France, Germany, Japan, and the United States. They, now by the 1990s, had a population approaching 100 million as the oil find became known, and quickly developed the aspirations to become a (if not the) dominant Spanish-speaking country of the world. The first discoveries appeared to be on the order of those in the Middle East, and Mexico used the export earnings from this oil to increase public salaries, hire more teachers, police officers, and government workers, and expand the physical infrastructure of roads, airports, rail, water, and electricity. It provided expansion of many aspects of the critical infrastructure needed for Mexico, such as building and extending existing roads and bridges, improving airports, and providing utilities, as well as funding for colleges and technical schools. Coincidentally it created some very great wealth among people in the know with the oil discoveries and the operations of Pemex, the state oil production monopoly. It made the union employees of Pemex the highest paid workers in Mexico and provided lucrative contracts for favored vendors. All of these funds were ultimately controlled by the PRI.

A Lucky Find

The history of the oil boom shows how accidental it was and indicates the rudimentary ability of Mexico to understand and use its natural resources. In the mid-1970s, angry shrimp fishermen led by Rudesindo Cantarell confronted the state oil monopoly, Pemex, in Veracruz. They complained about oil oozing out of the seabed, ruining their shrimping, and demanded compensation for drilling or piping actions of Pemex. Pemex had no wells in the area and the accidental discovery of oil by the fishermen changed the fortunes of Mexico. The source of the complaint was an unknown giant reservoir of oil that had long seeped some of the underground petroleum to the surface. That reservoir was named after the leader of the fisherman, Cantarell. When Pemex realized what the fishermen had discovered, it quickly began drilling and found, in the parlance of oilmen, "an elephant"—a huge, highly productive and convenient petroleum deposit.

Pemex is the sole supplier of all commercial gasoline (petrol/diesel) stations in the country. It was the state-controlled vehicle that President Lazaro created in 1938 when he confiscated the fields, pumping stations and refineries of American and British oil companies. Cantarell Field is the largest oil field in Mexico and one of the largest in the world.

Mexico has long relied heavily on Cantarell, this super-giant, for both domestic consumption and export. The volume of the production exceeded refinery capacity in Mexico and amounts of crude are moved to Texas and then brought back into the market as refined products for Mexican domestic consumption. In the first decade of the discovery and production, Mexico felt its oil riches would be the equal of the Gulf States of the Middle

East. However, the size of the find has proven less than the initial expectations as production continues.

Shrinking Output

In the early years the Cantarell field produced about 1 million barrels a day. Through technology, that production was boosted to a peak output in 2003 of 2.1 million barrels per day (65% of total Mexican production). It apparently held near that figure for two years and then began to decline sharply. Today the figure is roughly 900,000 barrels per day. The most troubling aspect is that the decline rate is accelerating, estimated at 2.5% per month currently, or 30% annually. It was producing 400,000 barrels a day in 2012. It appears that this field and others in the Gulf are relatively shallow and will "pump out" more rapidly than those of Texas, which now are greatly diminished, and those of the Middle East.

At the beginning of 2002 Mexico had the second largest proven oil reserves in the Western Hemisphere with 30.8 billion barrels (4.90×10^9 m³). However, according to Pemex, Mexico's reserves/production ratio fell from 20 years in 2002 to 10 years in 2006, and Mexico had only 12.4 billion barrels (1.97×10^9 m³) of proven oil reserves left by 2007. Mexico stands ninth in the worldwide ranking of conventional oil reserves, with only Venezuela higher in the Western Hemisphere (although Canada ranks higher if proven reserves of unconventional oil in oil sands are included).

The oil sector is a crucial component of Mexico's economy: while its relative importance to the general Mexican economy has declined in the long term, the oil sector still generated 14 percent of the country's export earnings in 2010, according to Mexico's central bank. More importantly, the government relies upon earnings from the oil industry (including taxes and direct payments from Pemex) for 35 percent of total government revenues. Therefore, any decline in oil production has a direct effect upon the country's overall fiscal balance.

The Mexican government has recently taken the unprecedented step of allowing foreign oil companies to explore for oil in Mexico. In a country that celebrates the 1938 nationalization of its oil industry as a federal holiday, it is clearly an act of desperation. In early 2011, Mexico held licensing rounds for performance-based contracts on oil blocks, allowing participation of foreign oil companies for the first time since the nationalization of the oil industry. The foreign firms will have no ownership rights over any oil they produce, but they are expected to provide Mexican fields with badly needed technological improvements.

Unless Mexico improves exploration success or has luck, the country may no longer be an oil exporter. It will be very difficult to replace the oil revenue that supports 35% of the Mexican budget. But promising offshore discoveries in Mexico will likely take decades to bring to production, according to Simmons (Simmons, 2008), due to the extreme depths and massive technical challenges of drilling and pumping the oil to the surface.

It may be too little too late to replace the rapidly disappearing Cantarell production. The effects are beginning to be felt both in Mexico and the United States. Replacing the 1.3 million barrels per day the US now imports from Mexico will not be easy (the United States imports 1.4 million barrels per day from Saudi Arabia by means of comparison, and slightly more from Canada). For Mexico, the problems run much deeper, as they must quickly diversify their economy or face wrenching economic and social dislocations. The adjustment period is bringing great change and tumult in Mexico, as well as across the border in the states of Texas, California and Arizona.

The Maquilas

The maquilas provided several desperately needed resources for Mexico. One was capital investment that built physical plants, provided sophisticated manufacturing tools, and created a tax base to extend utilities and transportation to the factories. This was an important gain for Mexico, as estimates in those years was that it required a dollar capital investment of $250,000 or much more to create each factory job as the costs of securing land, transportation access, utilities, manufacturing equipment, supervision and training are far larger than just the wage paid to the worker. The second resource was the job itself, and the earnings it provided for an urban worker. The job was what one must have to survive if one was not living in rural Mexico. These jobs also provided much better wages and a standard of living than was available in the rural areas. These attractive jobs had another unanticipated effect, which was to accelerate the movement of rural labor to the cities. The third resource was the training and education that a foreign manufacturer brought to the Mexican worker. Workers learned how to operate and maintain a variety of mechanical and electronic machines, the routines required of factory work, being supervised and learning to supervise—in short, the entire complex of knowledge, attitudes and skills for successful performance in a modern workplace. For many workers, with only about 6 years of education and impoverished environments often lacking electricity, running water, and other technological features, it was a cultural transformation.

Mexico also sought to build a stronger and more prosperous economy by increasing the size of its industrial sector. Like other countries it realized that manufacturing is an essential pillar of a powerful economy. Manufacturing, at least during much of the 20th century (unlike modern farming or tourism), could generate millions of well-paid jobs for those with only a high school education, a huge segment of the population in every country and certainly in Mexico. No other sector in the economy contributed more to the nation's overall wealth during that time. But as manufacturing weakens, the country becomes ever more dependent on imports of tools, food, computers, machinery and the like—running up a trade deficit that in time could undermine the currency and the nation's capacity to sustain imports.

A Risky Gamble

By the 1980s Mexico saw that its own national manufacturing sector would not or could not expand rapidly enough, and the country did not have sufficient numbers of innovative persons to create companies, nor the skilled managers and trained workers to achieve its desired manufacturing goals. Mexico then took a risky gamble, given its experience with foreign powers, including the United States, and began to create manufacturing partnerships with companies from other countries. The largest and most numerous ventures were with companies from the United States. These ventures were often in geographical zones where partially completed products could be imported into Mexico without tariffs. The products could be completed through the manufacturing and assembly process, and then sent back to the United States again without tariffs. These duty-free zones became in time the North American Free Trade Agreements (NAFTA). Thus, manufacturing through the boosting of expertise and the capital of foreign firms became a growing source of jobs, pride, promise, and income for Mexico.

Technical Education through Maquilas

Apart from the opportunities suggested by the discovery of large deposits of oil, there was a desire to make Mexico a manufacturing nation. Mexico's traditional sources of work were farming and fishing and there were not traditions of metalworking or large-scale manufacturing.

One exception was Monterrey, where public schools had strong science curricula that fed into college programs of engineering, physics, chemistry and geology. But in general, Mexico did not have the family traditions, trade unions or apprenticeships that could promote manufacturing. It did have ample natural resources to support manufacturing and a young but unskilled labor pool, as well as a group of young, relatively wealthy persons that had been educated in universities in Texas, California, Michigan and the Northeast. These persons had learned in classes how manufacturing interacts with the physical sciences and engineering, and the role of apprenticeships in creating a skilled labor force.

Pioneering Partnerships

Some citizens, particularly in Juarez, Chihuahua, Nuevo Laredo, Tamaulipas, and other border towns, began to approach American businesses about opening factories in their cities. To attract those factories, industrial parks were built to ensure utilities, equipment safe from theft, and available transportation. There was a ready labor force that only needed skilled supervisors and managers to set it to task. There were Mexican laws that forbade foreign companies from owning property, and there were restrictions and trade tariffs imposed by both countries on goods manufactured in the other country. But partnerships began to be developed, particularly on the border and northern Mexican cities with good highway and rail access to Texas.

In some cases a Mexican and an American jointly owned the factories. In other cases and over time, Mexico permitted full foreign ownership. These factories, which the Mexicans called *maquilas*, blended the inexpensive labor in Mexico with the tools, engineering and manufacturing knowhow of Americans to create a promising means for Mexico to develop a manufacturing culture. It was a tremendous advantage for the border cities, for a poorly paid and skilled labor force, and for lower costs for American manufacturers.

These developments might also solve the endemic poverty of the border cities, which depended upon providing low cost and often shadowy entertainment for visiting Americans. Juarez, for example, as early as the 1920s, was a major source of bootleg alcohol for the United States. These border cities were an embarrassment to the elites and emerging middle class of Mexico City. Industrialization was an alternative to bars, restaurants and bordellos, often in a "red light district," that were seen by many in Mexico to characterize its northern border cities.

Maquilas also served as a social and economic experiment for Mexico and the United States. Leaders in both countries were concerned with developments in the European community where easing trade restrictions and allowing labor mobility between countries promised future economic growth for Europe. The *maquilas* would test the integration of Anglo capital and managerial skills with lower-cost Mexican labor to create more factory plants that could effectively compete in the emerging globalization of the world's economy.

The *maquila* experiment laid the foundation for NAFTA, the broad set of agreements among Canada, the United States and Mexico to create a common market in the Americas. The idea seemed drawn from watching events developing in Europe where huge differences in wealth, education and social wellbeing existed, particularly on a north-south axis and then east-west after the fall of the Soviet Union.

Britain, Germany, France, and the Scandinavian countries were prosperous, highly educated and created a variety of innovations desired in a world market. Germany and (to a lesser degree) Scandinavia were known for innovations in manufacturing and technology, France for agriculture and Great Britain for financial innovations. Greece, Italy, Spain, and Turkey had younger populations and high levels of unemployment. Rather than continuing a tradition of five hundred years of wars among European countries, some saw an opportunity to blend the need for lower cost labor and an improved ability to compete in a global market by either importing low cost labor from southern Europe or moving factories from north to the south. Beginning after World War II, this notion matured into the Common Market and then led to a common currency, the Euro, and ending travel and commerce restrictions among the member countries.

The success of this activity was watched closely in Japan and Taiwan and in North America. In North America the response was NAFTA—The North American Free Trade Agreement. This experiment, created by the elites in the three nations of Canada, Mexico and the United States, has played out somewhat complexly. Here are two examples: one is the Mexican view of an emerging world of labor competition, and the second is an illustration of an early *maquila*.

Race Against China

I was in Mexico City at the UNAM campus in June of 1989 and noticed large crowds of faculty and students in classrooms and lounges excitedly watching television reports of the protests of Chinese youth against the Chinese government. When the Chinese army tanks began to seize control of the protestors in Tiananmen Square, applause broke out in the Mexican audience, followed by cheering. I was very puzzled by these emotional expressions. Mexico City elites and particularly UNAM intellectuals were the liberal core of Mexico. I presumed that there would be a sense of identity among Mexican liberals and young Chinese seeking to overthrow the oppression of the Chinese Communist state. In conversations with faculty and senior government bureaucrats during that week, I learned that a very different concern had animated what appeared as contradictory emotions. The Mexican intellectuals were seeing China and its vast labor pool of more than a billion workers as potential competition—a threat to Mexican labor in the emerging globalization of labor. Senior economic officials felt Mexico had only a 5 to 10 year window to industrialize its large potential labor resources before the world labor market would be hit by a billion new workers in China. If Mexican plants could be built and a Mexican workforce recruited and trained, then they would have labor capital in place to compete against the coming waves of even cheaper labor from Asia. The Tiananmen Square incident would provide additional years of advantage to the Mexican changes underway.

Unexpected Cultural Changes

The second example was a visit to a new *maquila* at an early assembly plant company, Elamex, in Juarez in 1986. The plant assembled floppy disk mechanisms for desktop computers. The product had been created and produced five years earlier in Minneapolis with labor costs of about $50 an hour. Then, two years later, the factory was moved to the Dallas area where labor costs dropped to $25 an hour; but now, in Juarez, labor costs were $3 a day!

The plant had two assembly lines, and all of the employees were young women. I found that most of the employees had moved from small towns and rural areas in northern Mexican states including Chihuahua, Durango and Coahuila, and had come to the city to escape lives of poverty, early marriage and caring for large families. They spoke excitedly of living in the large city, near America, shopping and buying things like make-up and designer jeans.

Under Mexican law factories have to provide medical care and I met the factory physician, also a young woman. I understood that part of the hiring procedures was a pregnancy test and the physician was to provide fertility control information and technologies to the employees. Under Mexican federal law pregnant women and those that have babies are entitled to substantial benefits charged back to the employer. This employer and my experience over the years in reviewing many such manufacturing entities have shown that efforts to avoid hiring pregnant women, as well as keeping of the number of employee pregnancies low, has been one of the controversial issues with the *maquiladora* program.

Substantial social policy, cultural and religious contradictions were and are involved in the Mexican experiment with factory work. One was the fact that birth control would limit the earlier efforts of the Mexican government to expand the national population. A second contradiction is the opposition of the Roman Catholic Church to the means of birth control provided by medical personnel. A third contradiction was disturbing the traditional role of women as remaining in the home or at the farm, not working in non-home settings with other men and women. Substantial conflict and misery may have grown from this contradiction. A fourth contradiction is the long remembered scars of colonialization by foreign powers and the fact that foreign companies owned these maquilas partially or wholly. In many instances the factory authorities were foreign nationals.

The promise of the *maquila* experiment was to provide companies, especially American companies but also manufacturers from Europe, Taiwan and Japan, a source of lower labor costs for manufacturing tasks. Never popular in the United States, especially with organized labor, the *maquila* was explained as an effort that would keep jobs near the United States that otherwise would migrate to other areas with large populations needing jobs and willing to work for low even lower wages. This included countries like Egypt, Turkey, and most importantly, India and China.

The advantage to Mexico was first jobs to help absorb the young and growing population that could no longer be supported by agricultural work or existing Mexican factories. For decades, tourism in Mexican resort areas and guest worker programs where Mexican workers would travel temporarily to work in the United States helped Mexico deal with surplus workers. Expanding factories were hoped to provide a higher wage to the Mexican labor market as well as building critical skills in manufacturing that would strengthen the Mexican economy.

Creating factory jobs is very capital intensive. They require specialized buildings, complex equipment, sources of high levels of energy particularly electricity and a cadre of engineers and supervisors. Estimates today are that it takes $100,000 to $1,000,000 of capital investment for each factory job created. A state of the art microchip fabrication plant may cost $4 billion dollars and yet employ only 2 or 3 thousand workers. Auto manufacturing plants run in the millions and yet through advanced manufacturing methods and the use of robotics each new plant requires fewer workers per auto built. The United States or Germany took generations to create such capital investments and thus industrial jobs. Mexico sought to jump start the process and skip so many years by permitting investment and ownership from other experienced countries to assist Mexico in building an industrialized economy. Jobs providing incomes for unemployed and underemployed workers decreased poverty, lessened welfare costs to government, generated tax and consumer revenues, made the government more secure, provided an external source of capital for industrialization, built critical labor force skills, and developed world markets for Mexican manufactured goods. Soon the *maquiladora* concept spread beyond the border cities to much of Mexico.

The Maquilas Today

The *maquilas* today are now part of the larger movement of Mexico through NAFTA to integrate into the labor and capital markets of the United States and Canada. As long as trade barriers fall and economic growth continues, the original experiment has great impact on Mexican society.

The *maquilas* produce a variety of products, and the impact on the American automobile industry is an instructive example. Lured by low labor costs, the Big Three auto companies General Motors, Ford, and Chrysler have been crucial to an industry that now makes up 3 percent of Mexico's gross domestic product and accounts for a fifth of its exports. The 13 plants run by Ford Motor Co., Chrysler LLC and General Motors Corp. account for more than 50 percent of Mexico's auto production. Mexico is heavily reliant on exports to the United States as a source of jobs and foreign currency earnings.

Three-quarters of vehicles produced in Mexico are exported, 70 percent of them to the U.S., according to the Mexican Auto Industry Association. Since the 1990s, wages as low as $1.50 an hour helped lure an average of about $2 billion per year in foreign investment in the auto industry, which now employs some 500,000 people, directly or indirectly.

The disadvantages of the *maquila* experiment have focused upon the threats to the culture and traditional social organization. A separate disadvantage was that the factories were built in cities with better transportation and thus worsened problems of inadequate housing, transportation, medical, educational, and retail services. This is true in the border cities but even more so in Mexico City, where air pollution and traffic gridlock is a daily fact of life.

Guest Workers
The oldest source of wealth, given the surplus labor created by Mexican national policy, was Mexican legal and illegal immigrants who worked in the United States, especially in construction, and remitted earnings back to families in Mexico.

Since the late 1800s Mexicans have gone north of the border seeking work. Ranch hands from Mexico have long been common, and migratory field labor began in the 1940s that would take entire families to Michigan and Washington.

One of two major areas of work that saw long term Mexican migration was in building railroads. Families would live in boxcars on rail sidings with men laboring along the tracks. Towns across the Midwest and West developed Mexican-American communities as some of this labor stayed in the United States, but in many cases some family members would return to villages in Mexico. A second area was large meat processing plants run by companies like Wilson and Armor. Like railroad workers, these migrants came to the United States in the 1910s, often fleeing the violence and poverty of Mexico, and established neighborhoods that provided connections for later generations to migrate to Kansas City or Chicago.

The largest scale of immigration occurred in the late 1980s and into 2001, with immigrants attracted by opportunities in the boom in real estate. Millions were absorbed in the semi-skilled and skilled building trades. Some returned to Mexico when the real estate bubble collapsed in 2005, but millions stayed because even a difficult American economy was better than the Mexican economy. In many cases these were individuals that had formed families and had children born in United States. Such persons thus were partially assimilated in two different countries.

The number of immigrant workers today is very great and likely is larger than ten million and perhaps thirty million. At any point in time one-tenth to as much as one-fifth of the Mexican laboring population is out of the country, mainly in the United States. Food processing, construction and service work absorbed most of these 10 to 30 million workers, as the agricultural worker pipeline was already full.

From 1980 until 2007 the United States was booming, and the Mexican workers spread out far beyond Texas and California, settling in cities and small towns all across the United States. Most of the workers were males and would send money back to wives and/or parents in Mexico and make treks back each year or so to visit families. While they often lived in proximity to other Mexicans they were influenced by the American culture and language and, like the factory worker in the *maquilas*, were a different sort of person than the humble, conservative, religious, and cautious Mexican farmer. Most developed some facility in English and increasing reluctance to return, as well as fewer ties with homes and relatives in Mexico.

The females that made the journey changed more than the males. The rights of women are far less assured in Mexico, and the young Mexican women in the States rapidly incorporated views of American women and their relative independence of males in where to live, shopping and entertainment. If they had children, they found that the American school system with children in school for 8 hours rather than 4, as would often occur in Mexico, meant the ability to create and sustain an identity beyond a mother at home. Like other American women, they would develop dual identities of workplace and home (Castenada, 2011).

With today's difficult economic conditions far less money is being remitted to relatives in Mexico, and that is less of a source of funds for Mexico. While immigration to the United States has sharply declined, those who are not American citizens may be reluctant to return to Mexico.

Tourism
Mexico as a nation has long promoted and welcomed visitors to its cities, ancient ruins and beaches. Most of the nation is semi-tropical to tropical and does not experience significant freezes or snow. Some northern cities such as Juarez, Monterrey or

Reynosa may see five snow days in a year, but central to southern Mexico has moderate temperatures year-round, with milder summers than the desert cities of the American Southwest like Phoenix. Beaches and waters along the Gulf, in the Atlantic south of the Yucatan, and those on the Pacific coast are as attractive as any in the world. Dozens of cities in Mexico, from Mexico City to Merida to Oaxaca, have thousands of modern accommodations, remarkable buildings, ruins, museums and regional music, costumes, and dances. All make for a very available and inexpensive vacations for the 325 million people in the United States and Canada and for tens of millions more in Europe.

Mexico serves as the 8th to 10th most visited country on the globe, and tourist income ranges to about one billion dollars a month. The source of wealth, coming from the improving transportation infrastructure, was especially pronounced with the expansion of tourism on both the most southern beaches of the Gulf of Mexico and areas all along the Pacific. Remote fishing villages were transformed into the model of the Acapulco of the 50s where large hotels, restaurants and shops were built to draw tourists and revenues from the United States, Canada and Europe. But as is true for most such service jobs in any country, the wages were just above the poverty level. Yet with a young and growing population every job and any job was an important added national resource.

Mexico saw the expansion of tourism as a source of external currency and jobs for a young labor force that often had some English skills, but many of the jobs would not require post-secondary college or technical school training. With many of the potential tourist sites in rural Mexico, tourism would be an important source of wealth for a population that existed largely with subsistence agriculture.

There was an area of advantage and an area of weakness to attracting more tourists. The advantage was that you would seek to draw tourists from wealthy countries and Mexico was next door to some of the world's most prosperous people, the Americans, and with air travel a convenient distance from Europe, another source of wealthy tourists. The vulnerability was perceived safety issues by potential tourists, so efforts needed to be made to address public health, improve sanitation in water and food, and eradicate diseases such as malaria, diphtheria and others that would discourage visitors.

Summary: The Seventh Fundamental Belief

Mexico committed itself to a rationally planned state during the latter part of the 20th century. It sought to inventory its resources and transform itself into a modern, suburban, manufacturing nation engaged in the world market. The belief of modern Mexico is one of entering the world of the cultures and social organizations of Western States like France, Germany, the United States, and Canada through a centralized plan. Mexico like China continues that strategy even as the world watched it fail with the Soviet Union. Mexico now has committed itself to the global market. It supports an urban population and increased government employees with oil exports. It promotes a tourist trade to bring dollars and jobs to dozen of remote but beautiful sections of its country. It has ended its centuries long caution with foreign owned and controlled businesses to accelerate the manufacturing base and training of its urban work force. It must seek and maintain friendly relations with the United States so that that country will permit migration of workers from a Mexican economy that cannot provide ample jobs. It takes these risks in a world market more turbulent than any seen.

Chapter 8: Modern Mexico-Four Regions

The reality of these four regions provides some signposts as tensions develop in the country. If Mexico continues on a trajectory toward a failed state, then the border region should break first with the nation. Next will be northern Mexico. Southern Mexico will be subject to increasing migration pressures from Central America. Mexico City will likely become destabilized with urban unrest.

Today Mexico is a complex society of 115 million. It is a young population with a median age of 26 years (compared to a U.S. median age of nearly 37.1), though it has for two decades had a sharply decreasing rate of population growth. It is the most populous Spanish- speaking country in the world; yet few of the population are of pure Spanish descent, but more accurately American Indian with lesser amounts of European ancestry, largely from Spain and Portugal.

Both nations are among the world's most populous, with Mexico having about 115,000,000 and the United States about 310,000,000 people. The U.S. population is substantially older, with a median age of about 37.1 years; by contrast, Mexico has a median age of 27.4 years. America is wealthy and well educated while Mexico is relatively poor, less educated and needing education resources.

It is one of the few countries of Latin America that is truly dominated by a population with mostly Native American Indian descent. This reality has long been an issue among Mexicans where it is often apparent that European physical characteristics are preferable to Indian ones among children and movie idols. Yet the ascendancy of those with Indian blood to political power dates back to Benito Juarez in the 1830s.

Population Components, Social Classes, the Economy

In Mexico today, the population is about 60% mestizos, 30% indigenous people, the Indian, and most of the remainder is white. The racial and cultural categories of *espanoles* (Spaniards born in Spain), *criollos* (Mexican-born, but with Spanish blood), *mestizos* (Spanish and Indian), and finally the *indigenes* (the Indians) are less serviceable today than in the 1600s and 1700s. NAFTA, modern communications, consumerism, and travel have lessened the distinction of *espanoles* and *criollos,* and more significantly, the *mestizos* are the bulk of the population. However, to varying degrees in the country, prejudice exists against Indian populations and Indian features.

Mexico has one of the strongest economies of the Americas. It is rich in natural resources including oil, many important minerals and productive fisheries on both the Atlantic and Pacific side. Mexico's tropical to semi-tropical climate is ideal for fruit and vegetable production. The Mexican transportation and communication system is among the most highly developed of Latin America, as are its institutions of science, technology and higher education. However, Mexico has limited arable land for crops such as corn, potatoes or wheat. Until two decades ago, Mexico was self-sufficient in agriculture, but today it imports substantial amounts of grain, chicken and beef from the United States. For example, Mexico is Texas' largest customer of its agricultural exports. This is both a consequence of population growth but also of urban migration lessening the number of persons involved in farming and farm production.

As in centuries past, geography plays a large role in the activities and outlooks of the Mexican people. Mexico has several very distinct geographical, economic and cultural regions, but four are of high importance: the federal district, the Indian south, the independent north, and the border.

The Federal District

Mexico City has a population of about 20 million, with another 10 million in nearby areas, and a regional culture often termed *chilango*. People from other regions of Mexico view the *chilango* as feeling superior, cultured and shaping the destiny of Mexico. *Chilangos* will often view persons from other regions of Mexico as provincials. It is not unlike the view that people for the East and West Coast of the United States have of the heartland, the "fly over country". Mexico City is the traditional seat of power in Mexico dating back more than 600 hundred years (Kemper, 2002). Mexico, or at least the denizens of Mexico City, has always exerted efforts toward strong centralization and that continues today, though without the exclusive strong single party rule which controlled the country from the 1910 revolution until the end of the 20th century.

The City

Mexico City is built on the bed of the lake that originally was the floating city of the Aztecs. Civil engineering through underground pumps and drains keeps the water that once filled the lake drained, as the city setting at about 6,500 above sea level is surrounded by high country—large volcanoes south of the city and mountains to the north. It is densely populated with some neighborhoods having continuous human settlements for over 700 years. It has 18 boroughs containing larger neighborhoods called *colonias* ranging sharply in wealth, with some being simply shanty towns residing on the rubble of the great earthquake of 1985. Only in the last decade has the streaming of rural people from central and south of Mexico to Mexico City partially subsided.

The City today accounts for about twenty percent of the gross national product of Mexico and includes the wealthiest ten percent of the Mexican population. While Mexico's politics are largely conservative, Mexico City's are liberal. Nominally Roman Catholic, religion in Mexico is hedged both by the role of the Church in the exploitation of Indians and the fact that Indian beliefs and practices have produced a Catholicism different from much in Europe or the United States.

The Hub of Mexico
Throughout its history, from Aztec times to today, all regions of Mexico have been bound by wealth, power and political sophistication to Mexico City. Even transportation and communication hubs in Mexico have reflected this central tendency, with the City serving as a hub for rail, highway and telecommunication landlines radiating out to all regions of the country. This centralizing power has been exercised through political control from the selection of governors down to city mayors. Government-owned business like banking, oil and communication provided positions to those loyal and funds to secure the support of the populace with subsidies to lower the price of foods like flour and masa for tortillas, and beans.

The Indian South
There are many forces that serve to challenge the power of the central state. In contrast to Mexico City and the northern regions of Mexico, south of Mexico City, with the exception of tourist spots such as Acapulco on the west or Merida to the east in the Yucatan, are where Mexicans of more fully and full Indian descent and culture are predominant. Here are the poorest, least educated and most traditionally rural of the Mexican population.

Continuities with the Indian Past

One challenge to the central state is the pull of traditional cultures never fully assimilated into the *mestizo* state. This is strongest in the Maya lands of the Gulf Coast and the southern states like Oaxaca, Chiapas and Tabasco. Spanish literacy is less, poverty is greater and illegal immigration of indigenous people from Belize, Guatemala and El Salvador create problems not unlike those in the southwestern United States from Mexican immigration. These immigrants are poorer, less educated and often in poor health. Perhaps 30 percent of the population south of Mexico City speaks traditional Indian languages of Zapotec, Mixtec, Nahuatl, and Mayan.

The Tribal Traditions

These are lands of traditional villages, often with strong rivalries and plagued by the loss of tribal lands to large farms. This loss of land to wealthy elites began to stir strong feelings of protest as early as the late 1960s (Trevizo, 2011), and the feelings were supported by both a liberation philosophy from some Roman Catholic priests and notions of personal salvation presented by Protestant missionaries. Indeed, an interesting feature of the south of Mexico has been the activities of these two religious groups. These areas are the seat of radical separatist movements in the 1990s against the central government in Mexico City. This has long been the land of the *surenos,* far more true to Indian beliefs than Roman Catholicism or Mexican nationalism. Now, with the growing narcotics traffic of illegal drugs moving north from South America, this introduces an important destabilizing force in the region moving along both the Gulf and Pacific Coast.

The Independent North

Regional differences are most pronounced and changing in the north where travel, media, trade, and currency provide a strong draw toward American culture. Many of the states north of Mexico City are arid and mountainous and were sparsely populated in pre-Hispanic times. As noted, the successful warrior characteristics of the Comanche and the Apache, and then the Yaqui to the western areas of the Chihuahua desert kept the control of Mexico from Aztec and Spanish eras weak and erratic as one moved north of Mexico City. Today, many of these states and larger cities beginning 200 miles north of Mexico City are often closely linked to the American side by business, travel and family ties.

Guadalajara, Torreon, Saltillo, and Monterrey have ready auto and air connections to the American side, and English is commonly spoken there as it is in the higher income areas of Mexico City. Monterrey is Mexico's second most wealthy and the highest educated city in the nation, known for manufacturing and strong institutions of higher education. Veracruz and Tampico on the Gulf of Mexico, like Zapopan and Leon, have an independence driven by oil production for Veracruz and agriculture and manufacturing for Zapopan and Leon, respectively. Manzanillo, Mazatlan and Los Mochis on the Pacific are rapidly growing ports with significant trade with the East including China.

Monterrey, Saltillo, Veracruz, and Tampico have for decades held close ties with the United States. Shopping trips to Texas cities have always been common, and wealthier Mexicans use medical facilities in Houston and San Antonio. It is traditional to have children acquire college educations, particularly in the United States.

The Border
The United States and Mexico share a 2,000 mile border with more than half, or about 1,200 miles, between Texas and Mexico. There are four Mexican Border States across from Texas: Chihuahua, Coahuila, Nueva Leon, and Tamaulipas. The prism to understanding much of Mexico and its relationship to United States lies in the four states (Arizona, California, New Mexico, Texas) of the American Southwest, the primary one

being Texas. The singularity of Texas resides in the nature of the border between Texas and Mexico, the adjoining Mexican states, and the history of that border region. The history of this region in both countries provides the context to understand the region today.

Examining a map of the two countries along the region where they meet advances an understanding of the border between the United States and Mexico. From the far western edge in California where San Diego and Tijuana are about 20 miles apart, the border extends eastward until one reaches the Gulf of Mexico and the cities of Brownsville and Matamoros separated only by a narrow band of water, the Rio Grande.

It is useful to think of the metaphor of geology and think of two large tectonic plates that are colliding at the Texas-Mexico border. The northern plate is the United States and the southern plate is Mexico, with the Rio Grande as the subduction zone where the two plates collide. Energies from this collision then radiate both north and south for at least 200 miles. Such a metaphor helps us to understand that cities like Houston, San Antonio and Austin in the United States and Matamoros, Monterrey, Durango, and Chihuahua in Mexico experience the perturbations from these collisions. The border is a zone about 400 miles wide, 200 miles south into Mexico and 200 miles north into the States.

The land is a high arid desert ecology that does not permit intensive agriculture, but rather is best used for grazing sheep and cattle (Dale, 1960; Graham, 2003; Jackson, 1986). The one exception is the region along the Gulf Coast, which can have heavy rainfall and is often exposed to hurricane-based storms. Because of the ecology, historically the population has been sparse, but the pull of the markets of the States has changed that centuries-old reality of large ranches and small villages in the last 30 years. The entire 200-mile zone on either side today has between 20 and 30 million people with almost all in urban areas. Far higher wages exist on the United States side, incurring continual Mexican migrations to the north. Indeed more than ever in its history northern Mexico is oriented toward the United States like the needle of a compass to its north pole.

Ties with the both sides are even deeper in the "twin cities" that extend in the east from Brownsville and Matamoros through El Paso and Ciudad Juarez, and to a lesser degree San Diego and Tijuana. The Mexicans refer to this zone as "La Frontiera." It is a transition zone between the two cultures, clearly neither Mexican nor American. With its rapid growth and access to the rest of North America, it may be the most rapidly changing part of North America.

Border Populations

The relations are most intense and complex on the Texas border as compared to New Mexico's, Arizona's and California's. Well-to-do Mexicans own homes on Padre Island or in the southern mountains of New Mexico. Houston and San Antonio with their university medical schools provide high quality health expertise to Mexican clients. Shopping visits include trips to malls in Houston, San Antonio, Austin, and Dallas. For more than 50 years Mexicans have kept bank accounts in the border states to protect against periodic weakness in the Mexican peso. Until the wars of the drug cartels began in the last 6 years, there were steady flows of shoppers and vacationers from states like Texas and California to border cities, the Mexican Gulf, the Pacific Coast, and far down the state of Baja California.

Indeed those Mexicans of the north are called *Norteños* and known for their lack of subtlety, their aggressiveness and more abrupt ways. Their skills with the land and the cattle they imported from Spain created the *vaquero* that, in turn, became the basis of the American cowboy. American notions of the

West with personal characteristics of independence, openness, entrepreneurial effort, and distrust of distant formal authority find resonance in the north of Mexico and produce a continual concern in Mexico City that America will again grab a piece of Mexico as it did in the 19th century. These fears are made real with the Americanizing influence of the *maquilas*, the power of American media, the waning riches of oil, and the new centers of power provided by the lucrative illegal drug trade to America.

Contraband: Threat to the Border Region
Since the 1980s, much of western Mexico has become a contested land as cocaine, methamphetamines, marijuana, and heroin are moved by land, air and the sea into the United States. These narcotics powers began to be evident in the 1970s, especially in the western state of Sinaloa where its capital, Culiacan, became headquarters for packaging marijuana and opium grown in its remote mountainous valleys and cocaine brought up the west coast for shipment into the United States.

Even as the United States was successfully disturbing the Caribbean drug route into Miami, a far larger and more sophisticated system of drug production and distribution was growing across the northern states and cities of Mexico. A similar pattern exists along the Gulf. Major entry points are at the twin cities, with Laredo and El Paso perhaps the largest. These gateways or plazas that are the bridges between the cities are the zones where competing cartels seek to control access to move illegal drugs to the north and dollars and guns back into the south.

Frequently, both Mexico City and Washington, D.C. write off the battles of the drug cartels and the growing brutality as a continuation of the wild and degraded nature of the border cities. Mexico City has never been in favor of these cities, as they have been seen simply as embarrassing tourist spots to serve the more base nature of the Gringos. They have also been long a source of concern as they represent a not so subtle incursion of American ways into Mexico. What this misses, with its view of the violence as a law enforcement matter, is that the extent, duration and brutality are now a challenge to the existence of the Mexican state itself.

The American response of bringing to bear its federal resources, including the military and the recent use of terms such as "surge," are redolent of American efforts in Iraq and Afghanistan. Northern Mexico or all of Mexico is not Iraq. In Mexico and certainly in northern Mexico and the American southwest are 500 years of contact and mutual trade. Men in armored vehicles wearing military uniforms and masks will not solve the problem. Soldiering and policing are two very different tasks, and to mistake one for the other can lead to disaster.

The problems derive from the failure of economic and civic development on the Mexican side. The distance and misunderstandings of Mexico City for its northern areas are part of the reason. The drug appetite of the American side is another part of the reason. Today the United States is dependent upon Mexico for oil imports. Mexico is dependent upon the United States for food imports. The drug violence tells us more of the failure of understanding and leadership of both sides than simply the failure of policing. This is an important and distressing development and we examine it more fully later.

Summary: Four Regions
Mexico is a country with four widely different regions. Mexico City is the cultural and power center. For five hundred years it has sought to centralize trade, business leadership, union controls, education, government, travel and media in Mexico City. Mexico City elites pride the City in its refinements and similarity to other world cities such as Paris, Rome New York City or Buenos Aires. Because of its wealth and services it is a magnet for the poor from Mexico as well as the ambitious

hoping to build a better life. With 25 million in the City and suburbs, all atop a volcanic active zone it has a precarious nature. A hundred kilometers south of Mexico City the Mexico of two hundred years ago continues. It is a region of Indian villages, communal lands, agricultural and fishing subsistence. North and west of Mexico City are the shipping ports on the Pacific feeding the global trade to Asia as well as important growing areas of tropical fruits and vegetables both for Mexico City and for export to the United States and Canada. To the northeast are important fisheries and the more important Gulf oil deposits and the Pemex refineries of Veracruz. The coasts are trade areas and the interior is one of mining, lumbering and ranching. The fourth region is the Border. It appears 200 miles south of the border with the United States and it a region of change for Mexico, perhaps the area of greatest change.

Chapter 9: Globalization: Surprises for Mexico

Globalization in several forms has been a dominant theme at times in the world since Cyrus, the Great of Persia, Alexander of Greece and later, the Romans, all empires, which pushed far from home to distant lands. In more recent times--since 1648--globalization was driven by the colonial powers of Europe. Late in the 20th century international capitalism as well as technological advances, and the search for cheaper resources including labor generated globalization. This phase of globalization is likely ending as plentiful oil and other resources critical for industrialized societies become less cheap, and with the United States spread thin with foreign responsibilities and mounting debts far less able to police the globe. Yet the impact of globalization continues to play out with unforeseen events. Some of those that first affect the American Southwest and Mexican Border are examined. These events will force new directions upon the United States. The directions chosen are not clear but what is chosen will have a substantial impact on the nation and its neighbors.

Expanding beyond one's borders is a recurrent theme among cultures of the world. Archeologists and researchers exploring the human genome think that *Homo sapiens* began in east Africa hundreds of thousands of years in the past and then migrated over tens of thousands of years through Africa, east into Asia and west into Europe. As early as 30,000 years ago and then again 10,000 years ago, there were migrations over the Bering Straits from Asia into Alaska, and those populations spread across North and South America.

A distinctly different form of migration over the globe began with the formation of cities and associated intensive farming cultures that used their created wealth and power to subdue other cultures. This was no longer a simple migration but movement into and control of new territory and people. Persia is thought to have been one of the first, then the Greeks and Rome, perhaps the greatest of antiquity. These entities spread their influence and often their control over other groups of people in an early example of globalization. Other ancient cultures engaged in limited dominance over others would include several dynasties in Asia, Africa and in North and South America. In all, the thrust of the global—or at least the relative—dominance activity came from the state itself.

Nation-States and the Impact of Globalism

After the decline of Rome in the 400s global powers were less evident, at least in Europe. But as the Dark Ages waned, the opening of the Silk Road and the desire for silk, tea, spices, china, tobacco, cotton, and other trade items spurred nascent global interests in Europe again. Like their antecedents, the initiative came from the state, though business interests were present such as the Great East India Company, Hudson's Bay Company and other English, French, Dutch, Spanish, and Portuguese enterprises involved in shipping as well as fur trapping and mining between Europe, Asia and finally the New World. The globalization that began with European hegemony from the Peace of Westphalia in 1646 saw a succession of nation states: Portugal, Spain, Netherlands, France, and England establish colonies in Asia, the Americas and Africa, and created the concept of the developed and undeveloped or underdeveloped world. That serial process among European nation-states exercising colonial dominance in the less developed world ended with World War I, resulting in a bipolar world with two superpowers and allied states arrayed against each other. One superpower, the United States, had a lower level of state involvement and control relative to the private sector and the lives of individuals. The other superpower bloc was first Germany allied primarily with Italy and Japan and then the Soviet Union, Eastern Europe and China. Both alliances had greater state participation and control throughout the society than did the American.

Modern consumerist nation states with large middle classes like the United States, Japan, Great Britain, France, South Korea, Canada, and Germany developed during the 20th century and have attributes that make them different than what they were in the 19th century, or other contemporary nations of today like Russia, China, India, Venezuela or Mexico. Germany, the last of the European colonial powers, came to nation-state conditions much later than England, France, Spain, Holland, or Portugal through the efforts of Otto von Bismarck in the last quarter of the 19th century. Through a variety of offices he welded the many separated kingdoms, cities and principalities of the Germanic Tribes north of France into a nation-state. Bismarck used public school systems to create a common language and understanding of cultural principles, and advanced the concept of the responsibilities and rewards of citizenship through the creation of programs of old age assistance and health and accident insurance. Strengthening public and higher education, he laid the basis for extraordinary advances in science by Germany in the 20th century and provided the most complete model of the welfare state (Bobbitt, 2003). Thirty years later in the 1930s, many of these state innovations were then adopted by other European countries as well as the United States and Japan.

Differences Associated With Modern Welfare States

The differences associated with such modern welfare states include higher per capita incomes, greater educational levels, more advanced physical infrastructure, better health, clear definitions of citizenship, and social welfare supports. Citizenship is defined by the state and typically includes rights and prerogatives such as voting, a national language and a court system. It includes state support and direction in education, health care, unemployment, and aging services. The systems of education, employment, language, taxation, and welfare are intended to create a common consensus of identity among the population. Income distribution is more even as compared to non-consumerist states, and relatively less income is spent on food and shelter with more available for non-essentials such as entertainment, travel and education. These civic advances pioneered by Bismarck in Germany greatly strengthen the state, its economy and the lives of the citizen. Per capita income rises, health and longevity improves, and in times of war larger, more capable armies can be deployed.

Relations between such states and those of the less developed world have grown much more complex throughout the 20th century (Wallerstein, 1982, 2004). In effect much of the third world becomes a client of first world states, providing raw materials and low cost labor. Those third world states do not develop advanced systems in areas such as manufacturing and education and are dependent upon the first world or hegemonic states for those products and services. Such relations are illustrated by those between Mexico and the United States.

A Different Globalization

A heightened notion of globalization coincided with the collapse of the Soviet Union and the ascendancy of American-style capitalism and democracy at the end of the 20th century. Advances in transportation, the Internet, computerized credit, stock and commodity markets, and peoples' perceptions made this globalization possible. It saw the opening of China and markets in India and Southeast Asia, and greater competition in markets for products and labor. It promised freer north-south trade in the Americas and general prosperity. It was additionally remarkable in the extent that much of the initiative came from global business interests, not just the designs of a nation-state.

In some ways the development of the European Common Market spurred Canada, the United States and Mexico to consider a similar arrangement for North America. Some European thinkers saw the far cheaper labor costs that existed in southern and eastern Europe as a potential resource to off-load portions of the high cost of their manufactured products by using this large pool of low cost labor. Germany especially was oriented toward being an export-driven economy and was concerned with competition from Asia for manufactured products. While Japan and Taiwan have substantial labor costs, those countries' ability to tap the high unemployment, underemployment and associated low wages in Southeast Asia, India and China sent shudders through much of Europe. The evolving Common Market was seen as a mechanism for tapping nearby low cost labor to survive in an emerging global economy.

This was coupled with the concept of "just in time manufacturing" where manufacturers utilized the comparatively cheap cost of oil-based transportation to hold very low inventories of raw materials at the manufacturing site. Then, the factory would utilize the transportation system to bring in the raw materials as orders appeared for the manufactured product. This reduced the amount of capital that would be tied up in raw inventory, thereby enhancing profits. As communication systems improved both within countries and across countries, manufacturers also found that not only could they avoid holding large amounts of raw materials, but they could also "out-source" some of the components in a manufactured item.

Rather than simply acquiring raw materials like metal ores, wood or plastics, the manufacturer would acquire components, actually specifying manufacturing standards of components and start a process of "out-sourcing" components and then doing the final assembly near the purchaser.

This example helps to illustrate the "out-sourcing" process. Early in the 1980s several garage tinkerers began to use the new integrated computer chips coming from manufacturers like Texas Instrument and Intel, placing them on small circuit boards and creating "homebrew computers." Several brands began to get traction and the Apple II was among them. After two or three years this fad began to get the attention of main line computer companies such as IBM, Control Data, NCR, Honeywell, and other names no longer extant. IBM doubted the fad would become a trend, but to safeguard a position in this new market, they set up a quiet operation in Boca Raton, Florida, far from its main manufacturing sites, to prepare a desktop computer. One of the components in the desktop computer was a device to read data and programs, a floppy disk mechanism. Rather than building their own factory to create floppy disk mechanisms, IBM turned to Control Data, a company that was building these devices for their own machines. In the 1970s Control Data built the mechanisms in Minneapolis-St Paul. Its labor costs ran about $50 an hour, including the wages to the employee, contributions to insurance, company overhead, and taxes. Sometime in the early 1980s, Control Data moved much of this manufacturing to the Dallas area where it cut these costs in half to between $20 and $25 an hour.

IBM misjudged the importance and size of the desktop computer market and it exploded as IBM brought its desktop, the PC, to market. It increased its contracts with Control Data for floppy mechanisms and Control Data looked to expand its factory. IBM was selling as many of its PCs as it could manufacture.

More Observations from a Visit To An Early *Maquila*

A small factory I visited in the summer of 1986 along an alley on an unpaved street three miles south of downtown Juarez showed me an early view of the *maquila* concept. The factory was in an old cinder block building and had two assembly lines running with equipment brought across the Rio Grande from the States. Work stations on these assembly lines were completely filled with young Mexican women from 15 to 25 years of age. I talked with one of the American owners (then the *maquilas* would have joint Mexican and American owners) of the factory and he said that all of the "girls" came from small towns and ranches in rural Chihuahua. They had come to the big city to have jobs rather than be mothers and housewives in some isolated, small dusty village. The women were dressed in new designer jeans and brightly colored blouses.

When I asked them about their work they spoke excitedly about the future and that they would not be trapped with children in poverty in some distant village. They spoke of missing family but felt like they were building a better world than their mothers and sisters who had not come to the city. When I asked them about dating and how their fathers and brothers and boyfriends felt about this new life, they became a bit guarded. Some of the more outspoken would say that Mexican men were too demanding, and they would have independent lives that their mothers never had. A few would note that married men would often have a younger girlfriend outside of marriage and they did not intend to get caught with that kind of marriage. Media from the states and now individual employment was bringing the "women's' movement" to Mexico. Clearly these *maquila* women would never be the Mexican women of their mothers' generation.

They chatted animatedly and worked quickly as the line moved computer mechanism components along, the same mechanisms being built that I had seen at a Control Data factory in St. Paul and then in a later visit in Arlington, Texas. When we sat down in the management offices I told the Mexican partner I had seen the same items manufactured in other sites in the States and asked him how his workers' productivity compared to those in Arlington or St. Paul. He said they were about half as productive but improving. He said one of the problems was that "the girls drink too much coffee in the morning and then have to stop the assembly line when they need to go to the bathroom." He said that the company now provides breakfast at the factory and works to limit the amount of coffee drunk. He also said that by Mexican Federal law, management is required to provide six months of paid leave if a female employee is or becomes pregnant. He explained that they had a female physician on staff that provided medical exams including assistance in birth control. He said that they gave exams upon hiring and avoided hiring pregnant women. I asked what the full hourly labor costs were per employee including wages paid to the worker, taxes and insurance. He said with pride that they were 50 cents an hour per employee. The employee was paid 35 cents and there were 15 cents for taxes, overhead and insurance. I ran the math in my head: 50 dollars an hour in St. Paul, then 20-25 dollars an hour in Arlington and now 50 cents an hour in Juarez! This meant no more jobs in either American city making computer components, and that the *maquilas* of Mexico would explode in number.

None knew the consequences this globalism would have for either country, including workers, and what it would mean for some of the lives of these young women drawn from rural homes to the big city on the border. Border life is very different from growing up in the interior of either country. Identity and social conflict are greatly increased at the margins between cultures.(Lâopez-Stafford, 1996; Paredes, 1958) It surely included a great change with far more freedom, financial independence and mobility than has ever been true for lower income Mexican women. Postponing marriage and children and shopping at the malls in El Paso would likely make them far different women than their mothers and they might be unsettling to their male peers. When I asked the managers of *maquilas* why I always saw a significant preponderance of female employees the answer was that women would follow directions better. The males were not compliant to the requirements of factory work. They did not follow orders well and were poor team members. This spoke volumes about the readiness of Mexico to make the jump to factory work. The arithmetic would be compelling for manufacturers, but few knew the consequences for the lives of these young Mexicans now becoming factory workers (Fuentes, 1996).

The developing tensions that factory work provided were sharply illustrated for me in a conversation with a Tijuana taxicab driver. I had flown in from Mexico City with Mexican Federal colleagues. As we headed to the meeting site, I chatted with the driver and asked if there were new *maquilas* in Tijuana, as I had visited several in Juarez. His mood noticeably shifted and he replied darkly that both his oldest daughter and wife worked at a plant that assembled auto parts. He said that they had much more money but his family did not respect him and that his daughter felt she should not turn her earnings to him but keep them for her uses. Aspects of that gender conflict are another one of the sad stories particularly of Juarez (Hill, 2010; Staudt, 2009.) and the changing roles of both sexes in Mexico. Dozens of bodies of young women have been discovered in Juárez as the maquilas developed and young women moved to the city. Few of the murders are ever solved.

Platform Companies
The arithmetic of global manufacturing has transformed many companies. Some manufacturers such as Nokia in Finland and

Dell and Apple in the United States moved toward becoming "platform companies" that did design work in the home country and then crafted a web of suppliers and transporters across the globe, always searching for the cheapest combination of raw materials, including manufactured components. At the retail level rather than manufacturing, Wal-Mart has a similar strategy. Such platform companies are very nimble and hugely profitable. They choose their multiple locations across the globe with an eye to where their markets are, the relative tax benefits in any jurisdiction, and multiple sources of supply for raw materials, components and labor. They are nearly immune to organized labor, which might pressure for higher wages and benefits, as much of the labor force is not where the corporate home is. Moreover, by using an out-sourcing model, if labor problems start to occur in one manufacturing site, they move assembly to a different labor market in another part of the country or to a different country (Uchitelle, 2009. July 21,).

Thus the "platform company" has the world as its oyster once it identifies or creates a market for its wares. Unencumbered with commitments and attachment to the local community, it sees itself as a citizen of the world free to roam to its advantage. The home, manufacturing and assembly sites are chosen with regard to relative labor costs, freedom from government restrictions, and lower taxation levels. Advances in communications, transportation and factory manufacturing make this new creature of globalization possible. It thwarts organized labor by being able to move its manufacturing away from situations where labor organizes. It thwarts environmental controls on manufacturing and resource mining by moving to areas where it finds less restrictive governments. It thwarts taxation by declaring its profits in subsidiaries in no and low tax havens. Unlike traditional farming and heavy industry, it is not tied to a specific location. Consequently, it moves the balance of power between itself and the state, much in the direction of the company. Part of the characteristics of the new globalization is the greater relative power of the global company and its ability to get various states to "bid" for its presence.

There are inherent flaws in the platform model in terms of the cost of transportation, the impact on the low cost provider countries, the domestic labor market of the home country, the enhanced power of "public service unions," control of intellectual property (Barboza, 2009), the middle class, and the local currency (Olson, 1982), but little of this was seen or understood in the opening years of the 21st century. Out-sourcing and perhaps the platform company became the model for world capitalism. Where it thrives, competition must take a similar form or perish.

Response to Globalization Pressures-NAFTA

Some features in North America make it ripe for such arrangements as this new sort of globalism provides. Canada has rich fisheries and vast and still untapped resources in petroleum, natural gas and many other minerals. It lacks manpower, access to world markets and capital. Mexico has substantial natural resources and extensive manpower. It lacks many forms of capital including educational, physical and world class manufacturing expertise. Other countries in Central America have similar conditions to those in Mexico, though they are much less developed. The United States has the world's best system of higher education, sophisticated networks of capital development, and deployment through banks, brokerages, and markets. It has world class manufacturing expertise but is hampered by high labor costs and increased depletion of natural resources in petroleum and minerals. A North American common market was visualized by the elites of business enterprise and government that would combine strengths and weaknesses of the countries in North America to face the powerful juggernaut of globalization. The response in the Americas is the North American Free Trade Agreement-NAFTA.

The ending years of the 20ᵗʰ century saw experiments across the globe in freer movements of capital, labor and ideas, and the United States was an intellectual and political leader in much of this activity including that on the North American continent. The United States-Mexico border provides a field laboratory to examine some of the effects of globalization, particularly at the margin of a hegemonic state and a low cost provider of labor and some raw materials, especially petroleum.

The Clash of Cultural Tectonic Plates

Borders between great societies are not narrow political or geographical lines but are often zones that shade back toward the core of each society. Metaphorically they are like the zones that are created when two of earth's tectonic plates meet and collide. Much of California resides on top of such an east-west zone where the Pacific Plate meets the North American Plate. As these two great slabs of earth and rock that float on molten substrata meet and grind against each other they generate immense pressures, produce upwellings that create mountains, plastic flows of volcanic magma, and quakes. Living in these zones is often exciting, unpredictable and sometimes dangerous. One zone created by these two tectonic plates extends from Alaska to South America. In the last thirty years it has generated powerful pulses, such as the great earthquakes in Alaska, San Francisco and Mexico City, that exceeded both the human ability to predict or control.

Such conditions also describe the social and cultural zone that extends about 200 miles to the south and north of the international boundary between Mexico and the United States, with about two-thirds of the distance of the entire border formed by the Rio Grande River. These two countries can be seen as two cultural tectonic plates pushing against each other along the Rio Grande and then west through the desert from El Paso to San Diego. Quakes do occur along this cultural tectonic, and in the last year on the Mexican side Nuevo Laredo, Juarez and Tijuana have been epicenters of such social quakes, leading to very high levels of social disruption, violence and death.

Border Zones and Change

Using another analogy, this time from biology: when two species come into contact at a border, heavy stresses occur in the margin zone. This zone is where the greatest rate of competition, innovation and adaptation is found. Biologists observe that speciation change is the result of the competitive pressures as well as the environmental differences when life is on the margins.

Contact in border zones between cultures has similar consequences. The contact can be very beneficial. The success of ranching in the west was first an innovation for arid lands created by Spanish and Mexican experiments with raising cattle including importing breeds that adapted to these lands. Ranching techniques including the cowboy derived from the Mexican vaquero and other skills associated with free ranging cattle in the demanding climate. American foodstuffs today include tomatoes, beans, corn, and chilies that originated south of the American-Mexican border. Centers of higher education were established in Mexico City a hundred years before colleges in New England, and Catholic orders including the Augustinians, Franciscans, Dominicans and Jesuits spread written languages among Indians of Mexico long before such education efforts were common in the eastern United States. The Spanish crown created highways, a Camino Real, which became patterns for highways and railroads in the American Southwest two hundred years later, with the evidence reaching San Antonio in Texas, Santa Fe in New Mexico and San Francisco in California.

Americans have similarly affected Mexicans and the effects are most notable in the north of Mexico where English is commonly spoken and there are strong spirits of individualism, entrepreneurship and even lavish shows of personal accomplishment. Independence and greater interest in civic actions are more common in the northern states of Mexico. Factories, shopping centers and electronic media with an emphasis on entertainment that shows the influence of Hollywood today permeate all of Mexico.

Cultures are fundamental rules and patterns of behavior developed from contact with the environment and other cultures. The Border Lands are the zones where the rates of change and innovation are the highest. They are lands of innovation, beauty and violence.

Major Changes in Both Countries as Part of the Globalization Process

Since the 1980s great changes have been underway in each society that have altered each and now are generating pressures that are flowing out of the collision zone between the two great cultural plates. From 1980 the United States has seen the collapse of the Soviet Union but not an easing of the burden of maintaining large standing military forces at many points in the world. The country is engaged in active wars in the Middle East and still bears heavy military obligations in Europe and Asia. The U.S. has "status of force" agreements with more than 90 countries, spending billions to maintain its position as the sole superpower on the globe. It has, furthermore, undergone great shifts in its economy, moving from a manufacturing nation to one that imports much of its manufactured needs.

The shifts away from manufacturing are remarkable. "Today the United States ranks behind every industrial nation except France in the percentage of overall economic activity devoted to manufacturing — 13.9 percent, the World Bank reports, down 4 percentage points in a decade" (NY Times, 2009). The four-year recession from late 2007 to 2012 has contributed noticeably to this decline. Industrial production has fallen 17.3

percent, the sharpest drop during a recession since the 1930s, and similar comparisons are available when levels of unemployment are calculated.

Service sector jobs have been replacing jobs in manufacturing. These jobs range from ones in banking, brokerage, and finance that pay amounts running into millions of dollars yearly for the wage earner to jobs in food service and retailing. Unfortunately most of the jobs in the service sector are not the sort found in high finance, but rather they are at or near the minimum wage and offer few or no benefits, including those for health care and retirement.

Initially the economic crisis in the first decade of the 21st century seemed to be about houses that did not sell. It has broadened. With Americans experiencing the longest periods of unemployment after losing a job since the 1950s, and with many high school and college graduates facing the prospects of few employment opportunities while seniors postpone retirements or are forced back to work, the economic crisis is being felt across the nation. It is more than likely the result of systemic changes in the American and world economy, including higher general levels of unemployment and generation of more jobs with lower levels of pay and benefits. Such a pattern has, however, been developing since 1970 with incomes flat to down for 40 years when corrected for inflation.

Mexico's Efforts to Build a Different Economy
Mexico's social changes since 1980 have been to fully urbanize and attempt to develop an economy that is industrial rather than agricultural. For much of the 20th century Mexico was a land of small villages and subsistence farming; yet the nation was self-sufficient in food production. However, decisions made as early as the 1930s changed the fundamentals of Mexican society and economy. In the 1930s Mexico expropriated foreign ownership

of oil production and flirted with alliances with Germany during World War II.

Driving some of Mexico's foreign policy in the 19th and 20th centuries was a fear of conflict with the United States and action by the States to appropriate Mexican land or to conduct military actions, such as those that had occurred in 1846, 1854, 1914 and 1917. Mexican leadership felt that its northern states, with their sparse population, were particularly vulnerable, and national policies were created to subsidize food and medical costs to encourage population growth. In poverty and rural climes where most work is agricultural and poor health conditions mean high infant mortality and shorter lifetimes, high birth rates are needed for the survival of family units and the society. Industrialization and increased educational levels are usually accompanied by far smaller family sizes along with decreases in morbidity and mortality.

The fact that reduction in family size did not occur in Mexico as industrialization and urbanization increased was partially because of this national policy consideration to create a much more populous country. Mexico's leaders felt that larger populations especially in its northern states would thwart American expansionist intentions into Mexican lands, and would make occupation difficult if they were attempted. This resulted in rapid population increases in Mexico, and by 1980 the median population age was under 20. Mexico moved from a country of about 30 million in 1960 to 115 million today, far outstripping the ability of the society to provide education, jobs, health care, and homes. Exploding populations and urbanization are two of the most important narratives of the Mexican experience in the last 50 years.

Texas shares a 1,200-mile border with Mexico that has a dozen legal border crossing points and a thousand that only the locals know. Trade is an important part of the crossings and has many old patterns and several newer ones. Among the older patterns are cow-calf outfits that move young animals born and raised on Mexican ranches across the border to be fattened and slaughtered for urban markets in Texas and then to the West and Midwest. Cheaper land and labor costs in Mexico makes this a viable business. Mexico does not have substantial grain harvests to "fat finish" cattle, thus a few months in a feedlot in the grain-growing areas of Texas and the Midwest materially improves the meat for the American market. A less known aspect of the business is the trade back into Mexico of raw hides from Texas feedlots into states such as Leon in central Mexico. There, large leather processing industries turn the hides into items like shoes, belts, jackets, and purses for French and Italian high-dollar brands that sell in the most exclusive stores in Rome, Paris, Tokyo, New York City, Dallas, and San Francisco.

Field labor, as it has for decades, crosses from Mexico in the lower Valley to work citrus, onion, peppers, and tomato fields and then north into the Midwest for other agricultural harvests including berries and apples. This is seasonal labor with migrants returning to Mexican farms and villages as well as South Texas in the winter. Invariably some stay in the United States working in meat processing, restaurants, hotels, yard care and other occupations with low skill levels or no or limited union rules to restrict immigrant employment. These are the 10 to 12 million Mexicans that become Mexican-Americans.

Several factors began to change this rhythm of trade between Mexico and Texas starting in the 1980s. One derived from the creation of OPEC in the 1970s as the United States moved from a net oil exporter to an importer. It was the first worldwide warning of Peak Oil and the slow shift from a century of dropping prices for all natural resources (including food and water) to one of rising prices. Coupled with this awareness of growing scarcity of oil was the discovery of a very large oil field in the Bay of Campeche off Veracruz in the Gulf of Mexico. While oil had been produced in Mexico since the 1920s, this new discovery was a giant and appeared to rank Mexico with Saudi Arabia in terms of promising oil reserves that could fuel prosperity in Mexico for generations.

Opening of the Political Process

The final change of great consequence was the opening of political process with the timid initiation of a civic space to discuss alternatives in political leaders and parties (Castenada, 2011; Contreras, 2012; Fuentes, 1996). Since the late 1920s there has been only one political party in Mexico, The Party of the Institutionalized Revolution (PRI). There were local, state and national elections. But at the national level the PRI candidate always won. That candidate for the Presidency and for many other offices was selected every six years in a highly opaque process within the PRI. The PRI and the state were the same and the state owned everything, including large businesses such as oil production, railroads, airlines, telephones, utilities, and television, and controlled the unions in all sectors. The political change that occurred was the capture of the Presidency by Vicente Fox of the PAN. PAN, the National Action Party, traces back to the Cristeros Revolt in the 1920s, which sought to reverse the 1910 Revolution and was long reviled by the PRI as a predatory Catholic machine intended to return the Mexican middle class to peasants requiring priests and caudillos to lead them. The campaign of 2000 and the loss of the Presidency from the PRI was the first experience of electoral choice in more than a hundred years.

Summary: Globalization Surprises

Globalization has engendered increased wealth but has been a catalyst for many unexpected things. One is a restiveness among Mexicans for the nation to address the extremes of wealth. Two is expectations for election alternatives and honest and fair elections. Three is exposure to foreign corporations of ideas and horizons new to Mexico. Four is a complex of ideas about what Mexico should become.

Chapter 10: The Soul of 20ᵗʰ Century Mexico-The PRI

To understand the Mexico of today we must examine the history of Mexican politics. For decades the PRI (The Party of the Institutionalized Revolution) maintained a vertical grip from remote villages up to Los Pinos, the Mexican White House. At the local level some towns would have a designated "red light district" where contraband was available, including prostitutes, drugs and gambling. Operators would "license" the business through the local PRI representative or, in some cases, law officer. The law and the PRI were often indistinguishable. To get almost anything accomplished in Mexico required somehow including the PRI. Larger businesses such as the telephone, television, energy and water utilities, railroads, and airlines were simply government-owned enterprises. The most profitable then and still today is Pemex, the oil production, refining and retailing monopoly. The human service fields including teaching, health care, and hotel and restaurant workers are controlled by unions and part of the PRI structure.

This control of the state began in the 1930s and reached its zenith in the 1980s. The PRI functioned much like the Central Committee did during the years of the Soviet Union. Elites in

Mexico City determined who the Presidential Candidate would be around the 4th or 5th year of the current President's term. Families and their associates would jockey to move one of their own forward. The candidate would typically have substantial education in elite Mexican universities, and frequently have a degree from the United States as well. In some cases the wealthy would advance one of their own for candidacy, but more frequently they would designate a rising star from government. A frequent route to the presidency was to leave Mexico City and become a governor in an adjoining state and then return for a senior post in a state enterprise, government office or political post. A similar process occurred in each of Mexico's thirty-one states. Often the more populous cities would provide a route to become a mayor and then a governor. That was more often a possibility in states more distant from Mexico City, as those states next to or near the Federal District were more likely to have gubernatorial candidates coming from Mexico City. In most cases the control of Mexico City was clear and as final as it had been for hundreds of years, at least as far back as the Aztec era.

All power in Mexico existed in Mexico City. All roads led to Mexico City as did air routes, telephone lines and power. At the center of the web, from 1929 to 2000, was the PRI.

Changes Coming

Beginning in the 1960s, several forces began to demand change and to lessen the control of the centralized Mexican government. One was simply the need to make the society more productive and innovative with less of the ossification and cronyism associated with a centralized system. A second was the increased awareness of the Mexican population, especially the emerging middle class, that the United States, Europe and Japan, all with higher standards of living, accomplished some of those standards via a more open marketplace of ideas than could occur in the fixed political arrangements of Mexico. Mexico was also influenced by the collapse of the Berlin Wall and then the Soviet Union in 1991, a paradigm of a command and control economy much as Mexico was. Forces that radiated in Europe, Asia and North America had powerful impacts in Mexico. Some of the forces came from advances in transportation and communication that permitted people to compare their lives with others elsewhere on the globe, This coupled with young, growing populations in many countries no longer scarred by World War II and increasingly the emergence of youth cultures weakened traditional ties in country after country. The result in Mexico was a renewed experiment with electoral democracy. The appearance of the PAN election, a conservative party in some ways with strengths in northern Mexico yet also one calling for free elections, and the decline of the PRI was also the beginning of an increase in private groups creating enterprises, rather than the Mexican State and the PRI.

The First Democratic Current Since the 1910 Revolution

Visible political change began to occur in northern Mexico in border cities like Juarez during the 1980s and 1990s. The city long closely tied to El Paso began to develop political practices influenced by American thought, including having several candidates, open elections, and a marketplace of ideas, candidates and political parties. The mayor in 1983, Francisco Barrio, was the first PAN mayor in Juarez and indeed of any major Mexican city. He later became the Governor of the state of Chihuahua. Other large landowners in border cities became attracted to the changing regulatory relationships between Mexico and the United States and began to build *maquilas* (assembly plants) that could use cheaper Mexican labor to assemble items for duty-free export into the United States. Jaime Burmudez, one of those landowners, became a leader in building these plants and served as Juarez Mayor after Barrio. Though he was aligned with the PRI, his ties in El Paso accelerated an electoral process in Mexico that drew from American culture, including having some level of competition among candidates and parties. He also supported the existence of a far larger private sector, as compared to the public sector.

A PAN President

By 2000 the climate in Mexico had moved strongly away from the appointed Presidential candidate of ten decades of the PRI rule, and for the first time an alternative party, the PAN, mounted a strong campaign and elected the President, Vicente Fox. Fox and his PAN successor, President Felipe Calderon, would break the old arrangements of petty crime, organized crime and perhaps, in time, political ties with the wealthy oligarchy of Mexico.

The result of the PAN election was part of a civic revolution in Mexico, a revolution long delayed and thwarted (Krauze, 1990; Preston & Dillon, 2004). The civil changes began with the 1810 Revolution that overthrew Spanish control but failed to establish a democracy as Mexican patriots looked to the United States as a model. European powers Spain and France, large property owners and the Roman Catholic Church thwarted the Revolution and reasserted a Mexico as a powerless, peasant regime. Electoral reform came again in mid-century with the election of the only Mexican President from the indigenous population, the Indian Benito Juarez in 1858. For a few succeeding elections democracy flourished, but with Porfirio Diaz' election in 1876 until 1910, it retreated into a dictatorship with the Church and a few large landowners as partners in total control. By the start of the 20th century 90 percent of the population was in dire poverty, existing as peons on lands owned generations ago by their forebears, but now owned by less than a hundred families and the Catholic Church. The 1910 Revolution again was thwarted by the PRI, which restored a dictatorship and took control of the population under the guise of continuing the Revolution.

The PAN victory in 2000 was a renewed attempt of a culture trying to break free from oligarchic, dictatorial control. The victors inevitably came into conflict with many of the structures of the PRI, which included corruption in the government as well as criminal gangs in many areas of Mexico, especially in the northern cities near the American border.

Even greater cultural changes were ushered into Mexican society with the election of PAN's Vicente Fox to the Presidency of Mexico. In a burst of democratic participation, arguably the first since the mid 1850s, the oligarchy of the PRI appeared broken and Mexico looked forward to dynamic multiparty democracy for the first time since a brief period after the 1910 Revolution. Until Fox's election, for about 70 years, one party had controlled all of Mexico from Mexico City to the smallest village, and had powerful interests in most businesses. Even shadowy or illegal activities, such as gambling, prostitution and the drug trade, were felt to be at least partially under the control of the PRI.

At about the same time the United States elected a President from a western state that appeared to understand and have close friendships with Mexico, George W. Bush. Both Mexico and the United States felt that these two Presidents seemed to come from similar backgrounds, and this would promote favorable conditions and greater understanding between the two countries.

Since World War I, an activist east-west perspective has dominated foreign policy in the United States. Presidents and the Washington establishment were focused upon Eastern Europe, the Middle East and Asia and huge garrisons of military, trade and embassy personnel based around the world focused upon this perspective. Some people, especially Mexicans and to some extent Canadians, were hopeful that the United States would now, with the dawning of the 21st century, move to a greater focus upon a north-south perspective, with the possibility the United States might be looking as well toward South America.

Failed Hopes

Such hopes were not to be. Many Democrats viewed Bush's election, unlike Fox's, as a stolen election. For the first time in the history of the United States the election was not settled by counting votes but by a ruling of the Supreme Court. This event would prove to be a warning of deep divisions among the American people, and Bush took office with bitterness and distrust between the two parties. The dust had scarcely settled from the election when there was the strike on the Twin Towers in New York City in late 2001 by persons from the Middle East using commandeered passenger planes, killing over three thousand people. Thus whatever the potential promise of improved relations with Mexico might have been, President Bush's attention reverted to traditional concerns and moved to the Middle East, Europe and Asia, and American foreign policy returned to its historical neglect of Mexico.

Yet while American attention was directed to Afghanistan and Iraq, a growing cancer was exploding in Mexico. That cancer was the movement of drugs from South America through Mexico and into Texas, California and other border states. It was overshadowed by the Middle East during both the Bush and Obama administrations, until violence in Mexican border cities rising from 2006 to 2010 forced recognition of problems to the south.

Summary: Shifting Political Winds

The PRI is the fullest expression of the authoritarian tendencies in Mexican culture. At least since the ending days of the Aztec Empire authority was narrowly focused in Mexico City with a hereditary elite. Cortez replaced it with the authority of the Spanish Crown and the Roman Catholic Church. That rule continued until the 1800s when Mexico caught the notions of self-rule and democratic participation that was sweeping Europe and North America. Democratic processes continued until the election of Porofiro Diaz and then authoritarian rule was re-established with Diaz, a few large landholders and the Roman

Catholic Church. 1910 brought the great revolution of the 20 Century. The earliest leaders were seen as bandits from the north, Francisco "Pancho" Villa and the south, Emiliano Zapata. The revolution returned democratic traditions, brought apart the large landholdings and distributed them to the peon classes, removed wealth from the Roman Catholic Church and returned the priests and nuns back to the rectories and nunneries forbidding the wearing of clerical garb in public and running public schools. The Church attempted a restoration in the 1920s leading to the Cristero Revolt and ended with the singular party that sought to maintain all of the values of the revolution, the revolution was intended to be continuous and an institution. The Party was the only party in Mexico and controlled all institutions and large businesses. All power and direction flowed from Mexico City. The PRI has defined Mexico since 1929 and lost control of the nation for 12 years from 2000 to 2012. It has returned and seems to seek to establish the Mexico of the years before the PAN period. Time will tell if the PRI can put the genie of political freedom and choice back in the bottle.

Chapter 11: Boom to Bust

Since the summer of 2007, sharper calamitous events have been manifested in economies throughout the world. The events began with the popping of real estate bubbles in several states of the United States, and in Ireland, Iceland, and Spain as early as 2005, followed by the discovery of excessively leveraged financial institutions in these same countries. Soon it was evident that similar leverage problems in banks existed in Japan, most of Europe, Russia, China, and India. The leverage does not stop with banks but extends to millions of families, state and local governments, and many businesses. Since 2000, central banks, large investment pools and regions in nations and many nations have borrowed far beyond their ability to repay.

Real estate is a burden for more than 20 percent of all persons with mortgages, as that group has loans greater than the appraised value of the home. Loss of home valuations and drops of savings and retirement holdings have significantly decreased the wealth of most Americans.

Put simply, many parts of the developed world including American public, private organizations and families are finding that they have been living beyond their means with incomes or sales and tax receipts falling below expenditures. It is most visible in California where cities like Vallejo, Stockton, San Bernardino, and Compton have been forced to declare bankruptcy and others are approaching that status, and the state has been issuing IOU's (warrants) to individuals and companies as it furloughs state employees each month. Municipalities in other states (Defaults, 2011) are finding that revenues will not meet expenditures and recently Jefferson County, the site of Birmingham, Alabama has suggested it might follow its sewage district into bankruptcy. Equally visible is the situation in Michigan where two of the nation's most iconic manufacturers, General Motors and Chrysler were plunged into bankruptcy and are now being bailed out by the U. S. government. Both California (the world's 7th largest economy if measured against nations) and Michigan, formerly two of the most promising American states, now serve as a warning of decline and critical decisions that may likely be faced by all states and in time the federal government.

The overall result of these economic reversals has been the sharpest decline in worldwide economic activity and the most severe unemployment levels since the Great Depression. In America, federal bailouts have produced government involvement in the economy matched to levels reached during the Depression and World War II. Household and government budgets are on tenterhooks, and all income classes are facing difficulties.

These global events have had sharp repercussions in Mexico and along the Border. With official unemployment statistics in the United States now reported to be 9.5 percent (if part-time and discouraged workers are computed, the U.S. rate is close to 20 percent), far higher levels exist in Mexico. The collapse of Chrysler and General Motors has had dire consequences for northern Mexican cities like Monterrey and Saltillo where major assembly plants exist for these and other auto manufacturers to serve the American auto market. The *maquila* experiment may be moving into reverse.

Home and commercial construction across the United States as well as restaurant and food production jobs have been large absorbers of surplus Mexican labor and one of the fourth or fifth highest sources of foreign currency earnings for Mexico. Now those employment areas are shrinking rapidly, sending many workers back to Mexico where even fewer jobs exist. Earnings returned from workers in the United States, petroleum exports, assembly manufacturing, and tourism are four piers of the foundation of the Mexican economy.

In the popular mind in both Mexico and the United States, Mexico is a rural economy, but that has not been true for two decades. It is predominantly an urban and young society. Significantly, in the last two decades it has gone from an exporter of agriculture to a net food importer. No longer able to feed itself, Mexico must depend on foreign export earnings, which grow more and more problematic, to purchase food from growers in other countries. While Mexico does not have the heavy individual household and government debt levels of the United States, both countries face immense problems in generating sufficient jobs for their populations, and especially jobs that provide incomes beyond subsistence existence. These are the kind of jobs that can sustain the middle class and that are so important to the economic and cultural health of any nation.

The events today are comparable in Mexico only to the 1910 Revolution. There was spill over violence then. Initially the army of Pancho Villa hoped for support from the Americans. When it did not come, he replied by raiding into the United States, with his last excursion in Columbus, New Mexico in 1916. The American response was to send General John J. "Black Jack" Pershing into Mexico to capture and punish Villa.

America built in the 1890s and grew over the years a huge permanent fort on the border near El Paso, Ft. Bliss. Even in the 1950s some would suggest that IH-10 was part of a strategic resource to be able to move troops and material across the length of the 2,000-mile border with Mexico. But in those years Mexican cities along the border were small from 10,000 to 50,000, making it relatively easy to contain disorder trying to cross the Rio Grande. Today there are about 2 million Texans in border cities and ten times that in the Mexican cities on the border. It is far harder to contain the violence and the refugees today than in 1910.

Today the United States remains in a deep recession, and Mexico far deeper. Unemployment in the United States is greater than 10 percent, though official government reports peg it as just below 10, and the level in Mexico is higher, reaching 20 percent or more in some areas. In both countries there are concerns about the accuracy of such statistics.

These economic problems occur in the context of worldwide challenges. Europe's Common Market that emerged out of World War II and knit together countries that had warred among themselves for 400 years became a goal for many parts of the world. It effectively used the higher educated, wealthier and creative populations of northern Europe and the lower cost labor of southern Europe to achieve higher standards of living for all and develop a powerful export system. The strength of the system contributed to the collapse of the Soviet Union and provided a model that was developed by Japan and Taiwan with Korea, India and China as the low cost labor states. That model was the incentive for the development of NAFTA in North America. But the success of the Common Market has become undone with excessive personal and government spending and a flagging commercial sector. That seems to also be a problem in the United States, Japan and China. The slowing of consumer markets in the United States adds to the challenges faced in Mexico.

A Century Long Prologue

Since the winding down of the Mexico Revolution of 1910 by 1920, the United States has largely ignored its neighbor to the south. Content to focus upon national development and then the involvement in two World Wars and a long Cold War, the U.S. paid little attention to Mexico. One prominent exception was strong concerns during the 1930s and 1940s when President Lazaro Cárdenas expropriated many foreign oil and agricultural interests, including American ones, and flirted with the Nazis to counter threats of retaliation or military seizures from the United States and Great Britain.

There were in the last two to three decades occasional reverberations from the south of Mexico around conflicts of land ownership, particularly by impoverished Indians and the indigenous tribes of some regions, that reached the American consciousness. But by and large Mexico was a forgotten neighbor by the *Colossus of the North,* as Mexicans learned in public school to refer to the United States (Riding, 1988).

Texas, more than New Mexico, Arizona and California—the other three states that border Mexico—maintained an interest through trade, travel and many families with both Mexican and Texan sides. It was commonly said along the border that Mexicans would have children in the States to secure American citizenship and Texans would have a child born in Mexico to be able to own ranch and timber land there. Shared agricultural interests were always present, and during Prohibition Texans turned to Mexican border cities to beat the prohibition on alcohol while still maintaining a strong Bible Belt presence back in Texas.

Having fought wars with Texas and the United States and having had American troops in combat roles in Mexico in the 19th and 20th centuries, deep fears of the Americans are part of the history of Mexico. Yet Texas has always had a special relationship with Mexico. It was the state that most Mexicans felt best understood Mexico and symbolized some of the similar values of rugged independence that characterized the people of northern Mexico, the *Norteños*. Indeed in 1971 Governor Preston Smith and Mexican President Luis Echeverria inaugurated the first office of any American state with a Texas office in Mexico City. This came shortly after President Lyndon Johnson resolved with Mexican President Diaz Ordaz a long standing dispute often viewed bitterly in Mexico between El Paso and Juarez on land along the Rio Grande between the two cities, and created the Chamizal Memorial to commemorate a pledge to a future of better understanding between the two countries.

Increased American Interest: Oil and Cheaper Labor
Two items triggered in the 1970s increased American interest in Mexico. One was the 1976 discovery of extensive oil deposits, the Cantarell, in the Gulf of Mexico not far from Vera Cruz in the Bay of Campeche. While Mexico had produced some oil early in the 20th century, this new find was said to rival those of Saudi Arabia's. Americans had just gone through the OPEC oil embargo and gasoline lines of 1973-75 with a related hostage crisis in Iran. Mexico was seen as a potential savior to the fickle and treacherous politicians and dictators of the Middle East and their use of oil to exert influence on American foreign policy.

The second item creating interest in Mexico was the growing success of the European Common Market in the 1970s bringing improved global competitiveness of manufactured items for German manufacturers through cheaper labor in Ireland, Spain, Portugal, Italy, and Greece, as well as similar growing competition from Japanese manufacturers leveraging cheap Asian labor in products such as electronics, appliances, autos, furniture, and industrial gear. Here the suggestion for American companies was that inexpensive Mexican labor could serve the same purpose as cheap labor in the south of the European Common market or in countries like Korea, China and Vietnam for Japanese exporters. By the time of the Clinton Administration this notion became the North American Free Trade Agreement (NAFTA) and brought American and other world manufacturers to Mexico to create factories to feed inexpensive manufactured items to the American market.

Accelerating Change

In the year 2000 events were in full swing. Mexico was experiencing waves of growth, increased prosperity, travel and demands for more consumer goods. World stock markets, especially the American market were at peaks and throwing off more investment into other parts of the world including Mexico. Mexican manufacturing surged significantly, including the NAFTA-type plants, the *maquilas*. The land port at Laredo became the world's busiest, with 18-wheelers rolling around the clock via superhighways in both countries—usually one every few minutes every day of the year. . There were more than a hundred and fifty million border crossings yearly in Texas alone. Oil was flowing from Cantarell and export earnings were filling government and private coffers in Mexico. Employment opportunities in the cities of Mexico accelerated migration from rural areas to its cities as Mexico City grew to more than 25,000,000 and Juarez doubled every decade since 1940 to substantially over a million. In these years Mexico changed rapidly from a largely rural nation, with most people employed in small scale and often subsistence farming, to an urban one. Now, rather than securing a living by farming, most Mexicans sought to hold jobs in cities.

During most of the second half of the 20th century all of Mexico had very rapid population growth, but the greatest was in the urban areas. Even today its median population age is 26 as compared to the United States' 35. The growth far outstripped Mexican schools' capacity to provide basic literacy and needed technical/vocational skills, much less higher and technical education.

Part of the efforts to attract *maquilas* was the hope Mexican workers could acquire desperately needed technical, manufacturing and engineering skills from the American, German and Japanese companies that were dominant participants in creating those factories. The promise of such jobs drew rural Mexicans to the cities, but many of the social controls of family, church and neighbors were lost with these migrations to Mexico's cities. Mexico's cities became youthful, crowded (especially with single youth and adults), and more volatile. The extent of the migration is stunning; by 2008, cities such as Juarez had only a quarter of the population having been born and raised there.

There were two additional boosts to the Mexican economy besides oil and export manufacturing. One was an explosion of tourism as increased tax revenues and earnings from oil exports permitted the nation to build the infrastructure to reach its fabled beaches on the Yucatan and along the Pacific. The second was the powerful draw of jobs in the United States as a world economic boom continued, with hard working Mexicans living and working in the United States and sending money home.

Something happened between 2005 and 2007 in the United States and Mexico. The loose money created by the Greenspan Federal Reserve to counter the economic downturn after September 11, 2001 and the bust of the *dot coms* along with deficit spending by the Federal government, local governments and citizens began to unwind. Many Americans were found to be simply speculating in the rising value of their homes, borrowing money from the inflated values, and increasing spending for vacations, autos and costly home additions. That pyramid process was starting to collapse.

Much of housing in the States proved to be a bursting bubble, ending the demand for Mexican construction labor for new housing. As American economic problems deepened, the market for consumer goods that drove the Mexican *maquila* phenomenon shrunk and so did *maquila* employment. Declining American incomes meant fewer jobs for low and semi-skilled labor from Mexico in the United States and increased concerns in areas like construction, food processing and restaurant work from Mexican competition with American workers.

In this economic vacuum only the billions available from the illegal drug trade provided jobs and aspirations for the unemployed rural and urban in Mexico, especially young males. The opportunity was always there, but with the population migration and economic hard times, the existing crime syndicates quickly expanded. This lit the fuse for the Mexican crisis.

The Mexican Crisis

Mexico has ceased in the last 30 years to be a society largely self-contained, rural and self-sufficient in food production and energy. It is a major exporter of energy and tropical foods, and an importer of manufactured goods and grains. It has taken the path of globalization, seeking to participate more fully in a world economy and increase the material standards of its population. Yet this participation opens Mexico to the storms of economic forces in global capitalism.

How prepared is Mexico to deal with a world economic decline, homelessness, and higher unemployment than has been seen since the Great Depression? How well prepared are the local, state and federal public safety concerns, courts and prisons of Mexico to deal with social disorder and crime? How well does Mexico trust its public structures and how strong is its civic health?

There are reasons to believe that most members of Mexican law enforcement are honest and hard working, but the substantial existence of corruption within threatens all. With drugs, kidnapping and protection as a source of great wealth and opportunity today in Mexico, there is little reason to expect in the near future a lessening of the violence or corruption. For Texans and for all Americans an important question is: will the violence stay in Mexico? The answer is that it will not. It is here already. The question of "spillover" is a bit of a canard.

What sense can be made of the events that we see across the Rio Grande? What meaning might be drawn from stray shots on the golf course in late 2009 on the University of Texas at Brownsville from Mexico as Mexican Marines pursued members of the Gulf Cartel to the edge of the Brownsville campus? What do the bullets in the summer of 2011 that hit the El Paso City Hall or buildings on the University of Texas at El Paso mean? Can we place faith and trust in declarations that these are random events and presage no movement into Texas? Or are these statements of assurances against "spillover violence" much like trying to control one's fear at night by whistling as one walks by a graveyard?

On December 26, 2004 a portion of a mountain slid into a deep undersea trough near Indonesia. It triggered a tsunami that raced across the sea, producing little visible movement in the open sea. In some beachside villages the ocean slowly receded but the shore seemed calm, perfectly safe. Only if one looked to the horizon could a great bulge of water, a massive wave be seen building and heading toward land. When the wave hit, great destruction occurred. Comparable deep forces have broken loose in Mexico. Many of the alert and wealthier of the Mexicans have fled to higher ground in Texas, but most of Mexico is poor and cannot readily come to the States. The forces of economic collapse and civic disorder will throw hundreds of thousands of those people against and across the border as violently as the Indonesian tsunami.

Refugee Outflows, Immigration and the Appearance of the Cartels

Several consequences from the growing poverty in Mexico are of concern for the United States. One is an increasing flow of desperate refugees from the cities and countryside of Mexico into the United States. With a population of approximately 115 million and a median age of about 26, Mexico has a relatively large number of dependent children; yet incomes are low for the average wage earner. The wage levels have scarcely changed since my first visit to a *maquila* about 25 years ago. El Paso colleagues report that the daily wage in Juarez is now less than 4 dollars, having been a bit above that level a year ago before the world recession.

To house, feed, clothe, provide health care, education and, ultimately, jobs is a huge task for the nation. With its educational system foundering even as public safety is collapsing, one must anticipate large percentages of a largely uneducated and semi-skilled Mexican workforce, and a population where many will leave or attempt to leave Mexico.

Such workers will earn little and are in great oversupply around the world. The initial impact of Mexico's problems is felt in the states of Texas and California. The size of the current immigrant population is quite large, likely greater than ten million, and is extending out along the Interstate highway system to other states. The second consequence is greater recruitment activity by the drug and human trafficking cartels in Mexico among the growing ranks of unemployed in Mexico and the border cities. Indeed Mexico refers to a current generation of "ninis—*ni estudian, ni trabajan*" (neither study nor work). The highest proportions of these rootless youth are in cities like Juarez.

The third consequence is increased dissension among unemployed and underemployed American workers who see illegal immigrants as threats to jobs and community services. In time, in Mexico and in the United States, this unemployment process coupled with homelessness and hunger will mean civil disruptions.

While the flow of immigrants seeking work from Mexico into the United States has begun to slow as the deep economic decline has reduced available jobs in home and commercial construction, yard care, restaurant work, and food processing, a new flow is beginning. This is seen in the growing numbers of "drop houses" where Mexicans and others from Central America will pay between $3,000 and $5,000 to get into the United States and then face additional extortion from those who brought them into the U.S. These are desperate persons seeking escape from poverty and violence. Whatever the conditions in the United States, those by comparison are worse in Mexico and those in Central America even worse.

A 5-year-old cartel war in Ciudad Juárez averaged about 11 murders a day in 2011, the year of the peak. About half that number occurred in 2012 as violence lessened. Under-equipped Juarez hospitals rush wounded persons across the border to El Paso's Thomason General (recently named University Medical Center and affiliated with Texas Tech and the University of Texas at El Paso), and then El Paso police and DPS officers are deployed to protect the hospital from continuing violence from Mexican gunmen while wounded Mexicans are treated. Facts are increasingly hard to obtain as death threats, kidnappings and killings have been directed against the news media in Mexico, and often government reports are viewed with suspicion.

Rising violence is underway in Mexican cities along the Texas border, including Piedras Negras, Nuevo Laredo, Reynosa, and Matamoros, spreading east from Juarez. The violence is between competing cartels and against Mexican law authorities. Among those killed has been the mayor of a wealthy suburb of

Monterrey, mayors in other Mexican cities and the candidate for governor of the state of Tamaulipas.

Mexico is beset with violence from cartels that challenge each other and law enforcement. More disturbing is that many have long suspected criminal complicity with local, state and federal police in Mexico. Such concerns were buttressed by actions by the Mexican President, Calderon, to remove local police in many cities (Juarez being the earliest large city). He sent Federal officers, then oversaw the removal of Federal police because of countercharges among the Federal police of some being collaborators with cartels to be replaced by troops of the Mexican Army.

The Mexican Army was hoped to be free of such corruption, but reports of Army-led violence caused Mexican President Calderon to depend upon the country's Marines. Mexican military organizations do not come under a common head like the U.S.'s Department of Defense, and the Marines as part of the Navy and the Army report as separate organizations to the President. One sensed a bit of a desperate search by President Calderon to find one part of the various parts of Mexican police and military authorities that he can trust to be uncorrupted by the cartels.

Summary: Mexico Enters The World Stage As Boom Goes To Bust

By the 1980s Mexico had grown from a land of small villages and farms to elements of a modern urban society. With the discovery of vast oil deposits in the Gulf of Mexico, the leadership had the resources to create the human and physical infrastructure of an industrial society. Oil and refiners, teachers and physicians and nurses unions were among the favored recipients. Oil workers controlled the flow of the oil exports that filled the coffers of the PRI and teachers, physicians and nurses were direct interfaces with the population and served to promote the programs of the PRI to the population. Government workers benefited as well with special programs for some police to establish criminal enterprises particularly in the cities on the border with the U.S.

But by tying the country to the world economy, the global down turn in 2000 and the real estate and bond collapse in 2008, hit Mexico with powerful forces. Authoritarian structures are the most durable in times of slow change. Rapid change makes de-centralized structures the more durable. The PRI is back until 2018 and Mexico is sailing on stormy seas of change.

Chapter 12: Unintended Consequence of a Democratic Mexico: The Cartels

The breakdown of the control of the single national party provided an opportunity for organized crime, the Mexican cartels, to grow explosively. The efforts to break with the past have come quickly and in many dimensions, with frightening effects. In 2007 Mexican President Felipe Calderon declared war on the cartels, and from 2007 to 2012 there were over 60,000 violent deaths in the war against and among the cartels. These were the reported deaths. Some observers think there are another 50,000 deaths not reported, and very, very few of the murders are solved.

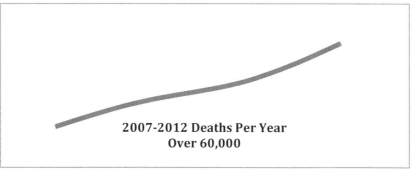

2007-2012 Deaths Per Year
Over 60,000

Figure 1 Deaths During Calderon's Efforts to Control The Cartels

To understand the growing waves of violence in Mexico and the implications for the United States we must look, again, at three factors in Mexico and the United States. These are the *economies*, *demographic* features, and *cultures* of each, but with the focus on Mexico. Unlike decades past, Mexico's economy is integrated with the world. Thus Mexico will be affected more than ever in its history by events in the United States, Europe, Asia, and the Middle East.

Major Mexican Economic Engines, Including Narcotics

Mexico is the third largest economy in the Americas behind Brazil and the United States. It is rich in agricultural, fishing and mining potentials with a young but not highly educated workforce. There are four major engines that vary in terms of the numbers employed, gross revenues, percentage of profits, and source of control of the sector. Now we must add a fifth, profits from smuggling drugs and related activities of the cartels. Below are the major engines, and the table outlines the economic impact of each.

1. Export of Crude Oil Primarily from the Bay of Campeche
2. Export of Temporary Workers (10 to 30 Million individuals)
3. Tourism and Services More than 70 Percent of Employment in Mexico
4. Assembly Manufacturing (*Maquilas*)
5. Drugs, Human Trafficking and Extortion

Export Item	Dollar Amount	Profit %	Profit
Petroleum	$130 billion	10%	$13 Billion
Tourism	$185 billion	8%	$12 Billion
Visiting Workers	$300 billion	10%	$30 Billion
Manufacturing	$100 billion	15%	$15 Billion
Narcotics	$50 billion	80%	$40 Billion

Clearly the area of highest profits and significant income for Mexico are activities associated with the provision and movement of illegal drugs, increasingly controlled by organized crime, the cartels, and rapidly growing ancillary crimes of kidnapping, extortion, cybercrime, and theft. Most of these activities had their initial greatest growth in cities near the American border.

Tijuana and Juarez are the most prominent. The two cities both had organized crime groups that went back to the era of American alcohol prohibition. During that time, they supplied illegal alcohol as legal drink in their bars and served as a source of shipping alcohol into California and Texas. Heroin was also available as Chinese immigrants grew opium poppies in the western Mexican states of Sinaloa, Michoacán and Guerrero during the 1940s to supply American medical needs when the war in the Pacific interrupted supplies from south Asia. From the 1920s until 2000 this illegal activity existed under the control and franchise-like arrangements with the PRI including local, state and federal government officials. However by the late 1990s drug consumption in the United States was drawing greater production in Mexico, and young farm workers were learning that they could undertake the risks of smuggling marijuana and cocaine and make more in a trip than in ten years of farm work. As efforts to curtail the movement of cocaine in the Caribbean succeeded, much greater opportunities emerged for Mexicans to smuggle drugs across Mexico and then at the key border cities into the United States.

The profits from all of the drugs are immense. They are far greater than any other line of commerce in Mexico, or probably the world. One of the challenges is what to do with all of the money earned from the United States. The June 15, 2012 New York Times Magazine (NY Times, 2012) offers an example, "The Sinaloa Cartel can buy a kilo of cocaine in the highlands of Colombia or Peru for around $2,000, then watch it accrue value as it makes its way to market. In Mexico, that kilo fetches more than $10,000. Jump the border to the United States, and it could sell wholesale for $30,000. Break it down into grams to distribute retail, and that same kilo sells for upward of $100,000—more than its weight in gold." The head of the Sinaloa Cartel, El Chapo (Shorty) Guzmán, is estimated to be worth several billion dollars. The largest cache of dollars ever recovered in a drug seizure, $206 million, was in the home of Zhenli Ye Gon, a Chinese-Mexican businessman who is believed to have supplied meth-precursor chemicals to the cartel. The vast money earned is used to pay persons all along the drug network, as well as politicians and law officers. President Calderon's top drug fighting cop, Noe Ramirez, was charged in 2008 with accepting $450,000 each *month*. (Ellingwood, 2008)

U. S. Customs Agents, Border Patrol Officers, beat cops, elected prosecutors, and the judiciary are targets for drug money to bend law enforcement to the efforts of drug traffickers. An early tactic in a community was to hire off-duty police officers for security work. The common ploy is to pay the officer in cash, as having too much cash is always a problem of the trafficker. Cash deposits to a bank bring IRS and other Federal scrutiny. When officers are paid in cash they may decide not to report the income and thus become twice hooked with the drug trafficker: receiving vast amounts of money for little services and open to blackmail when the money is not reported as income.

Efforts by the Mexican Government to Curtail Cartels

But with the 2000 elections the environment of the cartels began to change. The franchise arrangements that existed in some areas with law enforcement and in all cases with the approval of the PRI became unpredictable. The PAN presidency viewed those arrangements as both law violations and as a fund flow to PRI operatives, and a threat to democratic institutions. By 2006 a second PAN President, Felipe Calderon, declared open war on the Cartels and initially focused force on Juarez. At the same time a struggle had begun between the long dominant Juarez Cartel and a new force appearing from the west, part of the Sinaloa Cartel (Brands & Army War College . Strategic Studies Institute., 2009; National Gang Intelligence Center & National Drug Intelligence Center , 2009).

For the cartels as we have seen, control of key cities and sites (plazas) in the cities is like a fast food business such as McDonald's or Burger King seeking a key corner location or near an exit and entry ramp on an Interstate Highway. Location is nearly everything for them, and it is the same for drug smugglers, too. Drugs, unlike the five other major sources of wealth in Mexico, have an astonishing favorable ratio of cost of product relative to what it brings on the market and to those that sell. Estimates run between 50 and 90 percent profit. This means the business including the plazas where drugs are moved or sold is extremely lucrative, and the cartels will and can spend heavily to seize and defend them against all comers, including the Mexican authorities, rival cartels and the Americans. They will use a variety of tactics including psychological warfare such as brutally torturing, murdering and dismembering opponents.

They offer bribes to police and judges with the bribe and the warning of death if the person refuses. This is the source of the motto mentioned by law enforcement in Mexico, "plata o plumo" (silver or lead).

Since Mexico City started the effort to shut down the cartels, thousands have died. Most are said to be deaths among cartel members but thousands are innocent people, and those that were criminals are not enough deaths in all likelihood to deplete the cartels. More than half the Mexican population is in its earning years and jobs are difficult to find. Much of the population is young, unemployed, limited in education and skills, and willing to take risks. That is the advantage that a large youthful age cohort, a weak economy and an urban population provide the cartels in recruiting new persons to fill their ranks.

The Spiral of Violence at The Border
Mexico uses police and the military to control and interdict this flow of illegal drugs, but the Mexican cartels are so wealthy and powerful they not only war among themselves but with Federal forces. The city of Juarez across from El Paso by 2010 has had about 5,000 Mexican Army troops and 1,500 Federal officers since late 2008, largely replacing the municipal police force, but the high rate of violence has not been staunched. With shrinking national resources, Mexico draws many of these troops down starting in the fall of 2012 as other areas, such as Michoacán, are in play in a war between a cartel and the Mexican Federal government. Now with a new President elected in July of 2012 and with the return of the PRI there is a likelihood of a retreat from taking the fight to the cartels and one of accommodation as was the century long pattern of the PRI with the brief 12 year period of two PAN Presidents (Fox and Calderon).

Such conditions, where the cartels rather than the government control the exercise of violence, are the measure of a failed state. In many communities and some states in Mexico the government has simply lost control to cartels.

Youth and adults from the American side are drawn to the business of the cartels. In July of 2009 two American youths from Laredo were sentenced to life terms in American prisons for having been in the employ of a Mexican cartel and engaged in contract killings for the cartel (McKinley, 2009). Without jobs in Mexico and now with similar unemployment in much of the border areas of Texas and California, the apparent wealth and power of the cartels are attractants to poor youth.

They have spawned an admiring music following called narcocorridos that have performers wearing the clothes and carrying the preferred weapons of the gang members, including the chrome plated .45 caliber autos of cartel leaders, and composing lyrics that romanticize smuggling, violence and the general cartel life. The business influenced the popular culture. A new form of music developed from the country corridos or cowboy ballads in the ranch culture and was called narcocorridos. Bands appeared with popular records that recorded some of the "daring do" tales of the young smugglers, their sudden riches which they used to purchase new pickups and SUVs and the much desired silver-plated .45 ACP, as well as more formidable automatic weapons. The romantic ballads and bands serve as a recruitment vehicle for the growing cartels that were organizing the individual entrepreneurs into more focused and skillful smuggling operations. Video disks and tapes are sold at large swap meets on both sides of the border as well as figurines that represent Santa Murte, that is thought to protect narcotraffickers and Jesus Malverde, a Robin Hood-like character from Sinaloa.

The cartels, the music (corridos), the clothing, the autos, and the life styles of Sinaloa are powerful references for youth, particularly Mexican and Mexican American youth. They represent attractive alternatives to the life of the desert farmer or ranch hand, or rural housewife, or the student who stays in school. The outlaw image contributes to youth migrating to the cities and the very high school dropout rates among Hispanic youth. A challenge for Mexico and a challenge for the United States, as these cartel figures influence both youthful Mexicans, illegals and Mexican Americans, is to provide positive reference figures for these youth as the cartel path means a sure lost generation (Downes, 2009).

The cartels have also begun a subtle corruption of law enforcement on the American side (Kraft, 2009). The forces that radiate from epicenters such as Nuevo Laredo now carry far into the American heartland. Organized crime with ties to Mexican cartels now appears in almost every American city, and the products on the street—cocaine, heroin, high potency marijuana, and methamphetamine—originate or pass through Mexico.

Why Cartels?

Central to Mexico's challenges is the failure of the society to provide education and job structures to build a middle class. A populous nation of 115 million cannot have a middle class in the 21st century with educational levels of less than 12 years. A middle class in the world today is built on knowledge jobs, and education and skill training is critical. As a nation, Mexico still fights cultural battles between indigenous peoples and the

European- and now American-oriented elites that control its institutions and businesses.

Lingering influences from now-concluded state efforts through agricultural subsidies to encourage population growth, the theology and practices of the Roman Catholic Church, and family patterns of rural society still drive fertility patterns and family roles. A modern nation-state must develop social psychological attitudes among the citizens of self-control, achievement, a national language, skills in civic participation, and expectations of a rational determination of one's future. That is not Mexico. Mexico has never had a sizable middle class, though it saw the promise of one in the early 1980s. Oil exports, *maquilas*, tourism, and sharing in jobs in America were the promise. These have proven inadequate to the task.

As long as economic decline continues, conditions will worsen in Mexico. More areas will slip from being under the control of government authorities. Refugee flows will pressure American communities near the Mexican border with squatter camps appearing first in Brownsville, McAllen, Laredo, El Paso, Nogales, El Centro and San Diego and then far north of the border. Increased acts of violence will be directed at American law enforcement and then American citizens. Initially Texas and California will be besieged, but highways and railroads will speed the desperate people north and east. This began in the 80s but will reach far higher levels as time passes. Illegal drugs as a ready source of money will be a vexing problem, as well as associated violence.

Mexicans and persons from Central America desperately flee impoverished and violent communities and use a variety of means to get to the United States. Some of the persons involved in transporting these illegals are the traditional "coyotes," persons who will load a pickup and bring 6 to 10 people to a house in an American city with a local confederate who holds them.

However, as the authority of the Mexican government wanes, Cartels are entering this human trafficking trade even as they have come to dominate an illegal drug trade that comes to $50 to $100 billion annually. They are adding kidnapping to these businesses, but so far they are only preying on Mexicans and Central Americans. However, there is increased evidence of the activity against Mexicans living in the United States as well as American victims.

As Mexico spirals ever more toward a failed state, law enforcement personnel and their families as well as other civil authorities will become first order cartel targets in Mexico and in the United States. This is compellingly illustrated by a report filed by Dudley Althaus (2009) of the Houston Chronicle from his Mexico City office:

> *A senior municipal police commander, his wife and four children were executed and their home torched in a predawn attack Wednesday in the port of Veracruz. Jesus Antonio Romero had only recently been appointed operations chief for the joint police force of Veracruz and neighboring Boca del Rio. Both cities have become an underworld battleground as gangs vie for control of contraband traffic through the port and drug sales in neighborhoods.*

Some areas of Mexico will prove to be more capable than others. Cities like Monterrey, Saltillo, Durango, and other communities in the north may see more in common with the American Southwest than Mexico City. Already English is commonly spoken in retail shops, fast food sites, grocery stores, and restaurants similar to what one sees in Houston or Los Angeles. As violence builds and Federal power wanes, separatist movements are likely.

Globalization will not provide all the solutions for Mexico's need of jobs, education, houses, transportation, energy, health care, water… all the elements of existence. The United States does not have the jobs or wealth to be the solution or even an outlet any longer for Mexico's problems. Mexico is not ready to face that reality, and the United States does not understand the enormity of the challenges of Mexico, much less that of other problems building south of Mexico.

As globalization has been a mixed promise to Mexico, it has also been so for the United States. In the last decade much of the middle class that has long been the core of the American experience has slipped away.

Globalization for the United States has meant the loss of good jobs and benefits and substituting debt to maintain consumption. The nation today has seen income growth in the last decades only at the extremes, the very wealthy and the very poor (Saez, 2009). With 40 percent of the population paying no income taxes, the burden lies disproportionately on a shrinking middle class. America is a nation with too much debt and spread too thin in an effort to secure cheap oil to maintain patterns of transportation, housing and recreation that cannot be sustained. Core American values of thrift, hard work, deferred gratification, the importance of the family, service to the community, and a belief in the ability to create a better future are being challenged. Life will become much more a confrontation to secure food and shelter, and persons will need to learn to organize to help secure these essentials and security as well.

As these events occur in the Southwest, then other parts of the world will be unstable as well. Economic decline always creates population movements, and the availability of oil is critical to modern societies. Indeed, a few missiles fired south from Iran across 80 miles of the Gulf of Aquaba could curtail oil production and shipping, and would tie the American military down. If war were to become enlarged in the Middle East, such as action against Iran or by Iran, there is a prospect that the shipping lanes that move petroleum from Saudi Arabia, Kuwait and Iraq may be interrupted and Mexico's petroleum will be needed far more than ever for the United States.

Summary: Why Cartels Exploded In Mexico

Chapter 14 provides history and some of the forces that create and sustain cartels. They exploded in Mexico in 2006 because of larger change in Mexico that weakened traditional government controls and partnerships with organized crime. Rising numbers of unemployed youth growing up in urban areas without the traditional controls of family and rural society created waves of recruits for the "narco life".

The rapid increase of migration for work of Mexicans to the United States in the 80s and 90s blazed new trails for the cartels to use for trafficking of drugs and people. Lastly the PAN seeing the cartels having prospered under the partnership with the PRI acted to use the military rather than the compromised police to fight the cartels.

Chapter 13: Mexico: A Study in Contradictions

Photographs, paintings and posters help illustrate the popular notions of Mexico, today. The reality of the Mexico we know bears a heavy imprint of the past, including the means, betrayal and treachery Cortez used to overthrow the Aztec state, the interplay of Indian and European cultures, the march of peasant armies for land reform and against foreign domination, and ancient symbols of the past like Maya Temples in the southeast of the country.

Mexico: In the Popular Mind

The past shapes the modern, including the national cathedral in Mexico City built with stones from a ruined Aztec sacrificial pyramid, the statue of the angel in Mexico City, and enduring regional flavors such as native dress in Guadalajara, bullfights, sombreros, the Day of the Dead remembrance, and a welcoming poster from the government of Mexico with a saguaro cactus, sombrero, serape, and guitar. Below are the mariachi band and vaqueros and an aerial photograph of Mexico City, one of the world's great cities of more than 25,000,000, and some of the most beautiful beaches in the world on the western coast. This is the Mexico of the popular mind across the world and the face Mexico wants the world to see.

Mexico: The Hidden View

But there is another Mexico emerging from economic growth, more democracy, increased media coverage including private means via the Internet and the vestiges of a middle class. Mexico remains a country of singular monopolistic institutions, powerful regressive unions, authoritarian leaders, extremes of wealth and grinding poverty, and exploding passions. Long the dominant and autocratic Mexican political party, the Party of the Institutionalized Revolution (PRI) lost its hold on Mexico at the end of the 20th century. Genuine democracy began to appear in such persons as Vicente Fox, when in 2000 the National Action Party (PAN) elected the first Mexican President in modern times that was not a creation of the PRI (Fuentes, 1996).

While corruption and organized crime have long been a feature of Mexico, what was less known or popularly acknowledged in the rest of the world was the complex intertwining of the corruption with the agents of the Mexican State itself. The local cop who required "mordida" to fix a traffic ticket, arrangements for regulated alcohol, prostitution and drugs in certain restaurants, bars and clubs of the town, and the cabal that choose the nominee for the PRI every 6 years for the Presidency were all enduring features of Mexico since the end of the1920s.

American Ties

Relations with the United States are complex. Mexico is far more aware of the United States than the States are of Mexico. Mexico regards the United States warily and in the opinion of some Mexican elites, the misery that comes from the cartels and the drug addictions in the United States are long overdue and well-deserved. This is not discussed in public, but it makes collaboration between the two countries difficult. It is especially dangerous at the level of a law officer who finds he or she must collaborate with a Mexican colleague. That lack of trust is real, and what is also real is the high level of corruption in the Mexican government.

It is improbable that the United States can stop the actions of the drug cartels in Mexico. That is a Mexican problem made difficult because there is so much money available to the criminal organizations via moving drugs, kidnapping, extortion, and burglary. With a ready supply of young recruits into the cartels, often corrupt officials, and most importantly a citizenry that does not believe that honest government is possible, the actions of the cartels will continue. The demand for drugs from the United States provides a river of money that in many ways exceeds what either country has available to fight the problem. There are serious shortcomings with many of the proposed solutions to the violence in Mexico. Among the more unrealistic is closing the border. With Mexico as the States' third largest trading partner and with the U.S. being Mexico's largest trading partner, the border will not be closed. Closing the border destroys the Mexican economy and wounds an already wounded American economy.

As long as American drug consumption is high, money from drugs will fuel the cartels. Violence will migrate increasingly into the United States, coming first to Texas and California as cartels work on vertical integration of manufacture, transport, distribution and sales. In most instances local gangs in American cities will be the local franchiser. More corruption will appear in U.S. law enforcement, particularly in jurisdictions where law officers are poorly paid, as aided by the fact that in many jurisdictions, law enforcement, prosecution and the judiciary are part of the political process and more open to bribes. The map below based on highways alone provides a view to the complex trade relations via transportation of the two countries.

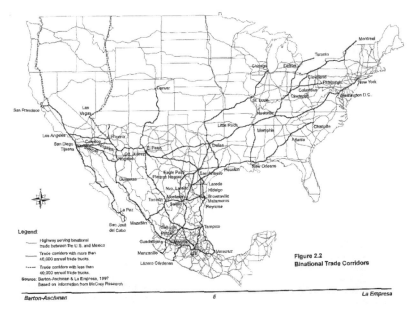

Figure 2.2
Binational Trade Corridors

Figure 2 Highway Trade Routes Between Mexico and the U.S.[i]

Cartel violence will be episodic with drug lords achieving some hegemony and then losing it through competition with rivals and government efforts. The pull of the cartels only recedes when good paying jobs are available and greater public revulsion against drugs and violence develops. Mexican cartels will continue incursions into Texas, Arizona and California. Most efforts will consist of partnerships with hardened gangs such as the Texas Syndicate, the Mexican Mafia in the Southwest, and groups like the Latin Kings in the Midwest and Chicago. To the extent old style Italian mobs exist in the eastern cities, they may look to the cartels for supply. Border gangs in cities like El Paso, home to a 20-year-old gang called Barrio Azteca, will serve as muscle and hired killers. Certainly major cartel figures may migrate to the United States, as consumer products are more readily available and they may simply be safer. There are already some reports of Mexican youth gangs migrating to Houston, as opportunities for theft are better than in Mexico City. Actual delivery of drugs to local consumers by the cartel is unlikely. Rather the cartel will prefer to work as wholesalers, leaving the risky part of the business to local gangs or individuals that make contact with customers and have a higher risk of arrest.

The Pattern of Collapse

The continuing Mexican collapse will follow a pattern. Violence will continue to rise in parts of Mexico beyond those cities along the border. That has already begun in Monterrey, Cuernavaca, Acapulco, and other Mexican cities. If local authorities cannot contain the violence, the central government will use either the Army or the Navy to match the heavy weapons the cartels have. When cartel hegemony is contained, the Federal government will use the Federal police to replace state and municipal police.

This will have mixed results as corruption has existed in the Army and the Federal police, and the central government must purge those entities. Army recruits tend to be drawn from low-income areas, and the Army has long been regarded with suspicion by the powers that be in Mexico City. Fuel, ammunition and guns are carefully rationed and installations kept away from centers of power. This is a result of a memory of history and the fact that elements of the armed forces were part of revolutions in the past. The fact that there have been several instances of corruption in the Army, including the Mexican Army linkage to the Zetas Cartel, supports this wariness.

This concern of military loyalty is not unique to Mexico. The United States has always maintained concerns about the loyalty of the military by having a civilian military head appointed by the President and requiring that military forces not be garrisoned in the Federal District. The Mexican Navy has long been free of corruption and has not suffered taints under Calderon. This is likely true because the Navy draws its recruits more from the more educated middle classes and often do joint training with the American military. But force cannot replace honest local authorities (including the judiciary) nor can it produce citizens that will support the rule of law

Oil, Not Cartels -The Greatest Security Risk

The cartels are not the most major security risk to either Mexico or the United States. For the United States the greatest risk, other than waves of refugees, is the loss of oil imports from Mexico. America imports 70 percent or more of the petroleum consumed, and the trend has increased as the economy grows and in-country reserves are naturally depleted. The largest source for imports is Canada's oil sands, but it is an expensive source. The second source is Mexico. As the following table illustrates, the other major sources are countries with stability problems or countries not friendly to the United States.

Major Security Risks-United States and Mexico

United States	Mexico
Must Import 70 Percent of Oil	History of Revolutions
Has Major Empire Interests and Attendant Enemies Susceptible to Fragmented Border	Great Wealth Disparities with Unemployment as High as 50 percent
Needs Secure Neighbor on the South and North	Potential Food Shortages in Urban Areas
Rising Unemployment	Failure of Oil Exports
High Debt Levels	Cartel Violence and Breakdown of Civil Order

The extreme fragility of the Mexican supply is not due to the disruptions posed by cartel violence, but rather the fact that Mexico is suffering rapid depletion of its largest oil producer, the Cantarell field (Malkin, 2010, March 8). When it was originally mapped, it was thought to be similar to one of the great Saudi Arabian fields such as Ghawar that has lasted for decades. While the Mexican oil is similar in quality to low sulfur, high quality oil from Texas, the field has proven to be shallow and Mexico is thought to lose its ability to export oil by 2014 to 2015. There may be other fields (especially offshore) to explore, but Pemex holds the monopoly and is notoriously incompetent and corrupt. If oil exports stop and they seem sure to do so, it removes the foundation of the middle class professions that have been built since the oil boom years of the 1980s, including medicine, nursing, teaching, and higher education. This creates a two-horned dilemma for the United States. Oil prices will likely rise, and Mexico will grow more unstable with many more attempts of Mexicans to migrate to the United States. Cartels will take advantage of the chaos to strengthen their ranks. Moreover, without oil export earnings Mexico will lose its major source of funds to import food to feed an urban population and to underwrite the middle class professions. Such forces only produce a more chaotic environment for the drug cartels to ply their trade.

Sequence of the Security Risk

1. Interruption of the Flow of Oil
2. Decline of Mexican Oil Fields
3. Collapse of the Mexican middle class paid by earnings from oil exports, primarily police, military, government workers, teachers, physicians and nurses

Crude Oil Imports for U.S. in Thousand Barrels per Day (Top 6 Countries)

Country	YTD 2010	YTD 2011
Canada	1,972	1,943
Mexico	1,140	1,092
Saudi Arabia	1,080	980
Nigeria	986	776
Venezuela	912	951
Iraq	414	449

Declining Production

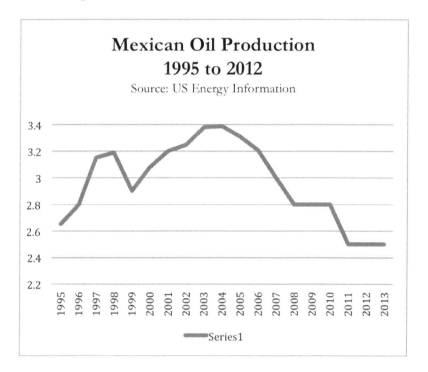

Figure 3 Oil Production

Economic Disasters Feed the Cartels

In this growing mire there remains one steady source of employment, and that is associated with the illegal movement of drugs and people from Mexico into the United States. Here is a source of potential wealth that does not require extensive education, ownership of arable land or expensive equipment. To get started in the illegal drug business requires daring, ingenuity, the ability to make contacts in informal networks, and a willingness to use brutality against one's competitors and the police. Here is rough and tumble capitalism at its coarsest as young men, working solo and in gangs, compete to control the trade in moving drugs and people into the United States. What happened in Juarez from 2006 to 2010 illustrates this. "The Chihuahua prosecutor general said Tuesday that within the

Juárez region there are more than 9,000 active drug cartel members. It is the first time a Mexican official has quantified the warring drug cartel organizations' membership. Carlos Manuel Salas, the state's chief prosecutor, provided the figures and other information in a statement.

> "'What happened is that the cartels entered into a conflict, and then organized crime began to get involved in common crimes. What happened when we confronted this is that the Juárez Cartel, which then had 500 people who controlled (their operations) throughout the state, added 5,000 gang members to its force,' Duarte said, 'and they brought weapons from the United States and began to fight the Sinaloa cartel that got hold of other gangs. In less than 60 days, this (Sinaloa) group had 4,000 armed members, and this is the challenge that the governor was faced with, but we are working each day to restore the peace to our state.'" (Valdez, 2011).

Dimensions in The Drug Trade

There are several major dimensions of the drug trade in Mexico. The first involves growing the drugs, including marijuana and heroin poppies, importing meth feeder chemicals from China, or transporting cocaine from Columbia, Peru, Brazil, and Venezuela by land and sea in Mexico and along its coasts. The second dimension is staging the drugs or people to get them into the United States, and each requires securing control and monopolies of areas (plazas) in cities like Tijuana, Juarez and Matamoros. There the bulk goods are assembled, American authorities are overwhelmed, tricked or bought off, and then people and drugs are smuggled across. The third dimension is securing trading partners in the United States to receive these imported goods. This may be individual dealers, unscrupulous employers, street gangs and, in some instances, members of Mexican cartels that have set up shop in the United States.

This market of illegal drugs and smuggled people is a huge market and the most profitable business in all of Mexico. It likely generates 40 billion dollars of profits annually, and the profits are used to buy law officers, military personnel, judges, and politicians. With these dollars military grade weapons are purchased including automatic rifles, grenades and combat vehicles. The profits are used to employ gunmen to protect the supply lines and eliminate competition. Gangs, termed cartels, have developed over the last 30 years that control the corruption in each region and yet compete with each other at the points of access to the American market. That is the reason that Juarez has become one of the world's most dangerous cities, with 10 people killed daily in 2010. Here is a recent depiction of the cartel activity in Mexico.

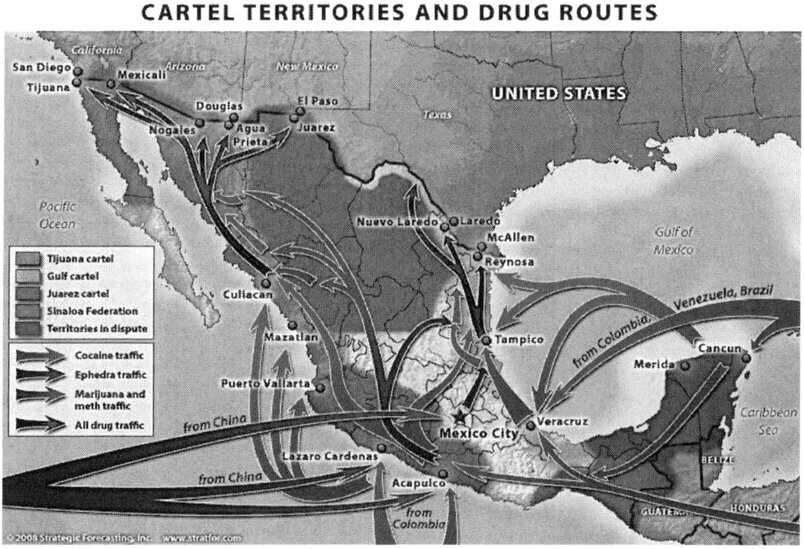

CARTEL TERRITORIES AND DRUG ROUTES

Figure 4 Recent Cartel Alignments and Drug Sources

These are a few of the dimensions of a failed/failing state on the southern border of the country. This is an existential event for Mexico and one with growing implications for the United States.

Summary: Mexico Two Views

Since the 1930s Mexico has presented itself to the world as a peaceful land of strolling mariachis, sombreros, cacti, stunning beautiful beaches and sunsets, cobblestone streets and an occasional man with a burro. Cities along the Pacific became vacation and retirement homes for Americans and Canadians as did traditional towns like San Miguel de Allende in the northern mountains. Existing simultaneously was a Mexico of shadows where anything could be bought if you had the dollars. Much of this began during American Prohibition as Mexican border cities like Tijuana, Juarez, Nuevo Laredo and Matamoros were sites where alcohol was readily available as well as other drugs, women and children for deviate gringo hungers. Mexico sought to present the first view to the world and to deny to itself the second view.

Both views could exist simultaneously as long as Mexico was not of great significance to the larger world. The discovery of oil made it important to the United States and its exploding population made Mexico more aware of itself

PART III-THE ROAD AHEAD

Chapter 14: The Origin of The Cartels

Organized crime occurs in most if not all societies. It serves a market that neither government nor the traditional business sectors serve. It provides services such as prostitution, stolen goods at prices below the retail market, gambling, illegal drugs, protection from theft and assault, directed violence at others, etc. Involvement with organized crime can vary with one's station in society. The poor often are ignored or irregularly served by the government and are more likely to be visible victims as well as participants in organized crime. Membership in youth street gangs can occur as a means of protecting oneself from others and also as an organized means to prey on others. Upper income classes may be less likely to be victimized as governments are often more responsive to the wealthy, and the wealthy also have the means to hire protection or neutralize some aspects of the activities of organized crime. If there is more than one ethnic group in a society, that may serve to increase the likelihood of exploitation of one group by another and provide conditions for organized crime. As an example in early American cities like Boston, Providence, Philadelphia and New York City recently arrived émigrés were often exploited by the existing social groups and in turn became involved in organized crime. The Irish and the Jews were often examples of such groups in the 1820s. Later waves of immigrants in the

1880s to the 1920s that became involved in organized crime included Italians, Greeks, French, and Polish.

Forces of immigration in Mexico provided the basis of organized crime in certain areas such as the states of Sinaloa and Nuevo Leon. Historians have contended that heroes of the 1910 Revolution began as rural bandits, citing Pancho Villa and Emilano Zapata. Other forces created conditions conducive to organized crime. Western Mexico is a significant supplier to North America of heroin. The source is the opium poppy, which Chinese immigrants brought to the state of Sinaloa in the 1880s. Sinaloa's proximity to California made it the legal source of opium and its derivatives, heroin and morphine, until the United States' Harrison Narcotics Tax Act of 1914, which tightly regulated the sale of opium in the United States. Legal opium production rose further as a result of World War II, which increased the demand for medical morphine, an opium extract. Since Japan controlled most of the world's opium supply, the United States turned to Mexico—specifically Sinaloa—for assistance. Although the morphine supply was a benefit to the military medical hospitals, the legal market for opium opened the door for more widespread illegal cultivation and distribution. Thus, the basis of part of the power of the current Sinaloa Cartel is the cultivation of the poppy brought by Chinese immigrants and grown for some years at the call of the U.S. military.

For the entire 20th century Mexican border cities, through organized crime, provided options for Americans who could not secure products and services in the United States or obtain them legally. During Prohibition, from individual states' laws in 1910 or earlier until the 18th Amendment in 1919, beverage alcohol was illegal and remained illegal until 1933 with the 21st Amendment that repealed the 18th Amendment. In northern cities gangs headed by notorious characters like Al Capone, Bugs Moran, and Lucky Luciano provided illegal alcohol, other drugs, gambling, and prostitution. In Mexican cities close to the American border providing alcohol during Prohibition was a lucrative business. It flourished in Matamoros, Reynosa, Nuevo Laredo, Piedras Negras, Juarez, and Tijuana, all large cities and near to populous areas in the United States. The drugs included alcohol, marijuana and opium. Prostitution and gambling were common as well, and many of these cities would have designated areas, "la Zona Rosa," the red light district or "tolerant zone," where bars and brothels were clustered. During this period from the 1910s to 2000s, these criminal enterprises existed in a convenient partnership with the municipal, state and federal governments in Mexico. The PRI controlled all levels of government and saw organized crime as a franchise that was granted to certain local gangsters with the provision that fees were paid to the PRI politicians. Mexicans, including those with strong religious or civic ties, simply regarded this as part of life and not something to crusade against.

Each of the border cities had its own set of families that ran organized crime. When there were disagreements within or between these crime families, they were settled within the families and on occasion with governmental intervention. For business to be good there could be little violence and violence could not be directed against "gringos," the most important customer. The prime spots to set up these businesses were near the gateways from the American side to the Mexican side. The Mexicans called them "the plaza", and for a gang to secure the plaza from the local government assured huge amounts of money.

As the American population grew and became more prosperous, these municipal level gangs also became more prosperous and began to move illegal product not just to the plaza but also to customers in the United States. This smuggling into the U.S. required two things not needed in the plaza business. One was a much larger amount of product. The second was the ability to get the product into the United States and to individuals that would sell it to users.

The Birth of the Cartels

Describing and tracking the Mexican cartels has generated a sizeable industry of book publishing and web sites. Terrorism directed at Mexican journalism has made the Internet in some cases the only public resource to describe events in many Mexican communities. The following descriptions of the changing world of cartels are drawn from these resources. Particularly useful are the works of Terrance Poppa, George Grayson, Samuel Logan, Howard Campbell, Ioan Grillo, and Sylvia Longmire (Poppa, 1990; Poppa & Bowden, 2010); Grayson (2008. May); (Grayson, 2010) (Logan, 2009 March 11,) (Grayson & Logan, 2012) (Campbell, 2009); (Grillo, 2011) (C. Bowden, 2002; Ford, 2005; Kling & Schulz, 2009; Longmire, 2011). An early travel log-type book before the violence reached fever pitch was Danelo's (Danelo, 2008). Useful as well are internet resources including the various wikis, dedicated sites such as Borderland Beat, Blog del Narco, Insight Crime, etc. Lastly, I am informed by conversations over the years with elected officials, citizens and law enforcement persons that grapple with aspects of cartel activity.

Several features describe the cartel world. One is that it is filled with conflict, and alignments and personalities change. Two is the great profits that permit the purchase of politicians, military members and law officers. Three is the high levels of un- and underemployment in Mexico and, increasingly in the United States, which provide a large base of recruits for cartel manpower. One must remember that Mexico has millions of young women and men with few skills and knowledge for jobs even while jobs are scarce. The drug trade provides a powerful economic promise and feeds a youth culture of "live hard, love fast and die young". This unpredictability, flamboyance and violence of those involved in the cartel life is changing the very fabric of life in Mexico and in those areas of the United States where immigration is highest and the cartels' influences most evident.

The Founding Cartel: Guadalajara

By the 1980s more sophisticated and larger networks began to develop among the gangs and the predecessors of today's cartels emerged. The birth of all *modern* Mexican drug cartels is traced to former Mexican Judicial Federal Police agent Miguel Ángel Félix Gallardo ("El Padrino-The Godfather"), who founded the Guadalajara Cartel in 1980 with Rafael Caro Quintero and Ernesto Fonseca Carrillo, and controlled much of the illegal drug trade in Mexico and the trafficking corridors across the Mexico-USA border throughout the 1980s. His former career as a Federal law enforcement officer is a pattern repeated again and again in Mexico and a stubborn feature of dealing with the drug-cartel wars.

Félix Gallardo started with smuggling marijuana and opium into the United States but was the first Mexican drug chief to secure connections with Colombia's cocaine cartels in the 1980s and Pablo Escobar, the most powerful of the Columbian drug lords (M. Bowden, 2001). In the 1980s the Columbians were the most active and profitable producers of drugs but mostly cocaine. Heroin flowed from Afghanistan and the Middle East much through France and other sources from East Asia as the Vietnam War wound down. Columbia moved the bulk of its product via boat through the Caribbean and into the eastern United States with Miami being an important receiving point.

Félix Gallardo was the Mexican connection for the Columbians. This was easily accomplished because Félix Gallardo had already established an infrastructure that stood ready to serve the Colombia-based traffickers of the Medellin Cartel. In the beginning years, Columbia sent the bulk of its cocaine to the United States via boats in the Caribbean. Félix Gallardo was simply another wholesale distributor for the Columbians, but as a former ranking Mexican Federal Police officer he knew both available routes and how policing operated to avoid detection and successfully move drugs through Mexico.

In Mexico, Félix Gallardo was the lord of Mexican drug lords. He oversaw all operations with his confederates and purchased the politicians who sold him protection. However, the Guadalajara Cartel suffered a major blow in 1985 when the group's co-founders Rafael Caro Quintero and Ernesto Fonseca Carrillo were captured, and later convicted, for the kidnapping in Guadalajara, torture and finally murder of DEA agent Enrique Camarena. Félix Gallardo afterwards kept a low profile and in 1987 he moved with his family from Sinaloa to Guadalajara.

According to Peter Dale Scott, a former Canadian diplomat, University of California at Berkeley English Professor, and antiwar activist, the Guadalajara Cartel prospered largely because it enjoyed the protection of the Dirección Federal de Seguridad (DFS) under its chief Miguel Nazar Haro, a CIA asset (Scott, 1972, 2000, 2010). Various sources contend that the CIA had a hand in the creation of the DFS, the closest Mexican analog to a Mexican national intelligence agency (Michel, 2004 February 23). After the assassination of DEA Agent Camarena and the resulting furor of the DEA and the Washington establishment, the DFS was merged into the Centro de Investigación y Seguridad Nacional (CISEN) in 1985.

"The Godfather" divided the trade he controlled, as it would be more efficient, less visible and convenient to dismantle in the occasional large-scale law enforcement initiative. He had learned that the attention span of the American public and the Congress was short and you survived and flourished by being more discreet and decentralized. In a way, he was privatizing the Mexican drug business while sending it back underground, to be run by bosses who were less well known or not yet known by the DEA. He had seen that occur in the eastern United States in the 1950s and the 1960s as the Kefauver Commission ran its course as did the efforts of Robert Kennedy when he was Attorney General (Fontenay, 1980; Kaiser, 2008).

Gallardo convened the nation's top drug traffickers at a house in the resort of Acapulco where he designated the *plazas* or territories. The Tijuana route was assigned to the Arellano Félix brothers. The Ciudad Juárez route would go to the Carrillo Fuentes family. Miguel Caro Quintero would run the Sonora corridor. The control of the Matamoros, Tamaulipas corridor— then becoming the Gulf Cartel—would be left undisturbed to its founder Juan García Abrego. Meanwhile, Joaquín Guzmán Loera and Ismael Zambada García would take over Pacific coast operations, becoming the Sinaloa Cartel. Guzmán and Zambada brought veteran Héctor Luis Palma Salazar back into the fold. Félix Gallardo still planned to oversee national operations, as he maintained important connections, but he would no longer control all details of the business. He would become the CEO of the Mexican drug cartels.

During the 1980s there was an explosion of cocaine on American streets, and an alarmed public resulted in successful efforts to interdict a supply coming through the Caribbean and to the east coast from Florida to New York. Military aide was provided to the Columbian government, and the Reagan Administration became concerned about threats from drug production in South America. The result was that much of the wealth and power of organized crime in Columbia, Peru and Venezuela was weakened; yet this presented an opportunity for the Mexicans (Reeves & Campbell, 1994; Reinarman & Levine, 1997). As the United States was able to interrupt the Medellin Cartel's flow of cocaine through the Caribbean in the late 1980's and then broke apart many of its operations in Columbia and Peru, relations with Félix Gallardo and this emerging cartel structure of Mexico changed. Effectively the Columbians were reduced to being producers of cocoa and the raw cocaine, selling at wholesale to the Mexicans that now controlled access to the American market, primarily moving the product by ground and air across Mexico to the American border.

Just a few years after this organizational coup, Félix Gallardo was arrested in 1989 and sentenced to a maximum-security prison in Toluca in the State of Mexico. His influence continues through the common use in the cartels of family ties to secure loyalties. Sandra Ávila Beltrán, who the media have dubbed "the Queen of the Pacific," is his niece from the Rafael Caro Quintero family and thought to be an important link between groups in Sinaloa and cocaine producers in Columbia. Family ties and the involvement of governmental connections in Gallardo's history illustrate a common theme among Mexican cartels and their resiliency and adaptability.

The Gulf Cartel
Perhaps the oldest and most experienced of the Mexican criminal enterprises is the Gulf Cartel, long operating in the Mexican States of Tamaulipas and Veracruz along the Gulf of Mexico and south of the Valley in Texas. It certainly may have very strange connections that go back to the Mexican 1910 Revolution, and potentially provides a very different look into the sources of Mexican cartels and may truly be the founding cartel unlike the one based in Guadalajara.

Intelligence Gathering
There is some thinking that Gulf Cartel began back in the 1930s and was created at the urging of British and the then-embryonic American intelligence service to create a network in Mexico should Mexico act on its threats to develop greater ties to Germany, Italy and possibly Japan in the run-up to World War II. Such notions tie back into the threats of Mexican President Lazaro Cárdenas when he nationalized Mexico's railroads and then the oil industry, inflicting damage on American and British companies in 1938 and 1939 (Ashby, 1967; Kiddle & Muñoz, 2010). This expropriation was wildly greeted by Mexicans as an

effort to expel foreign invaders and was compared to the defeat of French forces in Queretaro in 1867, the capture of Maximilian and the restoration of the Republic by Benito Juarez. Mexico, far more than the United States, is mindful of foreign invasions, having experienced war with Spain, France and then the United States in 1846-47. That war included American forces capturing Mexico City and a heroic but fatal stand of boys at a military academy at Chapultepec Castle, and the American occupation of Monterrey. Another example of American incursions into Mexico is the punitive expedition of General John J. Sherman through Chihuahua in search of Pancho Villa after he attacked Columbus, New Mexico in 1916.

Possible Role of Intelligence Operatives as a Progenitor of Cartels

During the 1930s and 1940s, the fact that Mexico sold petroleum to Germany and Italy added to the British and American suspicions that Mexico might ally with their enemies, particularly Germany. This was seen by the Americans and the British as Mexico leveraging a threat to provide shipping and submarine bases in the Gulf of Mexico near Tampico and Veracruz that would interfere with shipping of grains, petroleum, manufactured goods, and war material from ports like Galveston, Houston and New Orleans to Great Britain. These ports and the sea lanes through the Gulf and into the Atlantic were critical to the war materiel support and provision of food items for Britain as well as areas in Europe not under Nazi control even before the United States entered World War II, and grew in importance from 1940 until hostilities ceased in 1945. These Mexican ties with the Axis Powers provided the basis for rumors in both the United States and Mexico that intelligence operatives of Britain and the United States moved to create groups in Mexico to provide information about these growing Mexican ties with the Axis Powers.

The Zimmerman Telegram

These moves between Germany and Mexico in the 1930s were not the first time that Germany had sought to pose a threat to the United States via Mexico. A celebrated incident during World War I was the Zimmerman Telegram. The telegram was a message sent from the Foreign Secretary of the German Empire, Arthur Zimmermann, on 16 January 1917 to the German ambassador in Mexico, Heinrich von Eckardt. It was coded but intercepted and the code broken by British intelligence and provided to the American government. The telegram told Ambassador Eckardt in the event the Americans entered the war, to approach the Mexican Government for an alliance, with war equipment and funding from Germany. The quid pro quo for Mexico's participation was Germany would support Mexico regaining territories in Texas, New Mexico, and Arizona that had been lost to the United States in 1836 from the formation of the Republic of Texas, and in 1848 from the Treaty of Guadalupe where Mexico relinquished claims to lands west of Texas to and including California. The Ambassador was also directed to urge Mexico to help broker an alliance between Germany and the Japanese Empire. The Mexican President apparently was intrigued and directed one of his Army Generals to assess the feasibility of a Mexican takeover of their former territories. But, the General concluded the proposal would fail for these reasons:

- The Mexicans were not prepared or able to engage the United States in a war and win. They did not have a large standing army or navy or the ready structures to create such a military.
- Germany could not deliver on its promises of support. The British controlled the sea-lanes thus Germany could not get funding or war materiel to Mexico. The U.S. was the only producer of size of weapons and ammunition in North or South America.
- Any Mexican successes in this area would require it to face a heavily armed American population, most familiar

and skilled in the use of firearms in the former Mexican areas of Texas, New Mexico, Arizona and California, all English speaking, and a huge challenge to Mexican control.

Mexico did not act on the German proposal but it deepened the sense of official Washington as well as among many Americans of the potential threat to the Southwest posed by Mexican desires to reclaim lands in the southwest states of the U.S. Popular sentiment in the United States grew against Mexico and the incursions into Mexico by the U.S. Army to punish Pancho Villa (Doroteo Arango) (Andrew, 1995; F. Katz, 1981; Tuchman, 1979)

Thus for critical periods early in the 20th century there were active efforts by other nations to enlist Mexico as an ally against the United States. The motivations for the efforts grew out of wars between the United States and Mexico during the 19th century and those motivations and that history is critical to understanding Mexico and its view of the United States today.

The existence of commercial and military ties with Germany, Italy and to some extent Japan was used to checkmate invasion threats in the 1930s coming from the States or England seeking to restore oil fields and refineries expropriated by President Cárdenas, who was loudly applauded by Mexicans. Less documented were tales of Japanese agents establishing submarine supply bases along points on the Pacific Coast. (Miller, 1937, 1943) As an example, there were stories of one Texas Ranger, Rufus Van Zandt, who had long led hunting and fishing groups in Sonora and Baja California during the 1930s. (Roach, 1996) He was from north Texas and had trained at Camp Mabry in 1916 in Austin as a member of the State's National Guard and then became a law enforcement officer in the Texas Rangers. He enlisted in the Army when the United States entered World War II. Among some of the tales of Texas Rangers are those that Van Zandt organized groups of Yaqui

Indians to harass Japanese sailors and those supplying their submarines in bases at the tip of Baja California. Other tales included bases in other Mexican coastal states such as Chiapas. These stores, apocryphal or not, were based in a time when emotions ran high in the United States after the attack on Pearl Harbor by the Japanese, and gun batteries were placed on Pacific shores in several western states to prepare for Japanese invasion attempts. Japanese Americans as well as some German Americans were interned during World War II for fear of them being agents for a Japanese or German invasion. Agents from the British SIS and the emerging American parallel intelligence service were rumored to have assisted organized crime in Tamaulipas with market access in the United States in return for Mexican organized crime providing information about Mexico and certain Mexicans and their involvements and intentions with the Axis powers.

Mexico continued ties with the Soviet Union during the Cold War and provided a launching site for Fidel Castro and his brother, Raul, when they were released from a Cuban prison and then organized the start of an army to wage revolution against Batista. But Mexico grew hostile to the new Cuba and viewed it and its ties with the Soviets as a potential threat as well as competitor to Mexico in influence in Hispanic Central and South America. Yet the Soviets maintained a large presence in Mexico and, as an example, had one of the hemisphere's largest consulates in Ciudad Juarez, conveniently sited with visible presence to El Paso, Ft. Bliss and some parts of the missile ranges and atomic testing sites near White Sands, New Mexico.

The story about the presence of British and American intelligence operatives in the early alcohol and drug smuggling bands from 1910 through the 1940s and 1950s may be apocryphal, but there are many strange turns in Mexico-U.S. relations as well as complexities with the Mexican cartels. Clearly Mexico maintained all during the 20th century an edgy orientation toward its northern neighbor, and the political left in

Mexico would bait the Yankee tiger by suggesting stronger and bolder ties to enemies of the United States.

The presence of intelligence operatives in Mexico and a variety of efforts by the United States to secure information on adversaries takes many turns. (Marks, 1979; Trento, 2001) Though most Americans were not aware of it, the United States was and is referred to in Mexican public education as the "colossus of the North" and viewed as the major source of threat to the territorial integrity of Mexico. This is noteworthy in gatherings with Mexican intellectuals and their concerns that American scholars and officials may also be American intelligence agents. Indeed one of the burdens of an economy such as the United States is that American property and Americans are often at risk by operatives of foreign powers and terrorist groups. A friend, Fred Burton, tells a very personal story relative to this reality in his biography, *Ghost* about his years in the protective service for the State Department. (Burton, 2008)

These states, Tamaulipas and Veracruz, are perhaps the most important of all the locations on the Mexican border with the United States because Tamaulipas borders about a fourth of Texas from Brownsville west to Nuevo Laredo. Good highways run down the Gulf Coast through Tamaulipas to Veracruz, then Chiapas and to Guatemala. Increasingly Guatemala, due to its poverty and weak central government, is a favored point of cocaine coming in from Peru, Venezuela and Columbia to be moved into Mexico. With headquarters in cities like Matamoros across the Rio Grande from Brownsville and Reynosa, south of McAllen, large American cities are nearby with good highways and air connections to Houston. Houston became a large American depot moving drugs to Atlanta to supply the South and the Northeast.

Gulf Cartel Today

The Gulf Cartel's modern origins can be traced to 1984, when Juan García Abrego assumed control of his uncle's drug trafficking business, then a relatively small-time marijuana and heroin operation. The uncle, Juan Nepomuceno Guerra, operated out of a restaurant in Piedras Negras across from the Texas City of Eagle Pass about 100 miles south southwest of San Antonio. As García Abrego honed his talents smuggling marijuana and cocaine he moved downriver to Reynosa and Matamoros, far larger cities in the Mexican costal state of Tamaulipas. In a crowning achievement García Abrego brokered a deal with the Cali Cartel, the Colombian mega-structure that was looking for new entry routes into the United States' market after facing a clampdown on their Caribbean routes by U.S. law enforcement. It was an agreement that, from the business side, proved irresistible both for the Cali Cartel's leaders, the Rodriguez Orejuela brothers, and for the Mexicans. García Abrego would handle cocaine shipments via the Mexican border, taking on all the risks, as well as much as 50 percent of the profits. García Abrego also was a pioneer among the Mexican Cartels with his efforts not just to bring drugs to the border to sell to Americans or to border towns like Brownsville, El Paso or San Diego, but also to develop smuggling routes north of the border into many American cities. This was an important and serious innovation and blazed the path for most of Mexico's cartels today.

When García Abrego was arrested and deported to the U.S. in January 1996, the Gulf Cartel was reportedly pulling in billions in revenues each year, cash that had to be smuggled back across the border in suitcases, jets and through underground tunnels. In 1994 the United States Drug Enforcement Administration (DEA) believed García Ábrego was making as much as $10 billion per year in profit (Cockburn & St. Clair, 1998). This drug trafficking organization (DTO) built a wide-reaching delivery network across the U.S., from Houston to Atlanta,

New York to Los Angeles. It grew from border smuggling to supplying dozens of large cities and hundreds of small towns across the United States and used its funds to corrupt law enforcement. With the arrest of one of García Ábrego's traffickers, Juan Antonio Ortiz, it was discovered that the cartel would ship tons of cocaine in United States Immigration and Naturalization Service buses from 1986 to 1990. The buses made ideal transportation: as observers noted, they were an ideal conveyance since they were never stopped at the border. In addition to the INS bus scam, García Ábrego compromised members of the Texas National Guard having them move cocaine and marijuana from South Texas to Houston for the cartel.

His influence was seen in its imitators. Other kingpins, like Juarez Cartel head Amado Carillo Fuentes, alias "El Señor de los Cielos" (Lord of the Skies), quickly followed in García Abrego's footsteps and began demanding more control over distribution from their Colombian partners instead of settling for just a share in the transportation fees. As a result, by the end of the 1990s Mexican traffickers had built a series of cocaine, methamphetamine and heroin networks that rivaled Cali in size, sophistication and profit. And by paying off government aides, ministers, the federal police force, and even the attorney general's office, the Gulf Cartel was soon rivaling Cali in terms of political corruption.

García Abrego's heir, Osiel Cárdenas Guillen, then began to develop the Gulf Cartel's military wing in ways never envisioned either in Cali or in Medellin. Cárdenas recruited at least 31 former soldiers of Mexico's Special Forces to act as security enforcers, for at least three times their previous pay. They were expert sharpshooters, trained in weapons inaccessible to most of their drug-trafficking rivals, capable of rapid deployment operations in almost any environment, and they matched perfectly Cárdenas' more brutal, confrontational leadership style. Said to have received specialized training by the American military in urbanized and intensive combat, they introduced a far more brutal and focused violence into the Mexican Cartels. Cárdenas was arrested in 2003, after the U.S. Department of State placed a $2 million reward on his head. But his former protection unit, which soon began operating as an independent group known as the Zetas (a radio call sign from military training), is perhaps this DTO's bloodiest and most influential legacy in Mexico's drugs war.

The increasing violence in those cities has implications for Texas. Here is one disturbing example that portends the likelihood of far more serious "spill over" violence. In November of 2010 a unit of the Mexican Navy, the Marines, moved to capture Cárdenas' brother Antonio Ezequiel Cárdenas Guillén ("Tony Tormenta"), one of the leaders of the Gulf Cartel. The Marines engaged him in a firefight on the north side of Matamoros, and he was killed by the Marines against a chain link fence that forms the southern side of a golf course of the University of Texas at Brownsville. As the firefight raged over at least two days, the University of Texas moved to rush police officers from several of its campuses to Brownsville to form a "skirmish line" to protect the campus and students in the event that Cárdenas would enter Texas and the campus seeking refuges from the Mexican Marines.

Innovations of the Gulf Cartel

There were three new features that the Gulf Cartel added to the Mexican cartel world. One was shifting the power of cocaine distribution from the Columbians to the Mexicans. The second was moving from smuggling through Mexico and across the border to creating deliveries in several areas of the United States. Third was the introduction of "muscle" to control and exploit others with the creation of a military-like wing.

Los Zetas

A younger cartel that competes for the zones or plazas with the Gulf Cartel is the Zetas. The (los) Zetas were originally officers in the Mexican Army and the Federal Police. Some have argued that the U.S. Army at Ft. Bragg, North Carolina provided part of the training these men had. The first member of the Zetas was Arturo Guzmán Decena, a retired Mexican Army Lieutenant. He was hired by Osiel Cárdenas Guillén, successor to Juan García Ábrego, when García Abrego was arrested in Monterrey, extradited to the United States and sentenced to life in Federal prison in Colorado. To strengthen his succession to the head of the Gulf Cartel, Osiel Cárdenas Tuillen had Guzmán Decena recruit a force of other Army members and retired veterans. He recruited from the Mexican equivalent of the U. S. Army's Special Forces, the Grupo Aeromóvil de Fuerzas Especiales (*Special Forces Airmobile Group*, GAFE). Highly trained in a variety of combat scenarios and with powerful weapons, the first group of 31 former Army men provided a formidable force for the Gulf Cartel to consolidate its territories and destroy other gangs and police or Army units that opposed them.

As leadership changed in the Gulf Cartel and as los Zetas grew in experience by 2010, there was a rupture between the Gulf and its enforcers. Los Zetas emerged as a second cartel competing with the Gulf in Tamaulipas and Veracruz, and becoming a dominant force in the neighboring state to the west of Nuevo Leon and in the most western city of Tamaulipas, Nuevo Laredo. With their military training los Zetas are the most competent combat force among the cartels and, influenced by the brutality of la Familia, have made torture, beheadings and mass executions a calling card of Mexican cartels. Taking pages from Middle Eastern entities like al Qaeda, they post videos to threaten rivals, terrorize citizens and intimidate law enforcement. They contest for the plazas in Matamoros and Reynosa next to Brownsville and McAllen in south Texas and control areas near Saltillo and Mexico's greatest industrial city, Monterrey. Their violence there and on or near campuses like Monterrey Tech has fractured academic life and sent wealthier Mexican students fleeing to American universities.

The Zetas have pushed far south into Guatemala and west to Guadalajara. In Guatemala they have encountered a weak central government permitting them to establish hegemony over local government forces, and have also recruited from a feared special forces-type unit of the Guatemalan military, the Kailbles. The Zetas have adopted much of the psychological warfare first presented by a smaller cartel from Michoacán. The Zetas appear to control Nuevo Laredo, but are contested there by their former bosses, the Gulf Cartel, as well as the Sinaloa Cartel that has fought a 5-year battle in Juarez and appears to have prevailed there over the Juarez Cartel.

The Juarez Cartel

Organized crime has a history in Juarez extending back in time for more than a hundred years. Far from the control of Mexico City, it was home to bandits in the 19th century and a haven for early revolutionaries in the 1910 Civil War. Like other Mexican border cities it prospered during Prohibition as a source of alcohol, including some smuggling into the United States. Like its American twin, El Paso, Juarez sits at a desert mountain pass just before the Rio Grande starts a northward swing in New Mexico, rising to over 12,000 feet at its headwaters 530 miles north in western Colorado, near the small community of Creed. Juarez is the state of Chihuahua's largest city with a population of more than a million, though some reports are that as much as one-fifth of the population has fled since 2008 as the Cartel Wars flared and the Mexican government began to use higher force levels with military units to pacify the conflict.

Juarez was a leader in the *maquilas* concept with the efforts of Juarez Mayor Jaime Bermudez to attract American manufacturers to his warehouse developments, and today hundreds of American managers cross from El Paso each morning to factories in Juarez, returning each evening. Until the 1980s organized crime existed in a few red light districts to cater to Americans including soldiers from Ft. Bliss and students from the University of Texas at El Paso, New Mexico State University at Las Cruces, locals in El Paso, and tourists. Bars and bordellos were open 24/7; 365 days a year and alcohol, marijuana and girls were the basic trade. Heroin was always there, fed by poppy fields in Chihuahua and the more extensive farms in Sinaloa, but it remained a minor drug used only by hard-core addicts and not like the recreational drugs of alcohol and marijuana. The drug mix changed with the leadership of Amado Carrillo Fuentes. Like many other drug lords, Carrillo Fuentes was from Sinaloa and from an early age was schooled in the drug cultivation and smuggling trade. His uncle was Ernesto Fonseca Carrillo, one of the three leaders of the foundational Guadalajara Cartel.

As a youth he was sent by his uncle to Ojinaga, Chihuahua to oversee his uncle's cocaine shipments, and to learn about border smuggling operations from Pablo Acosta Villarreal "El Zorro de Ojinaga" (*The Ojinaga Fox*). Pablo was the perfect role model for Amado. He was born in Santa Elena, Chihuahua some 200 miles east, down river from Juarez. As a youth he worked in the farms, ranches and then oil fields of west Texas and eastern New Mexico.

Pablo's earliest smuggling was bringing the wax boiled out of the native candelilla plant for use in candles, waterproofing, cosmetics, etc. It was so valuable that most of those plants were stripped from the Texas counties north of the Rio Grande. The Mexican government outlawed its export and required those that gathered the wax to sell it to Mexican government agents. Pablo knew that much higher prices were paid on the American side and he developed the means of avoiding and bribing Mexican authorities and bringing the wax to the American side.

In the coming years he applied this knowledge of smuggling into the United States to marijuana, heroin and the most profitable drug, cocaine. Pablo, at his peak, was smuggling 60 tons of Columbian cocaine a year into the United States. He had moved his base of operations from the 300 people of the village of Santa Elena up river to Ojinaga where his uncle had based the cocaine smuggling. As it grew, much of the operation was moved even farther west to Juarez, and eventually Carillo Fuentes would come to inherit it.

Pablo Acosta was killed in an operation led by Mexican Comandante Guillermo Gonzalez Calderoni via a helicopter assault. The Comandante was traveling through Texas' Big Bend National Park with an FBI escort, and had obtained permission for Mexican armed agents to enter U.S. air space and use American military helicopters. After this feat Calderoni became concerned about his safety in Mexico, became somewhat of an American agent, and moved to San Antonio, Texas. There was some evidence that like many Mexican law officers he had long played both sides of the Mexican drug trade, and was eventually murdered in 2003 in McAllen, Texas as he sat with his driver in his car in front of his attorney's offices. The killer or killers were never identified.

Amado Carrillo learned the lessons of Pablo well, and that was the highly profitable cocaine trade and the need to work with the Mexican Federal government. You had to determine who to place on the payroll and how much money to pay. You had to be watchful of the rise of new competitors and how to avoid coming too much to the attention of the Americans. As he watched the growing industrialization of Juarez by the late 1980s, he began to apply those same large corporate strategies and revolutionize transport by the use of Boeing 727 airplanes to move cocaine from Columbia to Mexico, and then use his well-developed smuggling skills to bring it to market in the United States. For this he became called "El Señor de los Cielos" (The Lord of the Skies). Amado Carrillo was said to be worth 25 billion dollars but was haunted by the fear of capture by law enforcement. Credited by American law enforcement as being one of the most low-key, sophisticated, and diplomatic of Mexico's drug lords, he was felt to have connections to General Jesús Gutiérrez Rebollo, Mexico's top drug enforcement official.

Amado Carrillo died in July of 1997 in a hospital in Mexico City under controversial circumstances. He was undergoing plastic surgery to alter his appearance as part of his ongoing efforts to avoid capture by authorities. His brother, Vicente Carrillo Fuentes, has assumed control of this large cartel and has sought to initiate agreements with his brother Rodolfo Carrillo Fuentes, his nephew Vicente Carrillo Leyva, and Ricardo García Urquiza, and formed an alliance with other drug lords such as Ismael "Mayo" Zambada in Sinaloa and Baja California, the Beltrán Leyva brothers in Monterrey, and Joaquín "El Chapo" Guzmán in Nayarit and Sinaloa. Building agreements rather than competing was the strategy of Amado Carrillo.

By 2005 many of these agreements fell apart and the Juarez Cartel found itself in a violent struggle with the Sinaloa Cartel that continues to this day. Still immensely powerful and wealthy, the Juarez Cartel like the Gulf Cartel has an armed group to provide protection, actually two groups. One is led by existing and former Juarez municipal police officers and state police and is referred to as la Linea (the line).

The second is an El Paso street gang, Barrio Azteca that has evolved into a group that provides violence and protection on both sides of the border and is a recognized prison gang by the Texas Department of Criminal Justice. In addition to Juarez, the

Cartel is thought to be active in Culiacán, Monterrey, Ojinaga, Mexico City, Guadalajara, Cuernavaca and Cancún. In its conflicts with the Sinaloa Cartel, it is allied with los Zetas, the Tijuana Cartel and the Beltrán-Leyva Cartel.

The Tijuana Cartel

This cartel has long had an enviable location as the supply point for drug users in Southern California. With San Diego, a city of one million, about 20 miles to the north and the Los Angeles area 100 miles further north with over 17 million people, Tijuana with 1.6 million people is next to the largest American market for illegal drugs. Like El Paso with the large Army post of Ft. Bliss, research installations north in New Mexico at White Sands, and the Holloman Air Force base, there are several Army, Navy and Air Force installations in southern California, resulting in thousands of adventurous young people eager to cross the border into Mexico. With Hollywood nearby, aspects of its exploits and involvements in California have made their way into movies including Traffic (Soderbergh et al., 2002), To Live and Die in LA (William, 1985) and End of Watch (Ayer, 2012).

Like Juarez, alcohol, marijuana and girls were available since the end of the 19th century and accelerated during the Prohibition years in Tijuana. Miguel Ángel Félix Gallardo of the Guadalajara Cartel started the Tijuana Cartel by assigning it to his two nephews, the Arellano Félix brothers, when he was imprisoned. Those brothers were raised both in Tijuana and cities of Southern California and had wealthy and privileged backgrounds. They served as reference points for youth in both countries and promoted designer clothes and jewelry and expensive cars as part of a youthful "narco culture". Luis Fernando Sanchez Arellano, known as El Ingeniero (the engineer), now heads the Cartel. He seems to stay in power with the connivance of Mexican local and federal authorities and the Sinaloa Cartel. The Sinaloa Cartel is south of Tijuana and moves much of its drugs through Tijuana, and appears to pay a tariff but has little visible conflict with the Tijuana Cartel. That may be because the Sinaloa Cartel is locked into fierce struggles in Juarez with the Juarez Cartel and with los Zetas in Nuevo Laredo and other areas of eastern Mexico including areas under the control of the Gulf Cartel.

The Sinaloa Cartel

The wealthiest and perhaps the most powerful cartel today in Mexico is the Sinaloa Cartel. Like the other border Cartels it has its inception with the Guadalajara Cartel and Amado Carrillo. The current head and today's wealthiest Mexican drug lord is Joaquín "El Chapo" Guzmán. Unlike the Cartels in other areas, it exists in an area of Mexico with substantial agricultural productivity, including historical traditions of opium poppy and marijuana farming. The Sinaloa Cartel's advantage of producing much of its drugs is matched by the disadvantage of not having a border "plaza" to smuggle drugs to the American markets. Sinaloa has addressed this need by having partnerships with the Tijuana Cartel to use the land gateway into California.

Needing more access to the United States and particularly to the areas east of the Rocky Mountains, the Sinaloa Cartel has fought a bloody war to capture the "plazas" at Juarez and Nuevo Laredo. Those wars and the efforts of Mexican President Felipe Calderon have resulted in the high and visible levels of violence on the streets of Mexican towns, particularly Juarez and Nuevo Laredo. The Juarez Cartel opposes Guzmán in Juarez, and much of the original success has been able to gain control of areas west of Juarez leading into New Mexico and the Valley of Juarez, east along the Rio Grande. In Nuevo Laredo, the Sinaloa Cartel has encountered the most brutal of the Cartels, the Zetas, and has replied with equal brutality and the use of banners hung from highways bridges declaring intents and making threats.

It is based in Culiacán, Sinaloa with operations in the Mexican states of Baja California, Durango, Sonora, and Chihuahua. It is thought to bring into the United States tons of cocaine each year and many times that amount of marijuana. It is probably the dominant buyer of cocaine from Columbia and likely, since it produces its own heroin, the dominant smuggler of heroin. But its newest drug and perhaps the most profitable is methamphetamine (meth). Meth may be the direction of drugs in the future as it is chemically synthesized from several different starter chemicals and less expensive to create than traditionally grown drugs like marijuana, cocaine and morphine. At one time anhydrous ammonia and iodine and the antihistamine pseudoepinephrine were widely available in drugstores, and ammonia could be found at agricultural suppliers as it is used to provide nitrogen fertilizer. Federal controls restricted the availability of these chemicals, reducing the supply of meth. However in the last decade as world trade has increased, China has become a leading supplier of these chemicals and the Pacific Ports in Sinaloa, Colima, Michoacán, and Nayarit are convenient shipping points of chemicals and readily available for the Cartel.

La Familia Michoacán

Perhaps the oddest of the cartels is la Familia in the very impoverished state of Michoacán. It achieved notoriety with a brutal act probably copied from videos of executions of prisoners of al Qaeda including that of Daniel Pearl, the Wall Street Reporter, beheaded in Pakistan after being kidnapped in 2002 by Khalid Sheikh Mohammed. Apparently the leaders of la Familia saw the worldwide horror this produced and adopted it as a psychological warfare tactic to use on their rivals. At a dance club and bar in Uruapan in 2006, the cartel members tossed five severed heads onto the dance floor of the *Sol y Sombra* night club along with a message that read: "*The Family doesn't kill for money. It doesn't kill women. It doesn't kill innocent people, only those who deserve to die. Know that this is divine justice.*"

The Cartel seems to have begun as a group of vigilantes seeking to control bandits and drug traffickers in the state. The leader Nazario Moreno González, nicknamed "The Craziest One," mixed evangelical texts with self-composed statements to assist the impoverished residents of the state to improve themselves.

The Cartel members trained with the Zetas in the early 2000 but today are allied with the Sinaloa Cartel and against the Zetas and the Beltrán-Leyva Cartel. La Familia forbids its members to use the drugs it sells, emphasizes religion and family values during recruitment, and has placed banners in areas of operations claiming that it does not tolerate substance abuse or exploitation of women and children. According to Mexico Public Safety Secretary Genaro García Luna, members are recruited from drug rehabilitation clinics by helping addicts recover and then forcing them into service for the drug cartel or be killed. Advancement within the organization depends as much on regular attendance at prayer meetings as on target practice. The cartel gives loans to farmers, businesses, schools and churches, and it advertises its benevolence in local newspapers in order to gain social support.

Under heavy government assault it first disbanded and then split in 2011 into two groups, one using the la Familia Michoacán name and the second calling itself Caballeros Templarios, the Knights Templar. The Calderon Administration declared the Cartel was gone but both groups appear to be in existence today, reflecting the reality throughout Mexico that as long as unemployment is high and vast riches from drugs available, military and police force will not be sufficient to end the existence of cartels.

Other Cartels

The Pacific Cartel is variously described as a group in Acapulco, Cuernavaca and other areas in the state of Guerrero and southwest of Mexico City. Parts of it are the Beltran Leyva Cartel that was formed by four brothers and was a part of the Sinaloa Cartel at various points and led efforts to secure sites in northeast Mexico for drug transit into Texas. There it fought with the Gulf Cartel, its armed wing, the Zetas, and with the Zetas after they broke from the Gulf Cartel. It also refers to an ally of the Sinaloa Cartel headed by a person originally from Laredo and engaged in competition in Nuevo Laredo with the Zetas. Edgar "La Barbie" Valdez Villarreal, originally from Laredo, was the operator of its armed group known as Los Negros, formed by the Sinaloa Cartel to counter the operations of the rival Gulf Cartel's Los Zetas. Los Negros has been known to employ street gangs to carry out murders and other illegal activities. The group is involved in fighting in the Nuevo Laredo region for control of the drug trafficking corridor. Following the 2003 arrest of Gulf Cartel leader Osiel Cárdenas, it is believed the Sinaloa Cartel moved 200 men into the region to battle the Gulf Cartel for control.

Since 2010, however the Sinaloa Cartel has been allied with the Gulf Cartel in conflicts against the Zetas in Nuevo Laredo, Monterrey and Saltillo. The Nuevo Laredo region is an important drug trafficking corridor into Laredo, Texas, where as much as 40% of all Mexican exports pass through into the U.S. Following the 2002 Nuevo Laredo assassination of journalist Roberto Javier Mora García from *El Mañana* newspaper, much of the local media has been cautious about their reporting of the fighting. The Cartels have sought to control the media and often issue their warnings via posters hung on roadway bridges, called "narcomantas."

Knights Templar is an offshoot of la Familia and continues some of the quasi-religious aspects. The original Knights Templar was a part of religious military orders beginning in the 1100s in Europe and the Middle East. The members fought wars against Muslim armies and held important sites to both

Christdom and Islam, including the Dome of the Rock in Jerusalem. They acted as military escorts for European pilgrims journeying to the Holy Land to protect them from bandits and armed Muslim groups. The Knights Templar Cartel's slogans reflect some of the beneficent aims of the Knights of the Middle Ages even going far as issuing helmets and Swords!

Cartels of the Future

The forces that create Cartels include high levels of unemployment, vast profits from moving contraband, extortion, kidnapping, and opaque and untrustworthy governments. A wealthy market is needed, and the U.S. provides it. The PAN governments, Felipe Calderon more than Vicente Fox, used Federal power to attempt to remove Cartel leadership. It resulted in a bloody six-year term. With the 2012 elections, the PRI has returned to power. Past masters at using franchises, the likelihood is less violence, more small Cartels and increased movement of contraband. Some feel that the Sinaloa Cartel may become a controlling cartel like occurred in the 1980's with the Guadalajara Cartel, but powerful forces exist to splinter alliances. History may provide some information on the shape and patterns of the Cartels for the rest of this decade.

Salinas as Narco-controlled Prototype of the PRI

Looking back to what was a promising Mexican Presidential Administration, that of Carlos Salinas offers a caution. The answers to some degree are in the pages and videos of brutal murders, not just in border cities but also throughout Mexico. The wars among the Cartels are a function of the breakdown of shadowy traditional partnerships of corruption between parts of Mexican government, including law enforcement. This corruption may have reached to the Presidency in some administrations, as evinced by the rumors surrounding President Carlos Salinas de Gortari, his family and his associates during the years of the unchallenged domination of one political party, the PRI. Cartels poaching on each other's traditional domains was a part of the problem.

The Salinas episode of corruption is the most visible of any in the last half century. It serves as a filter when viewing Mexican politics and illustrates much of the reason of the lack of trust by Mexicans in their political institutions. Salinas, who was President from 1988 to 1994, had an undergraduate degree from Mexico's National Autonomous University and a Ph.D. from Harvard in economics. From the inception of his election he was viewed as a modern leader that would help Mexico emerge onto the world's stage. He signed the NAFTA accords for Mexico with Bill Clinton and Jean Chrétien of Canada, but the closing years of his administration were clouded with the arrest of his older brother, Raul Salinas, on a variety of corruption charges as well as huge financial problems caused by a peso devaluation to cover huge debts acquired by the Mexican government. The final months of his administration were additionally scarred by the assassination of PRI presidential candidate Luis Donaldo Colosio in Tijuana and, a few months later, that of José Ruiz Massieu. Ruiz Massieu was Salinas' former brother-in-law who was also the Secretary General of the PRI, and whose murder was never solved during Salinas' presidency. This was in spite of the fact that Mario Ruiz Massieu (Francisco's brother) was the Attorney General in charge of the investigation as Salinas' last year ended.

Salinas' older brother Raul was active in the Salinas administration while quietly amassing a fortune of 100 million dollars, moved with the assistance of Citibank to Swiss accounts. It has been contended that the wealth came from protection paid to Raul by the Cartels and the largest amount by the Gulf Cartel and García Abrego. Raul was convicted and sentenced to prison for masterminding the murder of Jose Ruiz Massieu.

Raul spent ten years in prison until his conviction was reversed in 2005 and he was released. No other person was charged with the murder. After his term Carlos Salinas moved to Ireland and spends most of his time there and in London and Spain with occasional trips back to Mexico. His youngest brother, Enrique, was found dead, severely beaten in his auto in the State of Mexico with a plastic bag wrapped around his head on December 6, 2004. These are markings of a contract killing and suggest some feud with a cartel. Many questions exist to this day of corruption issues within the PRI and the administration of Salinas. The saga of the Salinas administration, his conduct during and after office, and the involvements of family and friends provides a critical lesson in the fact that organized crime in Mexico is often not relegated to rural areas and shadowy sectors of society.

Summary: Post Calderon-Cartel Configuration

Cartels prior to the PAN era were relatively durable organizations. Calderon's attack on them, rather than the franchising style of the PRI, resulted in a fracturing of many and traditional alliances with aspects of the Mexican State. It is unclear if that process continues under the new PRI administration in 2013. By and large there are currently two major Cartels in Mexico, one dominating the eastern part of the country, the Zetas, and one the western part, the Sinaloa. The current patterns as mapped by the DEA are:

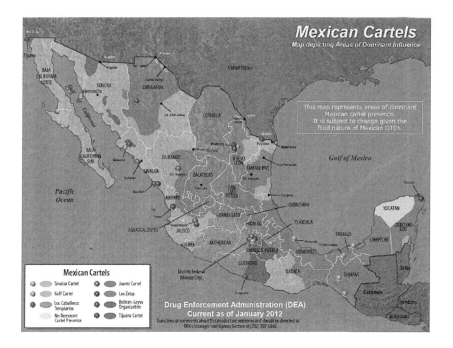

The cartels of the last decade or so are rooted deep in the culture and the economy of Mexico. They may to some extent have derived from international efforts to counter military threats of the United States and are for some Mexicans viewed as a bit of "payback" for lands that formerly belonged to Mexico. They will continue to exist as long as Mexico has its authoritarian institutions often pervasively corrupt that exclude so many common citizens as well as the promise of quick wealth for the millions of young unemployed and ill-educated men and women.

The charges of the PRI in the election of 2012 that the PAN administration caused or inspired the violence are inaccurate. The realty of Mexico is that it has been an exceedingly violent society during the 20th century. An article adapted from the El Paso Times drawing on official Mexican data illustrates that as the table presents:

Mexico Homicide Rates

Year	Rate	Total

1931	50.78	8551
1935	44.9	8098
1940	67.04	10175
1945	48.04	10782
1950	48.09	12403
1955	35.93	10782
1962	25.48	9493
1979	18.32	11862
1989	19.93	15399
1996	16.01	14508
2003	9.92	10883
2010	21.7	24374
2011	24.0	27199
2012	22.0	25712

Recent Mexican Presidents have had strikingly high levels of violence not simply violence being new with Felipe Calderon. Criticism of the violence of the Calderon era as unprecedented is not founded in fact with rates far higher in the 40s and 50s.

Homicides in Mexico in five administrations

President/term	Homicides First five years.	Rates	Highlights
Felipe Calderón (2006-2012)	79,956	14.5	Crackdown against drug cartels.
Vicente Fox (2000-2006)	49,862	9.78	First opposition party president elected.
Ernesto Zedillo (1994-2000)	69,698	15.1	Replaced slain candidate Luis Donaldo Colosio.
Carlos Salinas (1988-1994)	76,871	18.92	Got country to adopt NAFTA.
Miguel de la Madrid (1982-1988)	69,306	19.22	Drug lords begin power grab.

Source: El Paso Times research - analysis.   NACHO L. GARCIA JR. / EL PASO TIMES

The existence of violence is much greater south of Mexico in all of Central America except for Costa Rica, Nicaragua and Panama. Honduras in 2011 had the world's highest rate at 82.1 per hundred thousand and El Salvador had 66. That year

Guatemala had a rate of 38.5, all three countries south of Mexico with far higher rates.

Chapter 15: Spillover

Mexico and the United States have historical concerns about foreign influences and efforts of domination. The United States fought wars in 1776, 1812, 1850, 1865, 1912, 1941, 1951, 1968, 1974, 1984, 2001, among smaller events and maintains standing forces greater than any country in the world. Mexico has had substantial wars in every century of its existence with the possible exception of the 18th century. The two countries with very different histories and cultures regard the other with caution and concerns about a variety of spillovers from the other culture.

People

People, oil and cartels are three visible exports of Mexico. Not since the Revolution of 1910 to 1920 have such as large percentage of the Mexican population left Mexico mostly to the United States either to live permanently or to return in a few years when conditions improve. The numbers are far greater now since 2000 than the numbers in the Revolution and the totals are 34 million who identify themselves as Hispanics including those born in the United States, those who were born in Mexico and have secured citizenship and those that have not. Many have secured citizenship, many more have children with citizenship but about 6 million have not.

There are now over 40 million immigrants in the United States reflecting rapid growth of persons born in other countries and moving to the United States with immigrants from Mexico being the overwhelmingly largest. The height of the recent trend especially from Mexico and Central America was in 2008 just as the housing and mortgage finance bubble burst removing many jobs that were important attractants. Nevertheless the current immigrant flow is one of the greatest in many years.

Oil

The export of oil while not visible to the ordinary person is the most important of Mexico's exports earning significant currencies to permit a highly paid petroleum workers' union, funds for teachers, nurses and physicians across Mexico, many other government workers and lucrative construction contracts for Mexican firms. These employees are the key to the emerging middle class in an urban Mexico. Oil export earnings have provided the capital to improve the public infrastructure of roads, airports, energy and communication utilities. But like in the United States most of the readily available oil has been pumped and Mexico to continue to have oil exports must invest in exploration and refinement either by developing the research infrastructure in Mexico or permitting foreign contractors. But so far Mexico's concerns about the risk of foreign domination of such a critical national resource have resulted in slow progress in exploration and level to declining oil exports.

Spillover of Cartels, Members and Influence

The cartels themselves rather than government now by 2013 control significant areas of Mexico and the war among them and with the Mexican government has accounted for more than 60,000 deaths since 2006. If one includes missing persons, then the total is 100,000 individuals dead or missing since 2006. The cartels influence production areas of cocaine in Peru, Columbia and Venezuela, moving products through Central America with warehouses in these largely rural countries, as well as via boat and submarine in the Atlantic and Pacific, into Mexico and then via the "plazas' at points of entry into the United States.

All of the cartels extend efforts into the United States to deliver product either directly to users or build alliances with local street gangs to serve as the immediate seller. In addition to cocaine sourced from South America, Mexican cartels obtain or cultivate heroin poppies in states like Sinaloa, grow marijuana in several Mexican states and bring precursor chemicals, especially epinephrine and pseudo-epinephrine, for making methamphetamine from countries particularly China into Mexico. Mexican or Chinese chemists in Mexico then create methamphetamine for the American market.

All these illegal drugs flow through the plazas of Mexican cities at the border and fan out from Texas and California into all of the United States. It is a process that covers two continents, South and North America, and increasingly uses commercial trade structures, especially legitimate banking, to move its vast proceeds and profits. The cartels have long struck agreements with the governments, banks and business structures in Mexico. That pattern of accommodation is now occurring with international banking. The monetary fine but no criminal conviction of principals or agents at the London based bank, HSBC, in December of 2012 [*(Banker, 2013, February 6), 2012)]* active in years of laundering money including drug money for the Cartels is blunt testimony to the reach and power of the cartels and the immunity they and some partners like HSBC, the world's third largest bank, hold to government prosecution.

Examples of the Reach

The wealth of these cartels translates to power, ever increasing power, and their reach now goes south far beyond Mexico to Central and South America, and north deep into the American heartland as well as Canada and Europe. Here is a recent and well-detailed example.

Meth in the American Heartland

Methamphetamines, synthesized by a Japanese chemist in the late 19th Century and used by both the German and Allied armies to increase endurance in World War II, began to appear in rural and small town America twenty years ago. (Bonne, 2001). There it is referred to as "meth" or "speed". In those years the starter chemicals were available in agricultural chemicals (ammonia used for nitrogen), and drugstore antihistamines. Small labs were found in homes and garages to "cook speed". Slowly official Washington began to address demand suppression and achieved results by placing restrictions on the availability of the starter chemicals from farm supply houses and drugstores. Now the supply of the source chemicals comes from outside the United States, especially Mexico.

The reach is illustrated by Nick Reding in his book, *Methland* (Reding, 2009). Through four years of reporting he details the changing lives through the impact of meth in Oelwein, a small town in Iowa. The story is of the vanishing of educated young people from rural Iowa, as well as the destruction of middle-class jobs at the local packing plant. The agricultural conglomerates that have gobbled up Oelwein and similar farm towns may feed the world. However they parasitize the workers, creating a craving for synthetic stimulants that sap the appetite while increasing the body's capacity for labor in feed yards and packinghouses.

Reding observes in Oelwein that methamphetamine is not a recreation drug but a vocational crutch to support long working hours often at two or three jobs. In this town the impact of globalization is not prosperity but the destruction of jobs and unions that strive to have living wages but are being replaced by minimum wages and the ever-present threat that foreign workers will be brought in who are more malleable than local people. These places are the magnets for desperate immigrant laborers who as they search for agricultural work in states like

Iowa, blaze the drug smuggling trails that run up into the Corn Belt from Mexico.

Cartel Presences Across the United States

The map below is taken from a Federal source that illustrates the presence of the Mexican cartels in almost every state early in the development of the cartels, DEA, 2008. Meth is one of the newer drugs provided and growing in quantity. The others include cocaine, heroin, marijuana and traditional prescriptive drugs such as Oxycontin, diazepam (Valium, Librium), Fentanyl, SSRI uptake inhibitors (Prozac, Paxil, Zoloft), human growth hormone, Adderall, Ritalin, Rhohypnol; indeed a cornucopia of pharmaceutical substances that are mood altering while addictive.

The DEA estimates during the 2010 alone that 50 billion dollars of illegal drugs were sold in the United States and otherwise state this is the pattern and volume in succeeding years. Federal estimates are that there are at least 1,000 cities in the United States that show a presence of the Mexican cartels.

Significant portions of the money earned from the drug trade buy weapons, cars, jewelry, status and influence in Mexico and increasingly in Texas and California. It flourishes with a culture of early flashy wealth, young women for the young men, lavish parties and early violent death. We see examples of competing Mexican cartels seeking to establish footholds in American cities and developing as well franchise-type arrangements with local street and prison gangs.

Recruits From Texas
The presence of Mexican Cartels now with the historical pattern going back more than a century of Mexicans living in Texas and traveling back to families in Mexico creates new permutations that affect security in Texas. With almost 9,000 Mexican Nationals in the Texas Department of Criminal Justice there is solid concern for connections of some of these inmates back with the Mexican cartels in home communities. There have been killings in Houston and Dallas between Mexican cartel rivals since 2010. Kidnappings and extortion now occur of Mexicans and Americans in Texas cities as well as other states. There are criminal involvements coming from American youth growing up in our border cities then working as *sicarios* in México.

The most prominent recent example is the case of Edgar Valdez Villarreal (*la Barbie*), a popular former high school football player from Laredo who rose to hold high office in one of the most notorious Mexican cartels before his arrest in Mexico. (Grigoriadis, 2011) He began with a familiar pattern of most youth in Texas cities that grew up on or near the border. Youth would go across the river to Mexico to buy liquor without required identifications and with bars open all night long. The pattern from Brownsville to El Paso was youth starting in about the 9th grade growing up in this dual life of some time on the American side and some on the Mexican side. The pattern has only been disturbed in the last 5 years as the violence has become so frequent on the Mexican side to dissuade parents and in some case the youth to avoid being in Mexico or at least when nightfall comes.

The Upper and Middle Class Start to Abandon Mexico

The violence in Mexico is also disturbing residents that have lived in cities like Matamoros, Monterrey and Saltillo for generations. Both wealthy and upper middle class Mexicans intent on escaping the violence and chaos are buying homes and in many cases starting business in Texas cities like El Paso, San Antonio, Houston, Brownsville, Austin and smaller Texas cities. Sources say that there has been a virtual explosion of EVA1 permits issued to foreigners that provide permanent residence visas for persons and families that invest either $500,000 or $1,000,000 in businesses that promise to create a minimum of 10 jobs (DEA, 2012 June 12; USINS, 2012) Banking rules in the United States as compared to Mexico though increase the transparency of these persons and the risks to new immigrants from Mexico to Mexican organized crime even in the United States is a reality.(Hendricks, February 11, 2012)

In this migration are also cartel members that find they are safer in Texas than in Mexican states though there are occasions of violence between Mexican cartel members in Texas. Regular news reports of these incidents come from El Paso, Brownsville and Houston.

Cartel Activity in Austin and Texas

Americans and Texans have been reluctant to recognize the presence of Mexican cartels having crossed the Rio Grande. Two illustrations in the last two years in Austin and central Texas document the flow of cartel activity as drug distribution and money into legitimate business in the DEA-named Project Delirium involving a cartel from central Mexico, and a complex racing horse-money laundering scheme by the Zetas.

Project Delirium(DEA, 2011, July 21) was a national effort with a significant focus in Austin. Thirty-five people were arrested in the Austin area in a targeted attack on the La Familia Michoacán drug cartel in the summer of 2011. The Drug Enforcement Agency, Federal Bureau of Investigations, Texas Department of Public Safety and the Austin Police Department, along with other local law enforcement agencies, raided 11 addresses in Austin as part of "Project Delirium," an effort that involved 20 months of a series of investigations nationwide. Officials seized drugs, weapons and more than $150,000 in cash. Authorities said it is a significant blow to the cartel in the Austin area. Nationwide, officials seized thousands of pounds of illegal drugs and millions in cash including:

- $62 million in U.S. currency
- approximately 2,773 pounds of methamphetamine
- 2,722 kilograms of cocaine
- 1,005 pounds of heroin
- 14,818 pounds of marijuana
- $3.8 million in other assets.

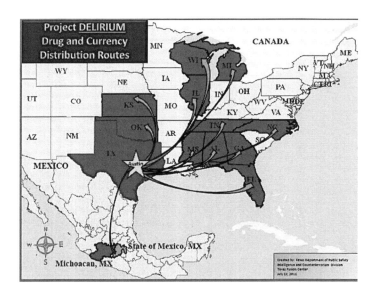

Michoacán is one of the poorest states in Mexico with a current population of about 4 million with another million thought to be living in the United States. Poverty in Mexico and the lure of jobs in real estate construction, restaurants and hotels in the United States saw great numbers of Mexicans from Michoacán leaving during the last two decades and living permanently outside of Mexico but maintaining ties to the state. In Austin much of the population was involved in working in and owning restaurants and those likely served as fronts for much of the drug activity as well as first jobs for recently arrived immigrants from the home state. Since restaurants have a substantial side to the business that is cash rather than using credit cards these business also provided useful conduits for "washing" drug money. Like the honest desire of Mexican migrants seeking work in the feed yards and packing plants in Iowa, restaurants owned by people from Michoacán provide work opportunities for others fleeing the poverty there but also serve as a cartel franchise to move drugs and cover for cartel members.

A different scheme was uncovered two years later with a direct intention of washing very large amounts of money earned by the Zetas Cartel. It was a quarter horse racing promotion that unfolded in El Paso, Ruidoso, New Mexico, and east of Austin and in Oklahoma. Essentially members of the Zetas purchased expensive racing horses in the United States with drug money, stabled and trained them in Texas with a major stable just east of Austin and in Oklahoma, raced them there and in New Mexico and simply laundered cartel money into a sport of American wealthy. Not satisfied with simply washing drug money by buying horses for cash, the cartel also was reported to fix races at Ruidoso thus enhancing the value of their horses as they won races. Apparently among those that raise, race and trace horses much of the business is done in cash and then nicely met the needs of the Cartel. (DEA, 2012 June 12) More crimes that appear to be those involving cartel activities include the planned killing of Mexican attorney, Juan Jesus Guerrero-Chapa, in South Lake a suburb of Dallas; (Todd Unger and Teresa Woodard; May 23, 2013, WFAA) the murder of the narco performer, Chuy Quintanilla, near Mission, Texas (Ildefonso Ortiz, April 25, 2013 The Monitor) to the recent conviction of Mansour J. Arbabsiar, a naturalized from Iran, who had lived in Corpus Christi and Round Rock, Texas who had attempted to hire a member of the Zetas cartel to bomb and kill the Saudi Ambassador to the United States in Washington, D.C. (Weiser, Benjamin, May 30, 2013, NYTimes) all illustrate the types of spillover violence coming from Mexico into the United States.

Public Safety Issues in the United States

The reality of substantial organized crime in Mexico and efforts of those crime entities to influence American communities become a factor first in two public institutions, municipal police and public school education. Both are fundamental institutions of American society and ones where most citizens encounter government. It is where visitors from other countries also have first interactions with American government. Visitors from other countries will bring the attitudes and concepts that operate in those cultures and will be a source of frustration and challenges. We examine how the threats will appear in both areas. Rapidly growing immigration and trade make contact with Mexico more complex.

As an example in 2002 I received a telephone call from Stanley Knee, the Austin Police Chief. Chief Knee asked if I could contact the Spanish Department at the University to see if there were any faculty that might prepare a short course in conversational Spanish for officers. In recent years he said officers were having more traffic stops and more home contacts with persons that spoke no English. He saw that it was becoming critical that there be some more officers fluent in Spanish. I contacted Professor Orlando Kelm of the Spanish and Portuguese Department who had just finished a language program for Dell Computers that was expanding its sales into Mexico and Latin America. Dell found a booming interest in its products and services in Latin America and needed to have staff that could converse in Spanish. While the Austin Police had a number of officers that were Hispanic, few felt comfortable with their Spanish skills particularly with persons that knew no English. At that time the Spanish surnamed percentage of the Austin Independent School population was 20 percent and Austin Police were just encountering increased numbers of persons that spoke no English. Today, a decade later in 2012, the Spanish surnamed proportion of the school district is greater than 60 percent and all police officers must be routinely prepared with Spanish knowledge. This rapid growth in the Hispanic population is partially a function of the Hispanic population in Texas being younger than the Anglo and African American populations, of larger typical family sizes but also of the significant numbers of persons that are immigrating from Mexico and Latin America into the United States and with Texas as the major gateway.

Stanley Knee made the point repeatedly in many conversations over the years he was Chief in Austin about how the nature of policing was changing. He felt that traditional department-based training or academic programs in criminal justice were not meeting nor would meet the need in future years. The reality of policing, particularly patrol, was becoming more and more a mobile and generic community solving profession calling for broad and in-depth education in many fields including health, anthropology and importantly leadership. Indeed we worked together for a decade, including Howard Prince, Stan Knee and me to create a prototype of such education.

The sudden increase in the presence of Spanish-only speakers and the impact on police patrol was a hint of challenges to come.

Police, Prosecution and Courts

The United States is a nation that has citizens on the move much of the time. Texas like most states in the United States with the exception of a few along then northeastern seaboard has a low relative level of public transportation and depends mostly on private autos with a limited flow of traffic on bus lines. Rail travel is mainly freight not passengers and commercial air travel accounts for a small amount of persons and cargo between Mexico and Texas.

This travel reality sets the conditions of how people come into contact with the police. The history of the police in the United States is a force hired, composed, funded and directed at the local level. This creation of local public safety authority reflects the colonial and frontier experiences of the 18th Century American populations and much of the direction is embodied in the Constitution and especially the Bill of Rights. The American Revolution was a war against centralized government, England, situated thousands of miles away and a government that was felt to be alien or indifferent to the needs of citizens. Powers of governmental authority were regarded as conditions to be carefully restricted and proscribed. Criminal statues and offenses were to be determined and adjudicated at the local or state level. Immediate law authorities such as the sheriff were elected, as was the local prosecutor, the county or district attorney. The military were kept separate from law enforcement and law enforcement codes, the criminal statues, were the responsibility of state legislatures not central authorities, the federal government. Police officers were expected to be known in their community and to wear distinctive attire to be identified as law officers. Clear separation of powers are required with one entity charged with being able to make arrests, a different one to hold persons charged for trial, a different one to conduct a trial and another if a guilty judgment was reached and a person was to be fined and/or incarcerated.

Contrast this to conditions that are observed in many areas of Mexico where the law enforcement function is performed by the military or police wearing military gear including using combat weapons and masks to make the officers anonymous. The argument is that this is for the safety of the officer as cartels routinely use the bribe of "plata o plumo," silver or lead, meaning accept a bribe or be killed to intimate and corrupt law enforcement. But this effort to protect law enforcement and the military personnel using uniforms with masks alienates the public from the officer making such officers appear threatening. The tactic of masks is further adopted by the cartels making legitimate authority and criminal entities appearing similar.

Funding in the United States of law enforcement is basically at the local level through municipal taxes, fees, sales and property taxes. The most immediate law enforcement officer, the sheriff, is elected at large. Most of the United States is now non-farm and municipal police officers hired by cities are the most common form of law enforcement. These officers typically have civil service protection and are directed by a chief hired at will who in turn is directly or indirectly hired by elected officials, mayors and city councils.

Elections and Corruption
The election process is intended to keep law enforcement directed and controlled ultimately by the citizen but the existence of elections and in many areas the need for expensive campaigns opens the possibility of bribes of elected officials. Heavy contributors expect favors and expensive campaigns thwart citizen controls. These local elected officials: sheriffs, prosecutors, county administrators and judges are one major area vulnerable to corruption. One of the core foundations of American democracy and the efforts to hold authority accountable at the immediate local level is also a major vulnerability to cartel influence. City council members, mayors,

prosecutors and judges are mostly elected and the fact that they must seek public donations opens avenues for bribery.

Police Officer Corruption

Based upon historical patterns and constitutional requirements, the basis and bulk of criminal justice responsibilities lie at the state and local levels. America has long had an ambivalent attitude toward policing. It comes from the fact that many persons came to this continent having faced exploitation from governments and viewed centralized political power with great caution. That is reflected in the design of the American system with substantial checks and balances and with the cultural and constitutional authority to define and prosecute crime residing with states and local communities. The American experience is having different levels of government with checks and balances controls the risks of too much power by the central state.

The police then represent a pivotal role in the culture between the people and the state. The police have broad powers over the citizen with the significant rights including using force, being able to stop and detain, conduct surveillance and initiate a criminal investigation process.

The most direct avenue of potential corruption is police and sheriff patrol officers. These officers have roles that bring them into regular contact with citizens as well as visitors from other countries. Unlike factory or office work the patrol officer is not under the direct scrutiny of a supervisor. Moreover the reality of police patrol work provides considerable discretion for the officer. While an officer will have standard working hours and a beat or patrol area, he or she will have a variety of activities that may be undertaken with some independent judgment. Does one watch for and pursue speeders or persons that appear to have tags on autos out of order? When does one follow or stop a suspicious person? When does one enter a place of business and which business?

Public safety officers must be carefully recruited, trained and supervised. Corruption takes several forms. One is simple attempts to bribe an officer at a traffic stop or to look the other way when an illegal act is spotted. Providing money directly to an officer when stopped in Mexico is routine and called *mordida*. Mexico is not alone in that situation as much of Latin America and Asia have similar patterns. Mexicans including Mexican police officers will defend the practice noting that police in that country are notoriously underpaid and the mordida is part of the franchise the officer has from his beat. In the United States such conduct is first order corruption and called *grass eating*. Officers that move from grass eating like using their badges to catch a free movie, getting half off for coffee or a meal to taking larger bribes such as several thousand dollars, special prices or discounts on housing, travel and cars are called *meat eaters*. Major police corruption starts not with receiving major benefits but with *grass eating*. While concepts like mordida are common in many parts of the world, they produce a caution, a warning of problems to come, a lack of trust in government and are anathema to American research and practice with police.

After Hours Work
Police work like Fire and EMS services is a public profession with a tradition of paid overtime work. In some cases it may be a result from being required to appear in court after a patrol shift. In other cases it can come from weather that requires additional police service or when there is some community event such as a parade, sporting event, etc. that requires additional service. While that is a tradition, the tradition can expose the officer to corruptive offers. After hours work is a frequent venue for corruption where officers are hired to provide protection for drug transports or to tip off traffickers moving contraband including people. Hiring off duty officers at convenience stores on routes that move drugs is a frequent

stratagem as well as hiring officers to provide protection for younger family members such as students away at college.

Police corruption is not new to the United States. During Prohibition alcohol was an illegal but sought after drug. Criminal gangs or cartels grew to import alcohol or source it from areas such as Appalachia where hidden stills could be located. The largest and most powerful cartels were in urban areas like Chicago where the Chicago Mob under Al Capone came to control or significantly compromise the Chicago police, public prosecutors and judiciary. A citizen group, the Chicago Crime Commission, was created to battle the mob and hired private police officers from Oklahoma and Texas to make criminal cases, turn them over to the FBI and used Federal courts for prosecution. Some areas have endemic occurrences of police corruption, Chicago, Detroit, the Bronx, Los Angeles, etc. and New Orleans is one of the most recognized. During much of the 1990s New Orleans police were poorly paid at about half the rate of comparable jobs in government and business. To meet living costs as much as 90 percent of the officers worked "details" overtime assignments for private businesses. Bars and restaurants were frequent sources of such details and inevitably contacts were made with the drug trade. Problems became so severe after several Federal convictions of officers that the Department was threatened to be placed under Federal supervision. A chief was hired, Richard Pennington, from Washington, D.C. and during much of his tenure was provided with protection from the FBI because of death threats felt to be coming from New Orleans police officers.

Austin provides a recent example of private pay leading to corruption concerns. In 2012 two municipal police officers were indicted and one convicted for receiving several tens of thousands of dollars in cash from a wealthy businessman from western Mexico for providing "protection" for his daughter a student at the University of Texas at Austin. The payments were sent in cash by air commercial carrier and the officer centrally involved in the scheme also failed to report the cash payments to the Internal Revenue Service. He was convicted and is serving Federal prison time for failing to report payments of in excess of $114,000 for security work. Another officer retired and 4 others were investigated. (Pitman, 2012 June 18; Plohetski, 2012, January 4)

Cases of this sort occur across Texas in municipal and county law enforcement offices and are the most visible parts of the corruption threat. (Martinez, 2013, February 11; Phippen, 2013, March 11; Shiller, 2013, May 17) News reports support that it occurs in other states as well (Phippen, 2013, March 11).

The reality of corruption among police may be the highest at the local level, the municipal police officer or deputy sheriff. That is a function of the fact that local officers tend to be local individuals and spend their career at one jurisdiction. While that reality supports that the police have community ties, it is the fact of those ties that may assist in creating conditions for corruption.

State and national police organizations are able to control the growth of local ties and the supervision challenges by rotating officers to different geographical locations. Some national police structures have developed during the 20th Century including the Secret Service, Treasury, Alcohol, Tobacco and Firearms, the FBI and DEA. But only the FBI approaches the role of being a national police and even there, numbers and budgets are far from sufficient to provide a national police force. The FBI also has roles to investigate law enforcement at the state and local levels and most states use the state police when concerns arise about the conduct of local police. But the assumption is that local, state and federal law enforcement work cooperatively and the levels are trustworthy to each other. Moreover the history of the last half century supports having officers that know their communities and build trust with residents. This is referred to as community policing. Federal and state agencies do not in most cases do community policing.

Persons hired and funded at the county and municipal level do the bulk of policing. Over the years various approaches have been tried to maintain officer integrity and yet have close relations with the public. Early in the 20th Century policing was in what was called the "political era" where officers were in close contact with citizens and elected politicians and often hired by politicians. Public concerns of cronyism with politicians and "influentials" led to a second era called "professional policing" that emphasized distant impersonal conduct by officers. That led to resistance and hostility toward the police and the isolation of the police from most community members. Policing is simpler in communities where all have common backgrounds. The most effective variety of policing is *community policing*, where officers work in partnership with citizens and neighborhoods to identify, prevent and solve crimes. That approach to policing means that officers are recruited with an eye toward the social norms of the community. Ethnicity, language, religion and politics are examples of social norms.

But the relationships between the officer and the citizen are complex and open to corruption. Sometimes friendships can skew the discretion of the officer to the favor of one person. The more serious is when friendships or commercial relations serve to direct the efforts of the officer. Many examples exist. Some businesses may find it useful to have police officers as part of the clientele. Restaurants and bars are examples where the presence of officers may more fully ensure the safety of customers and such establishments may grant free or reduced prices. In the study of officer corruption as mentioned earlier such acceptance of small favors is termed "grass eating". When officers receive more substantial payments or favors, that is "meat eating". However practice and science have shown that "grass eating" is but a step toward more serious corruption and must be understood as a continuum of loss of officer standards and a challenge to public respect. When police become corrupt they pose a crucial threat to other officers in that trust and integrity of one's associates is critical. Corruption is especially important to Federal officers as much of their surveillance and arrest process involves assistance from local police. This exists for a number of reasons including the fact that there is ten times or more the number of local officers than Federal and in many cases arrests requires the assistance of local officers.

Most officers employed at the municipal level do not serve "at will" but have some form of civil service review prior to being hired and during their employment. The chief is typically hired "at will" and may be supervised by a civilian, a city manager, also hired "at will" or a mayor, who will be elected. Elected officials are intended to be responsive to the will of the electorate but since they are elected, they are vulnerable to campaign funds offered to influence police actions. This is true as well for the historically oldest form of police in American communities, the county sheriff. In many states the criminal prosecutor (the district attorney) and in some cases the presiding judge are popularly elected. Like the mayor or the country sheriff, those are also venues that money and influence can be used for corruption.

Ensuring police honesty and integrity begins with careful recruitment of officers looking for individuals with a variety of extracurricular participation and careful examination for ties with gangs. Recreational choices are important especially those that would provide ties to illegal drugs. Once officers are hired efforts should be made to include them to be members of the communities where they serve. Policing by the result of stressful hours, events and concerns about retaliation is best met by working to integrate officers into the local community.

Departments must have highly professional internal affairs departments and all after hours work should have prior approval of the hiring department with full explanation of hours, location, hiring parties and amount of pay. Officers should not be permitted to work for bars, entertainment venues or settings in which they can become associated with or compromised by organized criminal activities.

Policing As Community Leadership
Critical to successful policing in these times is recruiting officers that become leaders not simple followers. In essence officers must understand the ways in which influence is developed within the ranks and from the outside and dedicated training and supervision provided to support a leadership perspective. (Knee, 2012; Lauderdale, Howard, 2007)

The current Austin Police Chief, Art Acevedo, provides a compelling illustration of a leader that ties his organization closely and continuously to the community. Born in Cuba and moved by parents to California during the tumultuous years of the 1950s, he is reflective of the pattern of immigration into the United States of millions of persons over the years. Knowing the importance of free and public institutions from the experience of his parents and his desire with theirs to make the transition to a new culture and life, he brings a very high level of dedication and enthusiasm to American life and his role as a community leader. Open institutions, ethical and committed to public service characterize his leadership and his requirements for service by all officers with the Austin Police. In a rapidly growing and ethnically ever more diverse community, he and his officers are one of the most trusted community institutions.

Corruption can challenge courts, prosecutors and corrections as well as police officers. Judges and prosecutors are elected and contributions to campaigns are a means for corruption. Mexican prisons are notoriously corrupt and often run by the Cartels.

The development of prison gangs and their control is a threat to correctional settings and may support serious continuities from prisons back to the street. (Burman, 2012)

Public School Social Structure and Norms

Public education is mandatory in the United States. Education is always dialectic between the teacher with the school and the child and the family and the community. In most cases the balance of authority is to the side of the teacher and the public schools serve as socialization mechanism to impart the goals, values, knowledge, skills and language of the culture. It is the culture's prime mechanism to explain and promote the civic culture. This socialization process is dependent upon the skills of the teacher and the support of the child's family and community. However if the community or a part of a community is not supportive of the values of the school then the socialization process is thwarted.

Schools provide the main conduit with the family of the moral values of the culture. The family is a more intimate teacher with the schools more broadly reflective of the culture. Grade schools will hold class elections, spelling contests and observances like Thanksgiving, Washington's Birthday, Lincoln's Emancipation Proclamation to teach core culture values much as the beliefs we cited in the Introduction. Mexico does the same and one of the more revealing examples is a child's play that Julia Preston (Preston & Dillon, 2004) recounts of her daughter's 5th grade class in a Mexican school. The play is called the Mouse Assembly and enacts a meeting of a group of mice that sought to organize to bring a tomcat under control that preys on them. The play features a chaotic meeting with none of the mice willing to plan or take responsibility on how to control or eliminate the cat. Near the end of the play the cat appears and grabs one of the mice and begins to eat it. The others flee in all directions with the emerging mouse crying, "Every mouse for himself!" Preston notes that the plays of her childhood in the United States always ended with an uplifting note and applauding democratic efforts. This Mexican play presents a cultural theme of authoritarian rule and the futility of resisting. The challenge of teaching the themes of the culture rests significantly on the public schools and it is likely an effort to teach a very different culture pattern for Mexican children becoming part of the culture of the United States.

Local property taxes and revenues from state government fund public school education in the United States. Local districts are established by the state and standards are set by each state for the curriculum, days of school, hours and teacher qualifications. The administration of each school district is conducted by a locally elected school board, which in turn sets the budget and hires the chief officer, the public school superintendent. Hiring of teachers and other school personnel (principals, school nurse, custodians, coaches) is the responsibility of the superintendent with varying degrees of school board involvement. Probably the most frequent involvement is the hiring of athletics' coaches. Construction of school buildings are made possible by long term borrowing of a district through the issuance of bonds and often a set percentage of property tax revenues are used to defray bond payments. The choice of books and the curriculum are usually controlled by a state board of education but influenced by the colleges that prepare teachers. Employers and national groups will push for the collection of comparative data on school performance as it is broadly recognized that proficiency in math, English, composition, civics, history, sciences, etc. are both critical for an educated workforce and an informed citizenry. With large percentages seeking to attend colleges and other postsecondary institutions comparative performance of students on college entrance exams also put pressure on schools to maintain performance. Some level of civil service protection exists for the teachers and usually teachers are not dismissed unless there is demonstrated failure to perform, criminal conduct or financial exigencies that require budget reductions.

Through much of the 20th Century the American public schools set international standards both in terms of the numbers of persons graduating from high school and relative performance scores of students. However overall educational progress by some measures reached a plateau about 1970 and some observers and scholars (Brooks, July 29, 2008; Katz, 2008) have suggested that that ceasing of the century long advance in educational levels and quality has negatively affected incomes as well as national progress.

If we compare American progress to that of Mexico, there are stark contrasts. With a median age of about 27 years the country has proportionally many more school-aged persons but much poorer educational performance than the United States or for that matter, Canada, much of Europe and Japan. In Mexico less than half of the students finish high school as compared to 75 percent for Brazil and 73 percent for Chile and 80 percent in the United States.

Central to understanding the failures of the Mexican system is one that is a private fiefdom of a few union leaders with one, Gordillo, that rose from a teacher to a king maker in Mexican politics for nearly 25 years. Her rise and exploitation of the education system teaches much about the Mexican system and how it serves an elite few at the expense of the system. The union, whose funds come from the central government and has been especially enriched by PEMEX oil revenues, has absolute control over who becomes a teacher and only the union knows how many teachers, schools and students exist in Mexico. The union has long determined who would become a teacher and positions were often viewed as an inheritance passed from parent to child or sold for a couple of hundred thousand dollars.

In late February of 2013 the head, Elba Ester Gordillo of the National Union of Education Workers, with 1.5 million members was arrested for the suspicious transfer of 200 million dollars to pay for accounts in America and Swiss banks used to purchase two houses in Coronado, California, art works, plastic surgery, credit card charges, shopping trips to a Neiman Marcus department store in San Diego, California and other alleged improprieties. Her daily spending trips in San Diego would be $3,000; three times what a well-paid teacher gets a month. ((http://www.lapoliticaeslapolitica.com/2013/02/after-arrest-of-teachers-union-leader.html), 2013b)

The experience of Mexican children in Mexican schools seems to follow them in terms of performance when they move to the United States. Dropout rates are above 40 percent and very few go on to attend college. Of all immigrant groups to New York, Mexican children are among the least successful.(Reitz, 2011; Semple, 2011) Nationally Mexican children lag all other groups in the first and second generation for school completion though substantial improvement occurs in the second generation from 7.4 to 12.9 years of education completed. (Reitz, 2011)

Transition Issues from Mexican Schools' Experiences to the United States

Forces that will not be supportive occur with subcultures in the community. Some subcultures are pre-existing either as a consequence of immigration patterns from decades and centuries past. Others come from immigration that does not participate in legal routes but occur typically with mass migrations.

Public schools do not make inquiries into citizenship status. Thus knowledge of family and home community may be lacking by the school and this may further the likelihood of groups opposed to community norms. Alienated communities today represent that likelihood and areas to recruit adults but especially youth into criminal activities. In these instances the public schools serve as meeting sites for opposed activity, areas in which gangs readily form and recruit new members.

Home schooling can be problematic. Parents through ignorance or inattention may agree to permit students to be home schooled thus removing them from the structure and socialization process of the public schools. An example I saw two years ago in a juvenile courtroom in Austin, Texas shows how far awry this trend can become. A 15 year old youth was in court and being questioned by a judge about his actions of kicking doors in during the day and taking appliances particularly large screen television sets and selling them. The judge asked the boy why he was not in school and he replied, "I am home schooled." At that point the judge had the boy's mother rise and respond to her question about how the mother did home schooling and what texts she used. The mother spoke in Spanish, knowing no English, and said she home schooled her son. The judge asked about textbooks and curricula and the mother said, "I have TV." The mother born in Mexico and perhaps with 6 years of education thought that having a television in the house was adequate for home schooling.

A more serious youth conflict at Austin schools occurred in September of 2005 that illustrates the tie that some youth have to violent areas outside of Austin but not that far away.(Proctor, 2005, October 28, 2006, April 4) Unknown to school and police authorities several gangs were active in Austin including in many of the public schools. The gangs and their conflicts came to the City's attention at 3:30 p.m. on September 23rd as Christopher "Woody" Briseño and his cousin, Adam Cantu got out of a school bus that had taken them from Austin High School to a school bus stop near Zavala Elementary, the nearest stop for them to walk home. A stolen Honda pulled up next to the boys and both were shot. Briseño died and Cantu survived the shooting. The killing was preceded the day before with a large gang fight at Austin High on Thursday. Few people in Austin thought of Austin High having gangs as the school has historically served the city's highest income areas, is situated on scenic property on Lake Austin (Lady Bird Lake today) and on a highly popular walking trail that goes along the Lake in the downtown. When questioned about the School's responsibility to be aware of the gang conflict and to call police and warn parents the School's principal said that there was, "nothing to suggest that anyone in AISD could have prevented this tragedy."

Some weeks later the students that were involved in the fight and did the shooting were apprehended two hundred and thirty miles to the south in one of the boys' hometown, Nuevo Laredo, the Mexican city across the border from Laredo. In April of the next year Manuel Cortez, a 17-year-old dropout received a life sentence for the murder. Three other Austin students, 15-year-old Pamela Ruiz, and her brothers Alan, 18, and Humberto, 16, were still facing murder charges. The conflict had developed because Briseño and Cortez were teasing Pamela and she complained to her brothers about the teasing. Part of the teasing consisted of comments about Pamela being a Mexican not an American. Ethnic tensions between Mexican Americans and Mexicans have long flown under the radar in much of the United States and in Austin, Texas. Alan Ruiz stole the green Honda used to follow the bus home and enlisted Manuel Cortez to do the shooting.

Other developments that occurred after the murder included the finding that Woody often wore red shirts and bandannas and was viewed as a member of a Blood set. People in his neighborhood and at middle school knew him as being involved in a group that called themselves, Bloods. A special group was convened by the Mayor, School Board, Police Chief, District Attorney and District Judges to study what happened and why.

Among the findings were that almost every school in Austin had visible gang activity but teachers, counselors and principals were either unaware or unwilling to acknowledge this. While the schools had a police unit that unit did not regularly communicate with the city police and thus the youth moved among homes, neighborhoods and schools often beyond the view and awareness of adults. A year after the killing both the City and the Schools began to take steps to address the problems that partially gave rise to the killing. However, the fact that violence in Mexico was already underway and has grown immensely in the last 7 years and the fact that that violence is visible to youth in Austin is something still not well understood in the City.

Cartel Influences in American Higher Education

How pervasive and sizeable the drug money is in Mexico is beginning to be documented. But its presence in the United States is only starting to be recognized. An interesting twist is the involvement of a popular assistant journalism professor and associate director of the Center for the Study of Latino Media and Markets at Texas State University in San Marcos, Sindy Chapa. The Internal Revenue Service filed a lawsuit in September of 2012 in a San Antonio federal court that seeks forfeiture of two houses owned by Sindy Chapa, 37. Ms. Chapa, a former girlfriend of Gulf Cartel controlled politician, Tomás Yarrington Ruvalcaba, a former Mexican mayor and governor owned a home in Kyle, Texas valued at $272,910 and one in McAllen appraised at $357,441. Ms. Chapa had been a media fixture years earlier in Matamoros with Yarrington and the IRS charged she had laundered some cartel money for Yarrington with the house purchases. News sources in Matamoros report that she apparently had three children with Yarrington.

This cases raises two issues. One is the penetration and corruption of one of America's most successful and valued institutions. Of all of the products of American culture none has more highly valued acceptance than American education and particularly higher education. Students come the world over to the United States to secure higher education degrees and much of the success of the institution is the strict emphasis on hiring and advancement via merit. Ms. Chapa may have great accomplishments as a teacher and researcher but her parallel involvements with her paramour in Tamaulipas opens the question of how she was hired and forces promoting her advancement. The second issue is the role of extramarital affairs in Mexican culture. It is often noted and certainly traces back to Aztec royalty and the large number of concubines kept by persons like Montezuma. Such practices serve to marginalize the role of women and pose substantial problems, not the least of which are communicable diseases.

Some years ago I was contacted by two oncology researchers at Texas Tech that were working to establish a medical campus in El Paso. They had created a uterine tumor registry in El Paso and wanted to create a similar one in Juarez. They had noted that genetic and environmental conditions were nearly equal for the two cities by had anecdotal information of uterine cancer rates many times higher in Juarez. I asked them as the registry was created how one would explain the shockingly higher incidence in the Juarez population. They said that one of the major causes of uterine cancer was exposure to venereal diseases including viral, fungal and bacterial vectors. They said their data indicated far higher extramarital contacts among Mexican men that brought those contacts to their wives and thus social patterns of sexual behavior dramatically increased cancer rates of Mexican women.

Police Response

Immigration and migration when running at high levels pose important issues in terms of preventing corruption and assuring access for persons into the institutions of the society. It also, when it occurs pell-mell, invites these kinds of challenges. This murder of a high school youth galvanized the Austin Police Chief Stanley Knee to think about how he might better prepare his police force to deal with a changing and complex community and one with a variety of ties to Mexico. One of his first acts was to create a Spanish language capability for all officers by having a University faculty member adapt a program he, Professor Orlando Kelm had created for Dell Computers as Dell began to expand sales in Latin America. Immediately all new officers had minimum skills in Spanish to deal with a traffic stop or a home call when people spoke only Spanish. In a strategic step he asked me and a colleague at the LBJ School to create a leadership philosophy and academy to prepare police leaders for the changing roles that would lie ahead.

Summary: What Can Be Done

At its most fundamental level to avert a failing state, Mexicans must feel safe in their communities and trust in public institutions. Rooted deep in the culture and psychology of Mexico is distrust, cynicism and, today, fear of basic public institutions especially the police and the courts. Every Mexican knows what *mordida* is and thinks of it when a police officer is seen. When the middle class, as it is now doing, flees Mexico to Texas or California, then the engines of economic growth for Mexico freeze. Until Mexico finds ways to create millions of jobs, until she can find the means to educate her millions, until Mexico can fund and ensure honest police and courts, until Cartels can be hunted down, disarmed and disbanded, until Americans stop feeding the Cartels from their drug addictions with billions of dollars of dirty money and weapons, Mexico will not be safe.

Nor will Texas. Nor will all of the United States. As Mexico fails in these immense challenges, Texas is the first of the American states to face severe consequences.

Steps To Address The Lack of Civic Participation

The consequences for Texas will be and already are large-scale legal and illegal immigration to Texas. Legal immigration is taking the form of Mexicans with financial resources buying homes and properties in Texas and using mechanisms such as special immigration visas (USINS, 2012) to secure residence for families by investing in businesses in Texas that promise to create employment. Persons with professional training will seek licensure in Texas and those with capital will transfer it into Texas. But adjustments must be made. Doing business in Mexico means paying off officials from the traffic cop to higher authorities. Local and state governments must be certain that transparency is maintained to ensure that corruption patterns are not transported to Texas or other states. Clearly the experience of Wal-Mart in Mexico in securing building and parking permits suggest this is an important concern for both countries.(Jenkins, 2012, April 24; WSJ, 2012)

State and local governments have several operational and legal mechanisms to prevent corruption and maintain governmental trust and integrity. In Texas a special arm of the Travis County District Attorney's offices is a dedicated watchdog for state agency and state employee corruption with effective criminal and civil statues. State government has an independent State Auditor that reviews agency practices and for over thirty years the state has used an anonymous survey procedure to query employees in almost all state agencies and customers and clients of many agencies that helps secure public trust in state organizations as well as promoting organization candor and improvement.(Landuyt, 1999; Lauderdale, 1999).

Public schools must encourage student and parent participation especially in extracurricular activities that build civic participation and awareness. Teacher conferences and PTA participation as well as encouraging voter participation are important activities to promote civic involvement with persons that may come with distrust toward government.

Ethical, effective governments are created through citizen empowerment and participation. Our research and service efforts for Texas government have focused upon strengthening through state and local agencies the development of public trust in government (Kelly, Landuyt, and Lauderdale, 2008; Kelly, and Lauderdale, 2003; Landuyt, 1999; Montana, 2008; Moynihan, 2009; Putnam, 2000; Uslaner, 2002, 2012). We term that social capital. Social capital must be built among members of government organizations and with the public. That must be a central focus in schools and local government as well wherever immigrants come into contact with the institutions of the community. Similar efforts must be taken to push governments in Mexico toward building trust.

If Mexico continues a spiral into violence there will be strong calls for American military intervention. That is not a solution. At best it can suppress violence but building a safe, civic society must come from the Mexican people and from strong support from the United States. This support will be difficult to achieve and sustain. Official relations between Mexicans and Americans are framed with the Mexican being cautious about American intentions.

Remember part of what a Mexican learns as a child is the loss of much of the land of northern Mexico to the United States. And in this context are three episodes in the previous century where Mexico considered alliances with Germany, Italy, Japan and the Soviet Union as counterweights to American influence in Mexico and Latin America. An additional challenge in developing agreements with Mexico is the cultural and psychological orientation of the Mexican to government institutions. Mexico relative to the United States has low levels of civic involvement. This means low levels of social capital that exists among persons that are not family related. Part of the reason for examining the history of Mexico is to understand how this caution with formal organizations developed and the cynicism that the Mexican often has to any government organization. This means for the American that relations between a governmental or business organization from the United States will develop slowly and in many cases certainty of working with Mexican partners will be a challenge.

Even within Mexico the efforts by President Calderon to find a dependable, non-corruptible force to deal with the cartels were revealing. In time he used the federal police and the Army less and less and depended on the Navy, primarily the Marines. The Marines as an organization are drawn more from the middle class and often do joint training with Americans. The 6 year term of the Calderon Administration tells us much about the complexity and yet the reality of developing working relationships with Mexican society, both government and the private sector

Chapter 16: American Fundamental Beliefs

We have used beliefs in understanding aspects of Mexican culture and psychology in the sense of generalized beliefs that underlie institutions and cultural orientations in that society. We have sought to identify those major features in the Mexican culture that serve to configure the society, its institutions and the individual's psychology. Beliefs are not independent of the history of cultural groups, migrations and conflicts and geographical resources and constraints. Rather from this mix they are created and serve as guides to a society. The following are some of the significant beliefs that characterize American culture, also termed memes, expectations, norms and cultural tendencies. Many are central to the American culture(Alden, 2008; Appleby, 2010; Goetzmann, 2009; McPherson, 1990; Miles, 1976; Skocpol, 2003; Turner, 1984).

Rules for Social Arrangements
Fundamental to the creation of the United States of America were different means to arrange relations among members of the society and how leaders were chosen. These means were radical and new when they came into being in the late 1700s and were a fascination and perhaps a foreboding for many in Europe. Beliefs are always intentions and the social reality at a

given time will vary but behavior and thought trend toward the belief.

Achieved not Ascribed Status

Individuals that held neither great wealth nor social station in Europe established the American state. Central to their beliefs were that cultural rules that fostered individual achievement and assigned social status based on this achievement created a more perfect set of social relations. This was part of the break with the political systems of Europe that was symbolized by the American colonial experience and the Revolution. The American Revolution was a challenge to royalty and land controlled by inheritance for generations. It sought to establish that one's station in life was earned, achieved, not dictated by birth lines.

A Republic or a Democracy

The American state has always held a tension between a Republic and a Democracy. Voting was variously restricted to men, people holding property, and by race. The design of the U.S. Senate and the House as well as the Presidential Electoral Commission reflects this tension. The existence of the third branch of the Federal Government, the Courts, are part of the structure of moderating between rapid change as can be done in a pure democracy where each member has a vote and actions are determined by a majority and other structures that delay or moderate change to moderate the momentary actions of the majority.

Today the tension is played out additionally in the use of proxies such as corporations, unions and political action committees that serve to expand the influences of a few not the majority. The government of the United States derives from the consent and actions of the people. The extent to which government can impose rules upon individuals and how it does so largely moves into whether the government is a Republic or a Democracy. It is actually both.

Representative Government
Rather than conducting a popular vote on every issue the American government operates through elected representatives at the municipal, state and federal level. It has over time created a fairly large institution of governmental employees charged with implementing the will of the representative government. The assumption is that the actions of the elected representatives and those of the government employee reflect the popular will.

The Popular Vote
The Popular Vote refers to the actions of an electorate and decisions are usually based on where the majority lies. The majority may be denied by rules of various bodies such as the elected assemblies, the Courts and trial juries. The U.S. Constitution and individual states determine who is a citizen and eligible to vote. But the action of voting is the mechanism to direct the actions of the government.

Divided Government and Checks and Balances
The framers of the Constitutional were very wary of a powerful, centralized government. They provided for a separation of powers and responsibilities between the central government and the individual states. They divided the central government into three parts: One to create laws and apportion resources, the Congress; one to administer the laws, the Administration headed by the elected President; one to consider disputes and maintain fidelity to the charter, the Courts. Each of these entities has mechanisms of appointment and revenue all toward having checks and balances among the three components. Additionally a set of rights were preserved for individuals and succinctly expressed in the First Ten Amendments to the Constitution, the Bill of Rights. The intent of these documents was to create structures to limit the power of a centralized state and make the state responsive to the people

Beliefs

An Endless Frontier

Early in the Colonial Period individuals found a largely empty land and immense natural resources. While existing Indian communities in some cases provided resistance, diseases that accompanied the colonists and their domestic animals as well as technological superiority eliminated these populations substantially before the middle of the 19th Century. This gave rises to significant American beliefs of an open land and an endless frontier.

The elimination of the original Indian populations rather than assimilation is a fundamental difference between the United States and Canada as compared to Mexico and much of Latin America. First immigrants in the 17th Century landed on shores in what is today Massachusetts and Virginia. Settlements over time spread along the Atlantic seaboard and further west. This experience developed American beliefs of a people that always had a frontier and moved toward unsettled and unknown lands.

Immediate and Future Orientation

Americans are optimistic and have an immediate as well as a fairly short-term future orientation. Most do not feel a great weight of tradition nor given to plans that run in the decades ahead. Americans set lofty goals and often the goals are reached. In some cases goals are reached but why they are set are not clear. Norman Mailer captures that aspect well in his description of the development of NASA and the effort to go to the moon in his book, Fire on the Moon (Mailer, 1970). Mailer notes, "The mind of the Wasp bears more resemblance to the laser than the mind of any other ethnic group. To wit, he can project himself 'extraordinary distances through a narrow path. He's disciplined, stoical, able to become the instrument of his own will, has extraordinary boldness and daring together with a resolute lack of imagination. He's profoundly nihilistic. And this nihilism found its perfect expression in the odyssey to the moon—because we went there without knowing why we went."

Knowledge, Science and Technology

Americans since Colonial Times have had a great faith in the power of knowledge to solve problems and have for more than a hundred years made large investments in public education with an emphasis on science and technology. Beginning with the Morrill Act of 1862, Federal policy and funding provided for college education and science extension to rural homes and farms. This commitment to education continued until by 1970 the United States had the highest levels of education of all citizens of any country in the world. The success of this orientation is reflected in standards of living, health, median incomes, patents earned and achievement of world prizes such as the Nobel Prize.

Positive and Optimistic

Americans generally are positive about their status and optimistic about the future. People expect to better their economic status during a lifetime and for succeeding generations to have a higher standard of living.

A Melting Pot

American Belief assumes that prior ethnic norms and characteristics "melt away" and citizens have a homogenous belief, appearance and language. To the extent that the use of a common language over two or three generations develops then that supports the "melting pot belief".

American Exceptionalism

At the country's founding the first President, George Washington, in his farewell address, warned the young country about international entanglements, cautioned prudence in alliances and borrowing by the government. His action in leaving his elected office set a tone for elected officials to regard a position as a temporary condition not a lifetime appointment.

Taken as a whole, North America is sheltered from much of the world with two great oceans. It has deep natural resources in arable land, abundant rainfall, productive forests and fisheries, a river system that provides ready and economical transportation through the heartland to the Gulf of Mexico and still holds vast deposits of minerals. These with a practical, hard-working people and deep intellectual resources have provided abundance over the decades and the country still can claim some of the American Exceptionalism that guided it through two centuries and made it unique among all the countries of the world.

One definition of Exceptionalism is the concept that America through its Constitution, people and unique institutions and bountiful land offered a radically new pattern to monarchies, oligarchies and other forms of society in the world and through much of history. This Exceptionalism permitted science, arts, business and personal achievement and independence to flourish in ways beyond what occurred with other forms of government in other areas of the globe.

The Limits of Exceptionalism

But, since the end of World War II the United States has acted as if it had no limits to its wealth, military power and thought it was unchallenged in its factories, science and leadership. That was incontestably true in 1950 but that is not true today. American leaders often refer to the current economic problems as a storm that will soon pass. Add some deficits in budgets, some government borrowing, and the old system will run again. The hard but real answer is that this is not a storm to wait out. This time it is different. It is now time for a reckoning of goals, resources and values. The reckoning must include how we will use available resources, what will be the jobs of the future, what is the proper role of the government to the local community and the individual, what can we pay for and how much should we properly borrow. That is the implied and most important dimension of the increasing threats on the southern border.

Strategic thinking is often forgotten for choosing tactics. To date we have chosen tactics without careful consideration of strategies. We jump to tactics such as providing more police, creating and enlarging state and federal law enforcement agencies, using the military instead of the police, offering cities as sanctuaries to the world's poverty and violence, training and equipping the police and the military in Mexico and other countries to the south, deportation and building a wall. These are tactics, not strategy, and some have boomeranged. For example, the equipping of Afghanistan resistance with Stinger missiles and training in the 1980's as Afghans fought a Soviet takeover of the country is now a significant factor in what we face in the Taliban and al Qaida.

The Zetas, which are the most brutal of the Mexican Cartels, were originally begun with deserters or others working additional jobs from the Mexican Army's GAFE that were trained in Special Forces tactics and similar to other Central American and South American units purportedly schooled by the American military (Grayson, 2008. May, 2010; Logan, 2009 March 11,; Thompson, 2005 September 30,). To date we have not had success on the border or in Mexico. When we arrive at a proper strategy then we can entertain tactical considerations.

Manifest Destiny

The United States has pursued for a hundred years since World War I, an east-west strategy to the globe when the best bet today may be north-south. The earthquake of cartel-driven violence on the border asks that question. This requires us to revisit the concepts of Manifest Destiny and the proper role of the United States on the North American continent. Part of the cultural makeup of the American people comes from the belief in Exceptionalism and Manifest Destiny. It is a culture that feels it represents the inevitable future of mankind. This has led the nation into conflicts around the world and often the role of the world's policeman. Such beliefs include impatience with the present and a readiness an eagerness to bring about rapid change (Bacevich, 2008; Engdahl, 2004). This includes discussion about using American military might to remove the violence in Mexico and suppress the cartels. This was part of the solution in the 1980's in Columbia and Peru and is being considered. However with the Mexican view of the historical efforts of the United States relative to Mexico that risks an explosive reply and not simply from drug trafficking organizations in Mexico(Contreras, 2009; Engdahl, 2004).

Summary: American and Mexican Resources For These Challenges

We have to answer the question of what are the farms, factories, cities and communities of the future. We now have only one non-government sponsored automobile manufacturer, Ford. The American taxpayer heavily backstops Banks and brokerages. Our retail stores are filled with goods manufactured abroad and China alone holds 2 trillion dollars of our borrowings. Almost three fourths of the petroleum we require is imported and often from lands that are hostile to us. What will our work be? How will we create the jobs to meet unemployment in the double digits today and the new workers that enter the labor force each year? How well can we educate our people? What houses, travel and health care can we afford?

Mexico must answer similar questions. They, like we, know the best jobs, and the safest communities come from a highly educated and free people. Each country starts from a different point; but the fate of the United States and Mexico is jointly bound in a hundred ways. Mexico is the second source after Canada for imported oil for the United States. Saudi Arabia, Nigeria and Venezuela are three, four and five. These three are hardly more stable than Mexico. Mexico is a leading customer of American agriculture and the number one purchaser of Texas agriculture exports. These are only a few of the essential ties between the two countries.

What if our worst fears come true and there is a dying much less a dead elephant, is on the doorstep? That is the topic to be addressed next. We will look at what may be the likely path for Mexico if it continues to devolve and the direct consequences for the United States. The chapter after that will include suggestions as to how the countries of North America might face these challenges through some ideas on building the leadership and community structures to meet the changes that are now starting to appear on the horizon.

Globalization has brought some benefits yet many surprises, the unanticipated consequences. Only when urgency is recognized and the reality faced, can these fundamental questions be considered.

Chapter 17: Mexico's Challenges

We return to the fundamental beliefs of Mexico to construct a likely agenda for the future. These Beliefs are significantly different from those of Americans. Repeating the Beliefs they are:

- The role of Malinche and betrayal, treachery and fatalism deeply embedded in the psychology of the Mexican;
- The unresolved dualism of the Indian and the European in the context of a mestizo society;
- The external locus of control presuming that life events cannot be influenced;
- The dependability of the family and the failure of civic engagement and political success and attendant fatalism;
- The heroic vision of the peasant;
- The fear of the North and invasion from outside powers;
- The now very populous state can transform itself from an agricultural to a modern consumerist society;
- That the state can use rational planning to achieve state goals of social and cultural change.

How these are met and solved will be part of the equation of how Mexico, in turn, addresses its national agenda. Mexico with its relatively young, poorly educated population provides continuous recruits to organized crime in Mexico until its economy recovers. But that recovery waits on the American one. One priority for Mexico is to control the power of the cartels and not cede regions to their control as exist now. American resources can play a careful, helping role but the responsibility is a Mexican responsibility.

Mexico's largest challenge is to secure its people's belief in being able to change and having an honest and transparent state. To master that challenge is an enduring puzzle with repeated failures for Mexico. For five hundred years heroes have emerged, reforms achieved and then heroes failed and reforms destroyed. Between these failed revolutions and the long effort of the Mexican people to reconcile the Indian past and European colonialism, there is a tendency to view the outside world with caution and distrust. That psychological inclination thwarts building the sort of civic trust and vigor that Mexico needs and rather lets the country repeatedly revert to its authoritarian past (Castaneda, 2011; Joseph & Henderson, 2002; Joseph & Spenser, 2008; Krauze, 1990; Preston & Dillon, 2004).

The elections in Mexico in the last two decades beginning in the 1990s have offered that promise of a democratic, transparent and non-authoritarian Mexico, but it may have been reversed in 2012 with the return of the PRI to the Presidency. Events immediately after 2012 in the next 6 years will be critical as will all of these choices coming up to this decade.

The Challenges for Mexico

These are the challenges facing Mexico today. One is the role of the Mexican state and the psychological orientations of the citizens. Since pre-Hispanic times much of the society has seen the state as externally imposed, controlled by various conquerors and a vehicle that exploits citizens.

The strategic dilemma for Mexico could be summarized through several points:

- A large, young population that has exceeded the agricultural capacity of the land to produce enough food and Mexican civic institutions to educate, protect and provide employment and community and social security;
- Declining oil output with reduced foreign currency earnings;
- Vulnerable employment in factories and the maquila sector as the world economy slows and manufacturing changes;
- Decreased remittances from citizens working in the United States because of the housing collapse and general economic slowdown;
- Stagnant tourist revenues owing partially to the slowing world economy and the perception of danger from Mexico's high crime rate.

Taming the State

The Mexican state will alternatively use force and subsidies to secure compliance. The citizen views the state warily as a corrupt vehicle from the local cop to the highest office. A dedicated and honest civil service is less well developed in Mexico than in many modern societies. Some promise occurred in the late 1980's with the departure of the Miguel de la Madrid administration which signaled the end of the monopoly power of the PRI that had dominated all of Mexico since the 1910 Revolution through its creation in 1929 and the appearance of alternative political parties in the south but especially in the north of Mexico. Vicente Fox and then Felipe Calderon of the PAN provided some hope of more viable political institutions that competed in a fair arena and increased the flow of competitive solutions to civic issues (Anderson, 2013, January 26,; Archibold, 2013; Castaneda, 2011; Contreras, 2009; Fuentes, 1996; Massey, Durand, & Malone, 2002; Meyer, Sherman, & Deeds, 2010; Payan, 2006; Preston & Dillon, 2004;

Stratfor Global Intelligence (Firm), 2009; Trevizo, 2011; Zúñiga & Hernández-León, 2005). Institutions survive either from coercion or trust. Neither is in adequate supply for Mexico today. Indeed the strength of *confianza* betrays the weakness of the Mexican nation.

Addressing Wealth Inequalities

A second challenge is the high level of poverty including a small middle class with a tenuous hold largely ensured by export sales of oil. Repeatedly in Mexican history the distribution of income has favored the very few with the greater percentage of the population existing in great poverty (O'Boyle, 2013, March 12). Oil and industrialization were the hope to correct this condition but progress has stagnated. Without a large and strong middle class, the government and the wealthy are at risk of economic decline and class-based conflict. The fact that many wealthy and even persons of moderate means fear kidnappings for ransom is an illustration of the decline in the Mexican state and its assurance of civic wellbeing.

Jobs, Jobs, Jobs

A third challenge is the need for more and higher paying secure jobs in the Mexican economy. Mexico will be unable to survive as the largely urban nation of today without economic engines to provide jobs, sustenance and thus security. While the last thirty years have seen great progress in moving from a rural and agricultural state with much subsistence-based agriculture, far too many factory jobs have low skill levels and pay. This has been much of the legacy of the *maquilas*, jobs of limited intellectual and skill content exported from the United States, Germany and Japan to Mexico, a cheap labor state. Many of the first maquilas were simply transporting outdated technologies soon destined to disappear and extended for a few more years only because of the very low wage rates for Mexican labor. Globalization of such labor has forced Mexico not to compete just with American labor that is paid by a factor of 10 or more per unit of work but with workers in China and India where wages are a fraction of already low Mexican wages.

The content of jobs today and the number of workers is rapidly changing driven by science and technology. In the 19th and accelerating into the 20th century, manufacturing jobs provided great wealth and employment for persons with less than and a high school education. That has ended. The first phase of the end was the movement of such jobs to low wage areas. Now those jobs are disappearing. From 1996 to 2006 manufacturing employment worldwide dropped by 16 percent. There are five general manufacturing areas: chemicals and traditional manufacturing (autos, appliances); local processing (rubbers, food and beverages, printing); energy; high innovations (computers, other electronics) and labor-intensive goods (toys, textiles, clothing). Most of these categories no longer are labor-intensive and those with the greatest value added have the lower labor inputs. (Manyika, 2012 November)

Mexico or any society must address how individuals and families can sustain themselves. In years more recent in Mexico than the United States, that was accomplished by persons living on farms and raising much of their food and trading limited products and labor for manufactured items. Mexico like its neighborhoods in the United States and Canada now has a population that will require jobs not skills living off the land. Without jobs Mexico or any society becomes a failed state.

Trade and External Earnings

A fourth challenge is the decline of producing oil fields to generate funds for the State and export earnings. Without these earnings Mexico can neither command nor coerce loyalty to the state. The large earnings from illegal drugs, the proximity to the American side where there is money and a market for the drugs and the readily available weapons that can be purchased in a

Houston or Los Angeles build an alternative government in the northern lands.

A fifth challenge is the current economic decline in the United States that has for many decades served as a safety valve for the unemployed of Mexico to find earnings in the States. During the real estate boom of the last decade millions of Mexicans have found work in real estate construction and related fields. With the bursting of the real estate bubble those jobs are gone either increasing unemployment of Mexicans in the United States or their return to cities in Mexico already with too few jobs.

A sixth challenge is the fact that the north of Mexico has always looked as much to the United States as to Mexico City as its center of gravity. As earnings from oil and manufacturing decline, the ties of the north to the United States will strengthen. The growth of PAN majorities in cities and states of the north challenge the powerful grip of Mexico City. The existence of drug cartels as an alternative to government gives pause to the assurance that Mexico can continue in the 21st Century and it did in the 20th.

Mexico's challenges are substantial and enduring. In the 20th Century it has made great progress in economic development and improving education, housing and health for greater percentages of the population. It has entered the global arena of labor and manufacturing and now is exposed to these forces seeing India, China and even Central American companies competing for manufacturing for lower wages than Mexico's. Its largest trading partner is the United States but that exposes the country more to the vagaries of the American economy. The violence, now endemic not just on the border but in much of Mexico, is the more visible indicator of a nation that may be failing. Past solutions have partial adequacy and desperate migration to the Southwest border is already producing alarms in many American states.

Summary: A Three Part Mystery For Mexico

As my recounting of friends and colleagues in Mexico some years ago, much about Mexico remains mysterious to Americans and perhaps to Mexicans as well.

Part One-What Is The True Picture Of The Economy?

Part of the mystery is that facts about Mexico's economy, its governments and much of its social organization are elusive and that may be deeply rooted in the anthropology and psychology of Mexico. That is part of what my old physician friend explained as I puzzled about trying to secure a population estimate of Mexican cities. My sense was then and is today that there are few "facts" about Mexico.

Today there is a dimension of this reality as well in the States. Unemployment statistics in the United States are illustrative. The Labor Department reported in December a national unemployment rate of 7.2%. However because of reporting and statistical adjustments over the last 20 years this rate underestimates what would have been reported in the 1980's. Today's rate appears to underestimate the underemployed and the discouraged worker. John Williams runs one popular Internet site that provides sharply different figures than those provided by entities like the Department of Labor and the Federal Reserve (Williams, 2008).

Nevertheless the disconnect between the citizen, including the intellectual, and the government is greater in Mexico than in the United States. This is a potentially perilous state of affairs for any nation if trust erodes in the government, its currency and its official numbers.

Part Two-The Labor Puzzle

A second part of the mystery is the fragility of the labor market in Mexico as expressed memorably for me by the paradoxical reactions of UNAM liberals to the assault at Tiananmen Square. It remains as vulnerable today. Mexico does not have the educational infrastructure to provide high school and college to most of its population. Millions of young Mexicans are neither in higher education or the formal job market. Mexico's labor situation is tellingly explained by the careers of its two most powerful union bosses, Carlos Romero Deschamps and Elba Gordillo. Deschamps heads the Pemex oil workers union and those workers have the highest wages and benefits packages of all labor in Mexico. Deschamps is also a senator in Mexico's Congress and with that status immune from arrest. He and his family live as the wealthiest in Mexico traveling in private planes and yachts with expensive properties in the United States (El Diario de Coahuila May 6, 2013). He does this on an official salary of 2,000 dollars a month.

Gordillo is similarly lavish in her spending with properties in California and known for her shopping sprees in the United States. Through his union Deschamps controls oil production and the access to the best jobs in Mexico. But while Mexico has potentially great wealth in oil the corruption in the union prevents the development of that critical resource. Gordillo's control is through her ability to mobilize her union membership of 1 and 1/2 million teachers and through them the children and their parents. Union reform must come first in Mexico and then serious improvement in education. Without education, especially at the higher levels, Mexico cannot generate an economy that provides high levels of jobs, income and thus wealth (Goldin, 2008; Heckman, 2008; Meyer et al., 2003).

Part Three-A Failed State On The Doorstep?

A third part is the whispered fear of persons long familiar with Mexico of what could be the American response in the face of a failed state in Mexico. To a great extent law enforcement in Mexico has been corrupt for decades by the standards of the United States, Canada or much of Europe. Municipal police officers have supported themselves with fines and in some areas an officer's beat is his franchise. There have been times and locales in the United States when this was true but it is more continuous and pervasive in Mexico. However in the last two decades the degree of corruption, violence, organized Cartels, money and direct challenge to the government is without precedent in a hundred years. Efforts to control the plazas, the roads and bridges that lead from Mexican border cities into the United States have rendered cities such as Nuevo Laredo, Juarez and Tijuana, combat zones with deaths in Juarez alone in 2011 running about 3,000. It is the visibility and urgency associated with this violence that is forcing the Mexican topic on the United States and the border question on Mexico City. As President Calderon sought to control the violence on the border, the result seems to be that the Cartels have moved to challenge the government, itself. High level officials have been killed and kidnapping for ransom long a fear of the wealthy in Mexico now appears at rate of 40 a week and afflicts the middle class as well as the wealthy.

So far the American response has been either increased police presence or failing that then the use of military forces and strategies. That is also the Mexican response. This is not promising and may prove paradoxical. Significant among the major violent entities of the Mexican cartel are groups known as Zetas. Some were former members of the Mexican army trained at elite military posts by the United States Army to improve command functioning and combat in asymmetrical situations. These are cartel members that have intimate knowledge of the weapons and tactics that the American military has evolved to use in situations like Bosnia, Iraq and Afghanistan. They are using these skills against Mexican civilians, police and the military with devastating effect.

Hasty solutions are the most likely to yield unintended consequences. The American response to date is slow and only beginning to develop. Other urgencies including wars in the Middle East, terrible storms along the Gulf and spreading economic problems have delayed recognition. Mexico's problems play more to immediate "bites in the 24 hour cycle of cable news" than to a considered long-term understanding of the cultures and economies of the two nations.

An effective response must include changes in the educational system in both countries, efforts to understand the very significantly different cultural outlooks between Americans and Mexicans, strategic choices in manufacturing directions and energy development, greater transparency in government at all levels, adjustments in saving and consumption patterns, restrictions and controls on certain trade and labor items and structured interventions in civic participation. Without such fundamental efforts, more police, soldiers, walls and helicopters run the risk of being only palliative.

With a crashing world economy, the bankruptcy of some of America's grandest banks, brokerages, insurance companies and even auto manufacturers, a challenged President in the United States, anger and fear building in American communities toward outsiders, rising unemployment, sharp oscillations in the price of oil and a deep apprehension of cartel violence on both sides of the border, the United States and Mexico must act judiciously and with all deliberate speed to address these issues.

Two events not under the control of the Mexican government will be more significant than any action that can be taken by government. One event is when and how completely the decline of Mexican oil exports occurs. This will undercut the middle class and the promise of a progressive, civic-minded bloc to build a modern state. The other event is the course of the economic decline in the United States. The Mexican economy is deeply intertwined with it and the promise of Mexican manufacturing depends on a prosperous American economy.

Migration out of Mexico will continue to take two forms. One is economic refugees but that will decline if the American economy is weak and antipathy toward immigrants continues to grow. As American conditions grow harsher Hispanic communities in the United States will be less welcoming toward Mexicans much as Mexicans are hostile toward immigration into their country from Guatemala and El Salvador. The second form of immigration is persons with sufficient wealth to purchase Resident Visas.

Already the major cities in Texas see "little Monterreys" where the Mexican economic and educated elite have fled. While economic refugees, the unemployed, are a relief valve for Mexico, these wealthy immigrants leave with scarce physical and intellectual talent from Mexico that are critical in creating job growth and modern organizations. If this continues, it will deepen the poverty and violence in Mexico. It may also serve to promote an effort in the United States to intervene militarily in Mexico. Such an event occurred with Cuba and a similar pattern may develop with Mexico. A failing state follows this sequence.

Markers of a Failing State
- Citizens Lose Respect for the State
    - Inability to maintain civic order
    - Failure to protect citizens
    - Diminished trust in state's institutions including police, courts and currency
- Failure To Maintain Geographical Integrity
- State Loses The Monopoly On Controlled Violence
- People Migrate Out-Texas Could Go From 3 to 10 million Mexican Migrants

Chapter 18: A Time for Clear Thinking

America's greatest strengths are in its institutions of civic participation, educational systems particularly higher education, openness, flexibility, balance of systems and innovation. The nation exists on a continent with two large oceans that protect it from ready invasion and has substantial natural resources. These cultural properties are the key to the great rate of American inventiveness and successful competition that guided the nation through the past three centuries and remain critically important today. A continuously educated citizenry is required to create both the jobs of tomorrow and to be ready to fill them. An educated citizenry has been and continues to be the most significant political strength of maintaining institutions controlled by the people.

Resources and Technologies

An initial key to prosperity on the North American continent was the ready availability of natural resources and for the last hundred years, the resource of oil. In the first American century great forests and open prairies with rich soils provided the building materials for homes and villages and for vast agricultural productivity. The prairie soils were so fertile that by the 1950s, they fed not just the United States but also much of the world through grain exports of wheat and corn.

Burning wood was a first source of energy but it was soon displaced by an ancient and denser form of wood, coal. Coal fired the furnaces that built industrial cities like Pittsburgh and Cleveland. It replaced wind and the clipper ships that sailed from Boston in the first era of an America made powerful through food export, manufacturing and trade. Early in the 20th century petroleum began to displace coal as a primary fuel source.

Oil has many advantages over wood and coal. It is a denser energy form and being liquid is more readily transported by truck, rail car and pipeline. It was bountiful in the United States and until the 1980s was pumped from west Texas, Louisiana and Oklahoma wells at a cost of 3 dollars a 55-gallon barrel. The great oil discoveries fueled the American economy that has the world's highest rate of energy consumption and now with imports underpins the great agricultural productivity of the United States.

Earnings from oil export in Mexico are critical to that nation as well and provides funds for agriculture imports and those earnings additionally are the basis of the Mexican middle class that are government workers including government agency personnel, employees of the state oil monopoly, Pemex, nurses and physicians, teachers, soldiers, courts and police.

The darkest time for both countries lies directly ahead as cheap, readily available energy that fuels all of modern life including globalization comes to an end. The geologist, King Hubbard, first noted the disappearance of cheap and easy to reach oil. He had spent a life in finding and producing oil and drew a simple bell curve to illustrate the relative costs and availability of oil in a given field as well as around the world. In the early life of a petroleum producing field, oil is near the surface and because of natural gas may not even require pumping but rather rises up the well through pressure. The relative cost and availability slowly increases for the first few years of production, peaks and then starts down a slope finally ending in either a fully depleted field or one with the remaining barrels too costly to retrieve.

Hubbard offered this normal curve-like explanation of the discovery and use of petroleum across the globe from the late 1800s until final global depletion projected around the year 2200. He and others estimate cumulative production exceeding the rate of discovery of new reserves ending around the year 2000. At the year 2000 and since then production exceeds the discovery of new deposits. From that point on oil will become more difficult to locate and more costly to produce. Like wood and coal before it, some other source of energy will be required.

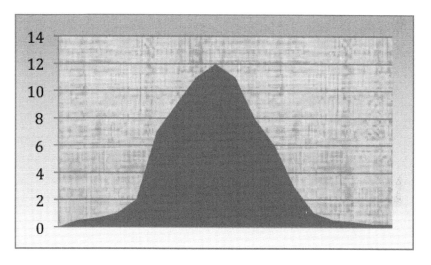

Hubbard and then others argued this is the worldwide pattern of the availability and cost of oil. This decline has been in place since the 1960's (Deffeyes & Ebooks Corporation Limited., 2008; Karl & United States. Minerals Management Service. Gulf of Mexico OCS Region., 2007; Malkin, 2010, March 8; Simmons, 2005) and as we addressed earlier is quite visible in Mexican oil fields.

In the last decade some of the forecast of Hubbard has been moderated by technologies to secure oil and gas locked in shale deposits both in depleted fields and in areas that were never oil producing before. The technologies of horizontal drilling and the injection of liquids (fracking) to free the petroleum has temporized but likely not invalidated Hubbard's thesis. Successful research in the United States in the last decade has greatly increased the supplies of domestic oil and natural gas through injecting water and catalysts as well as horizontal drilling to tap hitherto unavailable reserves. But this is a far more expensive source of oil with uncertain implications such as the use of water, its contamination and how long these new reserves will last. A constant factor that evolves with the exploration is EROI, the Energy Returned On the Investment, to find and produce any energy be it oil, coal, solar, wind or nuclear. The EROI ratio for oil has dropped severely and at some point it goes to 1 to 1. Oil will exist but the cost of getting will equal what is then made available. The one clear fact is that the world over including the United States will pay more for energy and its long time availability is uncertain.

Oil Brings A Surprise

But declining availability and rising costs have other meanings for the United States and Mexico. When oil hits about 150 dollars a barrel, a different calculus takes over in manufacturing and shipping and it provides a cost advantage to both the Mexican and American worker. Higher oil prices act as a tariff on imported and exported goods. Less expensive labor in India and China is checkmated with the shipping cost of raw materials to Asia and the finished goods then shipped to consumer markets. Both India and China have stark limits on available natural resources in or near their countries and are far from consumer markets in Europe, Japan, Taiwan, the Americas and Europe.

Already since 2007 more manufacturing and agricultural jobs are beginning to return in the United States and Mexico (Anderson, 2013, January 26,). But higher resource costs will create a requirement to do things differently. Homes will need to be constructed differently to conserve energy. Autos, electronics and basic industries will use processes including robots to lessen energy consumption and labor as well. A critical challenge for both countries is to address the current challenges, and at the same time take the steps toward higher local production and consumption. This will continue the process of the decline of the globalization. The pattern since at least the 1950s of greater globalization is changing to local development and that may be one of the largest new factors in the current century.

Perhaps the most striking increase in local change is a new wave of manufacturing developing in countries like Germany and the United States. It is termed additive manufacturing and grows out of computer-based design, lasers and the ability to make custom parts of any material including human tissue. It suggests that almost any thing including biological items can be "printed" locally rather than manufactured in traditional factories or laboratories. Such "one at a time" production promises products scaled to the local market need, less waste than in mass production and the ending of the long supply chains and warehouses associated with modern economies. Experts think the process is about where computing was in the 1980s as desktop computers began to appear as did laser printers (Markillie, 2012, April 21).

Impact of New Technologies
Fuller application of internet-type communication will have a profound impact on Mexico beyond manufacturing. It will be beneficial as candid informational flows will occur even as they do now in border cities where residents warn each other when violence flares using blogs, Twitter, Facebook and e mail, even as the Cartels intimidate and depress the traditional print and electronic media (Ortiz, 2013, March 11). Mexico has long had monopolies in the media that align themselves with current

political views. In recent years bombings of news outlets, threats and murders of reporters have made internet-based tools and the reporting on the American side of the border the information source for millions of Mexicans.

The idea of the vote, self-determination, free assembly and free presses were radical notions in the 1700's that were part of what created the United States. It has been suggested that the widespread use of the fax machine where people could exchange information outside of government channels hastened the downfall of the Soviet Union (Bajarin, 2011, March 7). Certainly internet-type technologies have accelerated the downfall of dictatorships across the Arab World though what will take their place is far from certain. As the Cartels suppress press reporting in Mexico including some papers declaring they will not report on such violence, Internet tools have taken their place and in some locations are the only available news source on violent activities.

Mexico's greatest strengths may be both its youth and its antiquity. Its greatest weaknesses are perhaps fatalism, a psychological sense of the lack of control over external events, paucity of civic trust, brittle response to change and institutional corruption. That will begin to change in the face of freer flows of information with more of it outside of state control.

Mexico does not have a strong, open civic culture and most Mexicans doubt that is possible for Mexico. Yet the experience of Mexicans working in foreign corporations from the United States, Japan and Germany may prove to create an opening there. After World War II, Americans like G. Edwards Deming from ATT taught Japan how to build quality, worker loyalty and participation in what had been an excessive authoritarian culture (Deming, 1986; Gitlow & Gitlow, 1987). A generation later, companies like Honda returned the favor to Americans in this country. Mexicans in the United States do not successfully create a Mexico in Iowa or even in Texas. People of Mexican descent, born and educated in Texas prove to be exceedingly independent, engaged in civic life, lacking in fatalism, preferring English and by the third generation wedded to American ideals of optimism and the importance of education. Yet this is a slow process and one that proceeds over generations. (Semple, 2011; Statistics, 2012, August 21)

Building Economies and Cultures in the 21st Century

The challenge for both countries is to realize that the vision of much of the 20th Century is no longer applicable. For Americans consumerism and the consumption binge is ending. The country will need ten and perhaps twenty years to balance the books of the excesses of the end of that Century built on public and private debts and the loss of manufacturing capability. The idea of an American Empire flung about the globe will end and with likely half of the national budget devoted to the military and foreign relations required to maintain that empire. Those resources removed from maintaining the global empire then become available for domestic ends.

Individuals, states, corporations and finally the federal government are facing the need to deleverage. Deleveraging means lessening borrowing to support consumption. Convenient credit via cards is an innovation of the last 40 years, a generation innovation. Using credit, leverage, to build wealth via housing was the final credit binge for the individual and the bubble burst around 2007. Municipalities and states binged on creating bonds that permitted borrowing for capital construction but also to pay current costs. It was leveraged based on the assumption of rising incomes of taxpayers and property values. Without the ability to borrow more money and with stagnant incomes and property values, individuals and governments have two choices though both have one identical result.

One choice is to declare bankruptcy and disavowal debts. Individuals can do that and the result is life or at least several years on a cash basis matching expenses to income. Legal mechanisms for bankruptcy are less available for governments, but they can shut down. That has begun in states and municipalities as books must be reconciled, expenditures must match incomes. Central governments like the United States have a tool to delay such days of reckoning and that is simply printing more money when revenues are not sufficient. That will work for a few years but the result is always the same: explosive inflation, discrediting of the currency and government collapse.

The other choice is painfully aligning incomes and expenditures. Priorities get set and some things are postponed or never purchased. That is the more rational choice. The classic story of the 20th Century of money printing is Germany in the 1920's as recounted by Adam Fergusson (Fergusson, 1975). The historical pattern of such manias and busts is best recounted by Carmen M. Reinhart and Kenneth Rogoff covering 800 years of a repeated social phenomenon (Reinhart & Rogoff, 2009). History always tells us that debts are paid and wild times come to an end.

Summary: Challenges for America

Among America's challenges is to move the focus from the Middle East and Europe to the North American continent. America must return to a place at the head of nations with citizen education and Mexico's challenge is far, far larger in that critical area. The infrastructure for public and private transportation demands attention and Mexico faces at least as large a burden with a more deprived population in the 50 million in the nations to its south to Panama as the United States does to Mexico.

America must, as it balances its books, separate consumption from investment. Borrowing for consumption always brings pain. Borrowing for investment can be successful if the investments are wisely chosen. The investment areas are clear: energy, public infrastructure, education, civic participation, agriculture, public safety, defense and health.

- Energy-Prosperity and population growth since the 1700's came from the successive exploitation of timber, coal and petroleum. The cheap and convenient sources are gone. Basic and applied research will be needed for decades to secure petroleum, natural gas, wind, solar, geothermal and nuclear. The strategy should be toward multiple sources with careful conservation in transportation, manufacturing and home consumption.

- Public infrastructure-This includes water, transportation, roads, railroads, airports, waste processing, pipelines, waterways and electrical grids. Most have been neglected and built on the technology of the 1950's and 60's.

- Education-From 1890 to 1970 America led the world in the average educational level of all Americans. (Goldin, 2008) The minimum was a high school education. The 20th Century was a technology century with basic science, engineering, business and government ushering in factory manufacturing, tractor rather than horse drawn farming implements, gasoline powered cars, electricity in factories, homes and farms, air travel, hundreds of new substances created from chemistry, the computer, radio, television, the internet, space travel, deciphering the human genome and nuclear power. All these basic and applied discoveries called for brighter and more educated workers and the nation responded keeping pace of workers with new required knowledge. Today America is losing the race with several countries having higher educational levels and grinding failures with some groups leaving school at high rates before even high school completion. As immigration continues education must include a focus on seeing that immigrants participate as all citizens in education and not create enclaves unassimilated in the civic culture.

- Civic participation-An unseen part of American wealth during the 20th Century were the high rates of civic participation from parents working with schools, to club and union memberships to voting. Americans, in general, trusted each other and were quick to come to each other's aid. People were generally optimistic and felt life's challenges could be met. A useful term for civic participation is social capital. Social capital comes down to trust and reciprocity. When social capital is high, there are high rates of innovation, better health and less crime. As late as 1970 America was as high in social capital as Mexico is low today. Social capital is built through social participation in the neighborhood, the larger community and the workplace. The current zeal for social networking software is an echo of a time when social capital was higher and specific steps are available to increase social capital. And social capital is the catalyst that propels innovation, education and prosperity. Specific steps are needed to teach civic participation in schools and colleges, foster it in the workplace and urge it in neighborhoods.
- Agriculture-The productivity of America's farms, grasslands, fisheries and forests has like natural resources been the starting point of the country's great wealth.

While all remain productive, single cropping, feedlots, questions about herbicides and genetically modified animal and plant strains raise questions. In recent years weather extremes have affected productivity. Much of fresh vegetables and fruits come thousands of miles from farms and orchards to urban markets. A changing energy matrix suggests that local production and marketing will become desirable and perhaps imperative.

- Public Safety-Crime, fire, accidents and illness are addressed by specialized professions that increasingly require highly trained personnel and complex equipment. Crime includes the police officer, the courts and the correctional system. For thirty years Americans have had a great fear of crime and expanded police forces and radically increased the numbers of persons incarcerated to the extent that the nation has one of the highest rates of imprisonment in jails and prisons. Most of those imprisoned serve their terms or are paroled and return to the community. Recidivism rates of 40 percent or so suggest a very costly burden and call for alternatives.

- Defense-In his final address to the American people, Dwight David Eisenhower warned of the dangers of a permanent military-industrial complex. The dangers were that vested interests would maintain themselves and create a great budgetary demand on the nation. In all previous years the United States had depended upon a largely volunteer military, mobilized at war and then scaled down. But with the Cold War the United States maintained a large ready military and assumed the protection of other states around the world including Europe, Japan, South Korea, the sea lanes in the South China Sea, the Mediterranean and Red Sea in the Middle

East and much of the Arctic. Today after removing Social Security and Medicare and Medicaid, half of the budget is for the support of the military. Yet in spite of this support homeless veterans as one example are a great national problem. The Southwest has an open border where contraband moves in both directions and citizens live in increasing fear. There are substantial reasons to return to required national service rather than a standing professional army and further the application of citizen involvement in efforts such as neighborhood watches as part of civic participation and responsibility.

- Health-The United States has the world's most expensive health care system but rank 16th in child mortality a measure of the quality of the system. Health access is irregular for much of the population and serious illnesses can bankrupt the individual. Efforts must focus upon preventive health, greater use of home care rather than institutionalized care and improved nutrition.

- Manufacturing-Once the marvel of the world much of American manufacturing has been cannibalized either by competition from foreign manufacturers with much lower wage rates or by American companies that moved abroad to secure lower labor costs. However mass manufacturing is ending with ever-greater robotic processes and lower rates of labor utilized. Mass manufacturing is being replaced by built to order and tools such as the computer, database of digitized forms and three dimensional printing remove the advantage of cheap labor. Indeed the promise of three dimensional, 3-D manufacturing is as momentous as the change from crafts to factories in the 18th, 19th and 20th centuries.

- Income Distribution-From 1890 until 1970 the American economy was striking in the extent to which wealth was distributed among all groups. Each generation was wealthier than the previous and even the generations of the Great Depression rebounded by the 1960's. However during the 1970's several new directions appeared. One was a decline that continues on the level of education in the total population. Middle class families began to require two outside wage earners to maintain middle class standards. Since the 1950's the family norm has moved from one adult working outside of the home to two and the rate of unmarried adults is at one of the highest levels in American history. Since 1979, the Congressional Budget Office reports the bottom 80 percent of American families had their share of the country's income fall, while the top 20 percent had modest gains. The real gains are in the top 1 percent — and, especially, the top 0.1 percent. That tiny sector receives nearly a quarter of the nation's income and controls nearly half its wealth. The reasons for this change are not fully explained. One line of thinking is that government has shifted economic policies to support the wealthiest and weakened the collective bargaining power of labor. The banking and finance sector has assumed more of the nation's wealth and yet when excesses have occurred with large banks and brokerages as happened in 2007, the tax payer bails the wealthy out. Banks must be shrunk and a cost of the bank franchise should be a requirement that they can go under. Another line of thought is that the movement of technology has substituted machines for labor so fully that it has suppressed the strength of labor, its ability to bargain for wages and decreased the numbers of laborers needed. Yet throughout the 17th, 18th, 19th and 20th technology moved at an ever more rapid pace but new jobs were continually created to replace the old ones. Yet through these centuries until the last 40 years new jobs were created to replace the old. That is not occurring today.

These items then are the major items on the American agenda for this decade. They must be addressed in the context of these alternatives developing in Mexico. Mexico's challenges are likely too great for it to continue without some form of continuing collapse.

Chapter 19: A Shining City On The Hill

In the years before the creation of the United States and in addresses by American Presidents including John F. Kennedy in 1961 and Ronald Reagan in 1984, the United States has been called a "city on a hill". The metaphor conveys the exceptional qualities that many view as the American culture and experience that includes not only prosperity but opportunities for high levels of achievement of all persons and particularly persons without status or wealth at birth.

Many factors contributed to the wealth and power that the United States developed over more than 200 years. Vast and bountiful natural resources were part of the mix. Small and responsive governments were part as well as the freedom from societies characterized by inherited wealth and status that many immigrants were fleeing in coming to the new world. Isolation, too, was important that freed the country of the concerns and involvements of the recurrent land wars in Europe and Asia. The isolation permitted the United States to avoid debilitating conflicts and the cost and cultural weight of large, standing armies. Indeed the Founding Fathers warned of foreign entanglements and urged isolation.

The *city on the hill* has long beckoned to poor and oppressed people and the promise of America continues today. It takes many turns.

In the 1980s I had a Fulbright student from Peru, Margarita Salas. Her father was an officer in the National Police of Peru and headed a unit that operated in distant villages controlled by the Shining Path (*Sendero Luminoso*), the Communist Party of Peru. He told Margarita to pass on to me an interesting observation he had made repeatedly when he interviewed young people that were members of the Shining Path. He asked why they were involved and what might they do other than being a part of an armed rebellion against the country. He found, as expected, that most were frustrated and angry about the grinding poverty in Peru and the lack of opportunity. When he would ask what they would hope for, he got a response more than once of the person wanting to get to Dallas, Texas. Somehow even in the remotest regions of Peru the popular soap, Dallas, and the connivings of JR Ewing were followed. He said he was told by youth in village after village that even a dishwasher was wealthy in Dallas! So, indeed, "the shining city" has long been seen by restless and ambitious people in other lands.

The Lure of the North

Mexican citizens have long been a part of the communities in Texas and from the 1821 to 1836, Texas was part of Mexico. During the Mexican Revolution beginning around 1910 there were substantial migrations from Mexico to Texas and for most of the years of the 20th century Mexicans would come to the States to work and then return. Thirty years ago I began to see Mexican adults in state prisons (Texas Department of Criminal Justice) in significant numbers suggesting population and economic problems pushing some groups in addition to traditional laborers to the U.S. On some research trips to the Huntsville Unit, the "Walls", I would see a special bus of

Immigration and Customs Enforcement, ICE officers sent to pick up loads of Mexican prisoners to take to Houston to fly by ICE planes back to Mexico City.

I noted, as well, that a far greater flow of illegals[4] was coming into El Paso in the early morning hours to work in construction. I had taught on this campus, the University of Texas at El Paso (UTEP) in 1967 and 1968 as well at New Mexico State, 40 miles to the west along IH 10. In those years, the Juarez population was about 300,000 and there was open desert south of the campus and west of the city of Juarez. The Juarez city dump was south and west of that area and south as well of Mt. Christo Rey of Juarez topped with a large concrete cross and sometimes a pilgrimage site for some persons. The border existed only in the minds of those people that lived on both sides and increasingly those on the Mexican side were not intimidated by the existence of a border.

I returned to lecture on the campus of UTEP in 1982 as part of an initiative conceived by the University of Texas at Austin's, Gerard Fonken, the Research Vice President, to assist the University of Texas at El Paso in developing its graduate programs and responding to the needs in El Paso, West Texas, southern New Mexico and Mexico's northern State of Chihuahua to create more professional programs in health and human services sciences. The State of Texas had great wealth pouring in from its oil fields and there was a building boom on the UTEP campus with elegant multistory buildings like the new University library only two hundred yards or so from

---

[4] The status and terms used to refer to visitors to the United States are varied and carry significant connotations. Immigration Services provides more than 20 different visas for people visiting, studying or working in the United States. Specific paths are arrayed for persons seeking permanent residence and/or citizenship. Those that have not acquired legal visiting permits are variously referred to as "illegals", "unauthorized", and "undocumented" among other terms. Mexico accounts for more than half of those in the United States without required documentation.

humble handmade adobe hovels across the Rio Grande in Juarez. I would lecture there, the UTEP campus, twice every month in two night classes that would begin late afternoon at 5:30 and conclude by 9:30 that evening. Sometimes in the evening but always in the mornings if you were on the UTEP campus at about 5 a.m., illegals would pop up out of the large drains that opened 6 feet above the surface in the Rio Grande for flowing storm waters into the river. The city of Juarez was only a stone's throw to the south and large, concrete flood control conduits, 10 feet or so in diameter, emptied south of the campus into the Rio Grande. People heading over would wade across the shallows of the Rio Grande and climb into one of the concrete raceways and follow it up to the UTEP campus. You would hear a bobwhite whistle and then an answer from another setting direction and location. The individuals, almost always men, would then catch a pickup to ride to a work setting in El Paso or Las Cruces, New Mexico.

By the late 1980s Juarez was nearly one million and was doubling in size each decade. No one knew the exact population because of the growth and the number of hand-built homes not registered by the municipal government. It was common for new home owners to appropriate some copper wiring and just split a utility line and drag electricity to a house and use a garden hose to do the same for water. This occurred on the outskirts of the city and in certain neighborhoods and some would have active protective societies that would keep city officials at bay when they would come to disconnect illegal ties to electricity and water.

NAFTA efforts were in full swing and industrial parks and small manufacturing plants were springing up across that city. Young people, particularly young women from rural areas of Mexico, were moving to Juarez to pursue factory employment and a different life than growing up on a ranch or in a small town. On most trips I would spend some time across the river in Juarez, Mexico at hospitals, police offices, welfare and social services offices helping my academic unit arrange field internships for our students. I knew the Juarez Mayor, Jaime Bermudez and his wife, Olivia and they would tell me that 100 to 1,000 people were arriving in Juarez daily and worried about how the City could provide housing, utilities, health services, education and jobs for the exploding population. But both El Paso and Juarez were excited about these developments and saw a future not as a windswept West Texas cattle town in the middle of the Chihuahua desert but as a manufacturing and world trade metropolis.

One summer evening I was there at 4:30 p.m. before my evening class and walked across the river to the Mexican side and stood in Juarez on a sandbar in the Rio Grande just across from the UTEP campus framing a hand-built adobe hovel in the foreground and the new several story UTEP Library in the background using a Nikon with several lenses for pictures to take back to Washington, D.C. to have emphasis points about the proximity and growing porosity of the border. I had watched individuals simply walk across for several evenings and decided I would capture some pictures to illustrate the situation. As I used the camera, I noticed that a Ford Bronco had stopped to my north on the UTEP side. I could see two men inside. They sat and watched for about ten minutes. Then one man climbed out of the Bronco and approached me as the other stayed at the wheel. As the guy walked down the grade, I could see from the bulge under his left side that he was wearing a gun and holster. I thought, "Oh, DEA or ICE." He asked in a threatening voice, "What do you think you are doing?" I replied, "I am taking pictures." He then said, "It is against the law to be there." I said that he was misinformed and that furthermore it was part of my research funded by the U. S. Justice Department.

As he visibly relaxed, I asked why he had approached me. He replied did I know what headaches this part of the border caused them, the Border Patrol? I said I suspected I knew and that was part of the reason for my pictures. I told him about watching the Mexicans pop up on the UTEP campus at night and I worried about what was going on and campus safety. He then called his partner down, they were Border Patrol officers, and they talked for an hour about how the Mexicans would send 5 guys at a time about 300 yards apart across that section between UTEP and Smeltertown along the Mexican border to the west. At best they would grab two but the other three "mules" would get across with their drugs. He said they were both very frustrated, often frightened as people on the Juarez side with high powered rifles and scopes were watching them and that Washington would not listen! He gestured at one large adobe house some 300 yards to the south and said they were observing someone in that house with binoculars and a gun with a scope watching us. They would have talked all night had I not had a class I needed to teach and my growing unease that we might indeed be in the crosshairs of a scope in the adobe to our south.

That was the starting years of the veritable flood of drug mules that began in the 90's and continues today and drives Mexican gang problems now hundreds of miles north of the Rio Grande border.

I took my pictures and this story and many other examples and testified to legislative committees of the State of Texas and to dozens of meetings with Federal officials all during the 1980's and 1990's. No one was really worried and few understood, it seemed. I concluded that those that did understand did not see a problem. Republicans saw the illegals as cheap labor and as a tool to bust unions. Democrats saw them as likely future voters. All felt the wealth of NAFTA would cure any problems.

I made my last trip to Juarez in the summer of 2003. My research had kept me from teaching in the El Paso program by then and many of our efforts were now being done by faculty at UTEP. One of our Austin faculty, Donald Blashill, had left our School and took a faculty position at UTEP continuing placements we had developed years earlier for internships including those in Juarez. We went over the second afternoon, and he and I argued about whether he should continue to have placements over there. In many neighborhoods you would see young men hanging out that would lock eyes with people traveling through the area with threatening gazes. Locals were calling these youth, "halcones", (hawks) and they were employed by local drug gangs to watch for competition or just any intruders. Some wore tattoos, which was unusual for Mexican youth. Juarez was changing from a large town filled with rural people to an urban area marked by gang territories. It looked more dangerous than the Bronx that I worked in as I completed my dissertation or the south side of Chicago or east LA. I told him there was no way I would have students in Juarez, Mexico. By 2006 it would become hell and no place for anyone!

The lure of the North has been strong in the Americas for the last half century. For a hundred years the North was a source of seasonal jobs for Mexicans who would return to villages in Mexico. Informal pathways were developed with contacts for work and a place to stay. Economic conditions are not improving for the 40 million plus in Central America and the United States stands as a beacon for those that hope to escape. Some years ago Austin had a program for the homeless in the downtown area and one of my former students, Richard Hendrickson, ran the facility. He noted as the real estate boom brought more Mexican immigrants to Austin looking for work that many would end up at his facility. He asked one how he found the facility and the man said he got the address and phone number from graffiti in the bus station in Saltillo.

Countries South of Mexico

A reckoning of the forces driving immigration, legal and illegal in North America, fails if only Mexico is examined. There are more than 40 million people living in eight countries south of Mexico that must be a part of the understanding of immigration to Mexico and then the United States. These are the countries of Belize, Guatemala, Honduras, El Salvador, Costa Rica, Nicaragua and Panama. Their pasts have much similarity to Mexico's in that remnants of ancient Native American cultures still reside there and all have suffered under colonialism. In all those countries, incomes are irregularly distributed and only the barest of a middle class exists. Violence is higher in these countries than in Mexico with the exception of Costa Rica and Nicaragua. Guatemala has the highest rate in the world and El Salvador is number three. Violence has grown in all but especially Guatemala as the Mexican drug cartels channel increasing amounts of cocaine from Peru, Venezuela and Columbia into Central America and create holding facilities particularly in Guatemala. With much weaker economies than Mexico all countries feed immigrants into Mexico with most headed to the United States. I will use commonly available data with narrative from the CIA site for these summaries of the Central American countries of most likely relevance, Guatemala, Belize, El Salvador and Honduras.(Agency, 2013)

Guatemala

Guatemala is the most populous country in Central America still filled with traditional Indian communities and much of the land held in common rather than surveyed and titled to specific persons. It is in many ways the significant country south of Mexico and the land transit point for all of Central America and South America to Mexico. Belize borders a small area of southeast Mexico with a coastline on the Atlantic with few roads that cross north to south through Belize to Mexico. A thousand years ago this land was filled with the prosperous city-states of the Maya but today with a GDP per capita roughly one-half that of the average for Latin America and the Caribbean, it is viewed as profoundly poor. Agriculture accounts for nearly 15% of the gross national product and absorbs half of the labor force. Key agricultural exports include coffee, sugar, and bananas.

During the 1980's the nation as well as most of the countries south of Mexico were racked with violence as competing groups sought hegemony to control each nation. Guatemala like Mexico struggled to create elected governments but was repeatedly thwarted with dictators and military overthrows. The 1996 peace accords, which ended 36 years of civil war, removed a major obstacle to foreign investment, and since then Guatemala has pursued important reforms and macroeconomic stabilization. The Dominican Republic-Central American Free Trade Agreement (CAFTA-DR) commenced in July 2006 and spurred increased investment permitting diversification of exports, with the largest increases in ethanol and non-traditional agricultural exports including increased exports of fresh fruits and vegetables to North American and European markets and some steps toward manufactured products.

Guatemala's economy is dominated by the private sector, which generates nearly 90% of GDP. Agriculture contributes 13.3% of GDP and accounts for 26% of exports. Most manufacturing is light assembly and food processing, geared to the domestic, U.S., and Central American markets. Over the past several years, tourism and exports of textiles, apparel, and agricultural products such as winter vegetables, fruit, and cut flowers have boomed, while more traditional exports such as sugar, bananas, and coffee continue to represent a large share of the export market.

The United States is the country's largest trading partner, providing 37% of Guatemala's imports and receiving 38.5% of its exports. The government's involvement is small, with its business activities limited to public utilities--some of which have been privatized--ports and airports, and several development-oriented financial institutions.

While CAFTA-DR has helped improve the investment climate, concerns over security, the lack of skilled and educated workers and poor infrastructure providing highway and rail transportation, airports, electrical and water utilities all continue to hamper foreign direct investment. The distribution of income remains highly unequal with the richest 10% of the population accounting for more than 40% of Guatemala's overall consumption. More than half of the population is below the national poverty line and 15% lives in extreme poverty.

Poverty among indigenous groups, (original Indian-Native Americans) which make up 38% of the population, averages 76% and extreme poverty rises to 28%. 43% of children under five are chronically malnourished, one of the highest malnutrition rates in the world. The previous President, Colom, entered into office with the promise to increase education, healthcare, and rural development, and in April 2008 he inaugurated a conditional cash transfer program, modeled after programs in Brazil and Mexico, that provide financial incentives for poor families to keep their children in school and get regular health check-ups. His successor, President Perez Molina has pledged to continue these efforts.

Common and violent crime, aggravated by a legacy of violence and vigilante justice, present a serious challenge. Impunity remains a major problem, primarily because democratic institutions, including those responsible for the administration of justice, have developed only a limited capacity to cope with this legacy. Guatemala's judiciary is independent; however, it suffers from inefficiency, corruption, and intimidation.

Given Guatemala's large expatriate community in the United States, it is the top remittance recipient in Central America, with inflows serving as a primary source of foreign income equivalent to nearly two-thirds of exports or one-tenth of GDP. Economic growth fell in 2009 as export demand from US and other Central American markets fell and foreign investment slowed amid the global recession, but the economy recovered gradually in 2010 and will likely return to more normal growth rates by 2012. President Colom, in his last year in office, faced opposition to economic reform, particularly over a long-delayed tax reform and an IMF-recommended reform to strengthen the banking sector.

Education is free and compulsory for the first 6 years but only 30 percent finish the 6th grade. About a third of the population is illiterate and the mean years of schooling completed is 4.1 years. Rates of illiteracy and low levels of education are highest in the traditional Indian communities with illiteracy there of 60 percent.

Belize

With a population of slightly more than 300,000 and only in the last 30 years receiving independence from Britain as formerly British Honduras, Belize is the most sparsely populated country of Central America. It is a largely agricultural land until recent years largely dependent on forestry with some mining and fishery activity. It has the least developed infrastructure of any country in Central America. English is the dominant language.

Belize has compulsory education through the 9th grade and an illiteracy rate of 5.9 percent. Yet the quality of education is questionable with students scoring poorly in the grade levels in competition with other countries.

It has little developed transportation structures with few rail or highways running north-south. Most of the development is along coastal and islands on the Atlantic. Other than Costa Rica English rather than Spanish is the dominant language.

El Salvador

The smallest country in Central America geographically, El Salvador has the third-largest economy in the region. In the last two decades, El Salvador has made considerable progress in social and economic transformation, undertaking significant social sector reforms that led to improvements in social indicators. These reforms contributed to an increase in the country's Human Development Index--which aggregates measures of life expectancy, adult literacy and school enrollment, and income per capita--from 0.524 in 1990 to 0.674 in 2010, and a decrease in the share of households living in poverty by 23.2 percentage points, from 59.7% in 1990 and 36.5% in 2010. El Salvador ranks 105th in the Human Development Index worldwide.

Much of the improvement in El Salvador's economy is a result of the privatization of the banking system, telecommunications, public pensions, electrical distribution and some electrical generation; reduction of import duties; elimination of price controls; and improved enforcement of intellectual property rights. Capping those reforms, on January 1, 2001, the U.S. dollar became legal tender and the economy is now fully dollarized. However, El Salvador's economy remains strongly linked to world and U.S. economic cycles. From 2000 to 2010, the Salvadoran economy averaged 2% annual economic growth, with GDP receding by 3.1% in 2009 due to the financial crisis and recovering only to 1.4% growth in 2010. El Salvador was expecting 1.4% economic growth in 2011, lower than previously anticipated. These rates of growth are decidedly below the Latin American average, and the Government of El Salvador is determined to reverse these trends by laying the groundwork for a development model built on a new cycle of investment and economic growth through the Partnership for Growth (PFG) initiative.

Years of civil war, fought largely in the rural areas, had a devastating impact on agricultural production in El Salvador. The agricultural sector experienced significant recovery, buoyed in part by higher world prices for coffee and sugarcane and increased diversification into horticultural crops. Seeking to develop new growth sectors and employment opportunities, El Salvador created new export industries through fiscal incentives for free trade zones. The largest beneficiary has been the textile and apparel (maquila) sector, which directly provides approximately 80,000 jobs. Services, including retail and financial, have also shown strong employment growth, with about 63% of the total labor force now employed in the sector.

Remittances from Salvadorans working in the United States are an important source of income for many families in El Salvador. In 2011, the Central Bank estimated that remittances totaled $3.6 billion. UN Development Program (UNDP) surveys show that an estimated 21.3% of families receive remittances.

Under its export-led growth strategy, El Salvador has pursued economic integration with its Central American neighbors and negotiated trade agreements with the Dominican Republic, Chile, Mexico, Panama, Taiwan, Colombia, and the United States. In 2010, Central America signed an Association Agreement with the European Union that includes the establishment of a free trade area, which is expected to enter into force in 2012. In 2011, El Salvador signed a Partial Scope Agreement (PSA) with Cuba. The Central American countries are negotiating a free trade agreement with Canada and Peru. Exports grew by 18.4% in 2011 and imports by 19.1%. As in previous years, the large trade deficit was offset by family remittances.

In 2006, El Salvador was the first country to ratify the U.S.-Central America-Dominican Republic Free Trade Agreement (CAFTA-DR), which has bolstered the export of processed foods, sugar, and ethanol, and supported investment in the apparel sector amid increased Asian competition and the expiration of the Multi-Fiber Arrangement in 2005. From 2005 to 2011, Salvadoran exports to the U.S. increased by 27%, while imports from the U.S. increased 84%. In addition to trade benefits, CAFTA-DR provides trade capacity building, particularly in the environment and labor areas, and a framework for additional reforms on issues such as intellectual property rights, dispute resolution, and customs to improve El Salvador's investment climate. As it has promoted an open trade and investment environment, El Salvador also has embarked on a wave of privatizations extending to telecommunications, electricity distribution, banking, and pension funds.

U.S. support for privatization of the electrical and telecommunications markets markedly expanded opportunities for U.S. investment in the country. More than 300 U.S. companies have established either a permanent commercial presence in El Salvador or work through representative offices in the country. The U.S. Department of Commerce maintains a Country Commercial Guide for U.S. businesses seeking detailed information on business opportunities in El Salvador. Illiteracy rate is 20 percent with compulsory schooling through the 9th grade.

Honduras

Honduras sits on the Atlantic side of Central America and with El Salvador on the Pacific side are the keystones south of Guatemala. Beyond there is the relatively stable state of Costa Rica, and then Nicaragua and Panama. The dominant language is Spanish and the population is about 9 million. Honduras, with an estimated per capita gross domestic product (GDP) of $4,200 in 2010 (PPP), is one of the poorest countries in the western hemisphere, with about 65% of the population living in poverty. While 2010 estimates project GDP to have grown by 2.8%, Honduras' GDP fell by 2.1% in 2009. Reasons for this contraction included the worldwide economic downturn and the political crisis surrounding the forced removal of President Zelaya from power. Previously, the economy grew by more than 6% per year from 2004 to 2007, and by 4% in 2008.

Historically dependent on exports of agricultural goods, the Honduran economy has diversified in recent decades and now has a strong export-processing (maquila) industry, primarily focused on assembling textile and apparel goods for re-export to the United States, as well as automobile wiring harnesses and similar products. Despite the recent economic diversification, there continues to be a large subsistence farming population with few economic opportunities. Honduras also has extensive forest, marine, and mineral resources, although widespread slash-and-burn agricultural methods and illegal logging continue to destroy Honduran forests.

Because of a strong commercial relationship with the United States, Honduras was hit hard by the international economic downturn, especially in the maquila industry, where orders were estimated to have declined about 40%, and where about 30,000 workers lost their jobs in 2008 and 2009 out of a pre-crisis workforce of 145,000. The maquila sector began to see an upswing toward the end of 2009 as the U.S. economy stabilized, and it has begun re-expanding its employment base. Over one-third of the Honduran workforce was considered either unemployed or underemployed in 2010.

Roughly 1 million Hondurans have migrated to the United States. Remittance inflows from Hondurans living abroad, mostly in the United States, are the largest source of foreign income and a major contributor to domestic demand. Remittances totaled $2.8 billion in 2009, down 11.8% from

2008 levels; that is equivalent to about one-fifth of Honduras' GDP.

The Immigration Debate

A decade ago Texans first began to be concerned about the changing demographics of their state. The state demographer, Steve Murdock (Murdock, 1996), extrapolated interim census estimates and suggested by 2030 or so Texas would become a minority-majority state. The most populous ethnic group would be persons of Mexican descent and would become the majority.

Murdock focused his report on several attributes of Mexican Americans in Texas and similar characteristics of Mexican citizens. Among Murdock's points and extrapolations were that Mexican Americans had the lowest levels of school attainment and highest levels of school dropouts of all ethnic groups in Texas. Lower educational levels mean lower incomes and perhaps higher crime rates. Importantly Mexican Americans were less likely to vote, participate in civic organizations, own a business, serve on juries, school boards, etc. They were as a group in Texas like Mexicans in Mexico and that as a culture very wary of civic engagement. Murdock concluded that without cultural change, Texas in 2030 would be more like northern Mexico, more populous, less educated, younger and poorer. Such findings have substantial significance when viewed through the lenses of theories of social participation and innovation (Putnam, 1996; Putnam, 2000; Putnam, 1996; Sampson, 1988; Skocpol, 2003).

Murdock argued that if educational achievement and civic participation for that ethnic group did not change, then Texas would become a less educated state, a poorer state and one with greater rates of crime. Murdock's report was controversial, rejected by many political leaders and disturbed by others.

Implications for Texas

With Governor Bush and Albert Hawkins, the Governor's Budget Director my research group held after every legislative session, a Governor's Conference on Excellence, seeking to get state leaders to prepare to address challenges for the coming two years and use opportunities for state achievements (the Texas Legislature meets only every two years). In 1999 we included Steve Murdock on the program and Robert Gates, who was the interim dean at the Bush School at Texas A&M, was the moderator. Murdock reprised his argument about the negative consequences that could come to Texas if increased Hispanic numbers were not coupled by greater educational achievement and civic participation.

In the question and answer session there were a few polite questions but no debate or high interest. After the program concluded, Professor Gates and I returned to my campus and over coffee discussed the day. He asked me if I was disappointed in the lack of concern about Murdock's presentation. I said I was not surprised and that I had had many experiences that made me think that Texans did not look closely at things in Mexico. I related to Gates an experience that a colleague, Guy Shuttlesworth and I, had that provided an example. We had taken a large group of nursing home owners to Guadalajara as a weeklong educational program and at the owners' requests had provided a tour of the single nursing home in Guadalajara run by the Catholic Church. The Texas nursing home owners were astonished at the second most populous city having only one nursing home and how meager were the services and crowded conditions. Guy and I were at pains to explain to the owners that there were no comparable Federal programs to fund nursing home care in Mexico and it was up to the families or the Church to care for the elderly.

Professor Gates shook his head and said, "I guess I see. Do you know what I thought of during today's presentation by

Murdock? I thought of my experience in Iran during the 1970s when the Shah held power and I was in charge of the targeting of missiles aimed at the Soviet Union to protect against potential strikes on Iran, Saudi Arabia and other countries of the Middle East. During those years Iran was going through demographic change with slower population growth of groups tied to the Persian culture especially in Tehran and more rapid growth of poorer, less educated persons and deeply involved in Shia Muslim beliefs."

Gates noted that those demographic forces were an essential part of the overthrow of the Shah's government and the appearance of a militant and anti-American Iran. Professor Gates and I ended our discussion wondering what indeed might lie ahead in the next 2 or 3 decades for Texas (Lauderdale, Landuyt, Hawkins, Barton, 1999). He asked as a parting if I intended to make Texas home given our discussion. I replied that I would be thinking of our conversation and asked him if he would return from Washington to College Station and the A&M campus, as he was sure to be part of the Bush Administration if Bush won the Presidency. He smiled and said, "What do you think?"

Components of the Hispanic Population

The growth of the Hispanic population that Murdock focused upon two decades ago has two components. One is those individuals born in Texas of Hispanic descent. In the 1700s the population of Texas was Indian-Native Americans. Cultures in eastern Texas were often from the Caddo culture that had villages, agriculture as well as hunting and fishing. The Caddo culture gave way in central Texas to more migratory cultures including the Apache and a recent even more migratory culture, the Comanche. Hispanic cultures were limited to villages surrounding Spanish Catholic missions such as at San Antonio and El Paso. El Paso and north up the Rio Grande were village and farming cultures, the Pueblo. Significant Hispanic populations developed in Texas after its war for independence from Mexico and the subjugation of the Comanche. Such Hispanic populations did not experience political governance from Spain or Mexico but from Texas and the United States. Thus their cultural orientation and socialization were as Americans but from Hispanic roots.

The second component of the Hispanic population is <u>persons born in Mexico</u> or other parts of Latin America. Mexico is far and away the largest contributor of Hispanic migration and immigration to the United States and currently it is estimated that 10 percent or more of the population of Mexico resides in the United States. During the late 1800s Mexicans began to migrate seasonally to Texas for ranching and farming employment and then with the war in 1910, great numbers migrated to live permanently. Temporary residence was encouraged during the First and Second World Wars as military drafts reduced American population for work in agriculture and factories. That tradition of migratory, temporary residence established early in the 20th Century continues to this day. The rate of migration and immigration appeared to decline about 2001 but has increased since 2006.

Hispanic cultures in Texas until recent years were characterized by higher rates of family formation and size than the Anglo and African American cultures. Several reasons have been suggested for why family size dropped with Anglos a couple of generations before Hispanics. They include moving to urban and suburban settings where children are less of an economic resource in farming to better health and more education. Better health reduces deaths at childbirth and during the first few years of life thus reducing the need to have more children for family survival. Better education with more equal rights for women especially with the availability of birth controls results in women having fewer children and postponing when children are conceived. Hispanics have lagged Anglos in the United States on all of these developments and this is true as a nation in Mexico. Those factors along with immigration from Mexico laid the basis for the transition in Texas of Hispanics becoming the majority population.

Other components of the Hispanic population are persons not born in Texas or for that matter the United States but immigrants from Latin American countries that include North and South America and the Caribbean. The national origin of the largest number of Hispanic immigrants is Mexico. It is estimated that the Hispanic population in the United States in 2010 was about 53 million with 33.5 million that trace their ancestry to Mexico. Those of Mexican origin have the lowest median age among the various components of the Hispanic population at 25 years while Hispanics of Cuban origin have the highest median age, at 40 years exceeding the national median age of 37 years. The Pew Hispanic Center provides a widely accepted estimate of 11.2 million illegal immigrants in 2010 with likely half or more from Mexico.[5] Citizens from Mexico, illegal immigrants from Mexico and then illegal immigrants from Guatemala and Honduras, in that order, have the lowest educational achievements of all groups in the United States.

Closing Comments

The story of Mexico and the United States and the border is a long story and one that is not near an end. Because of decisions in the 20th Century to grow its population Mexico struggles today with the need for jobs, education, health care and housing that exceed what it, as a state, can produce. Part of the consequence as been migration of Mexicans to the United States either to seek temporary work, education, health care or to permanently move to the United States.

---

[5] http://www.pewhispanic.org provides estimates of changing characteristics of Hispanic population and other contemporary issues.

For decades the nation of Mexico has been barely on the radar screen of the United States pushed aside by Europe, the Middle East and Asia. But in recent years attention has begun to be paid to the border of Mexico. Part of the reason for the notice is the cascading violence that began in the northern cities of Mexico and now has spread throughout Mexico. Less recognized is the "fall out or spillover" occurring in the United States from conditions in Mexico. The violence has reached such a crescendo that discussions have begun about whether or not Mexico is a failing state or, most serious, a failed state.

A part of the debate is to examine how radically different the demography, job levels and education are between the north and the south of North America. As word spreads among the youth of these countries to the south of the United States increasing numbers take the chance to head north for more prosperity and in recent years for safety as well.

Thus one must look at immigration in terms of the pressures that drive immigration, the growing violence in most of these countries including Mexico, the fact that much of the violence is organized now by drug cartels and the fact that today the United States in terms of our economy does not have the jobs to offer several million Americans much less many millions more of persons migrating to this country from Mexico and Central America. This is apart from costs that are born by the community in terms of providing education, health care and protection.

One fundamental issue that has developed in the United States since 1970 has been the declining real wages for many jobs. This has resulted in a downward movement of the economic condition of most American labor. Globalization in the next two decades accelerated that process.

Lower real wages are part of the picture. The second part is the failure of the American economy to simply generate jobs. That failure is not restricted to the United States but is a common issue in Great Britain and Europe. Youthful unemployment in Greece of 80%, in Spain of 55%, in France of 26% and in Italy of 36% indicates the worldwide failure of job development! Such failures mean that the United States is every year less able to provide for its population and has shrinking chances of providing economic mobility, health care and education for the tens of millions of Mexico and Central America.

A recent series from the NY Times (Cave, 2013) provides some detail about illegal migration today. It notes the illegal crossings, which are likely in excess of a million yearly, are in the context of 350 million legal crossings annually with 365,000 apprehensions last year. A second observation is that the smuggling ruses of drugs, humans and other contraband are complex and entrepreneurial including trucks appearing to be FedEx or oil field service vehicles and drug smuggling groups using homemade tire strips to deflate tires of pursing Border Control trucks.

Such reports do not detail very important additional needed information including:

- What are the profiles of individuals coming across such as country of origin, health conditions, reasons for crossing, age, moving contraband, etc.? The appearance of articles on drug resistant TB among illegals is an example that makes profile information important, very critical.

- What are the reasons some areas are easier and some more difficult to control? Part of this answer is simple in that the Valley is unique along the 2,000 mile border with miles and miles from Brownsville to Del Rio and

Eagle Pass and then again El Paso where there are heavily populated areas side by side along both sides of the border. There is where control is now most difficult and where apparently the most inequity exists in Federal funding parity.

- What are the organizations in Mexico and the U.S. that support illegal crossings? Mexico has for decades been notoriously inhospitable to illegal immigrants from Central America. With the exception of Costa Rica the countries immediately south of Mexico are far poorer and more violent than Mexico?. Why do immigrants risk the 800 miles or so through Mexico? Their numbers are a measure of the desperation in those countries. What are the numbers and characteristics of the illegals from other parts of the world? How do they make the transit to Mexico? What is the role of the Cartels? Who runs the cars, trucks and drop houses on this side to receive the immigrants? Where are the neighborhoods where they land?

- What institutions on the American side are particularly vulnerable? Emergency medical rooms will be and are hit hard. They serve as primary medical care for illegal immigrants. So are local police and sheriffs' departments. Effective policing requires people's willingness to call and report crimes and assist police in solving the crimes. But illegal immigrants come with very negative attitudes toward all police as well as the fear of being tuned in to the Immigration Services. Colleges such as UT El Paso and UT Brownsville with their open campuses and 24-hour operation provide ready cover for people moving through. In years past having taught at UTEP, I would watch illegal immigrants come through the large water viaducts from west El Paso running under the campus. They emptied into the Rio Grande from the barrios that line the south side of El Paso and the men and some women would then pop up from manholes on the campus and then fade into the city.

• What is the flow north in Texas? Houston and the IH35 corridor are heavily trafficked. What are the consequences? Occasional contraband intercepts in Austin and central Texas on the north-south highways are a small reminder.

The American economy is struggling to produce sufficient jobs and youth unemployment especially for minorities is high. In August of 2012 the Department of Labor (Statistics, 2012, August 21) reported "The number of unemployed youth in July 2012 was 4.0 million, little changed from 4.1 million a year ago. The youth unemployment rate was 17.1 percent in July 2012. The unemployment rate for young men was 17.9 percent, in July 2012, and the rate for women was 16.2 percent. The jobless rate for whites was 14.9 percent, compared with 28.6 percent for blacks, 14.4 percent for Asians, and 18.5 percent for Hispanics." The burden of youth unemployment is even starker in Europe as this chart drawn from the ECU details. Like the United States relative to much of North America, northern Europe has countries with stronger economies and better employment conditions.

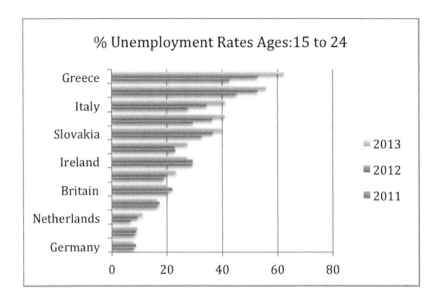

This is an explosive development for the future as jobs are critical for support and socialization! The burden will be on neighborhoods with unemployed youth on the street and police running from call to call.

Immigrants compete for these jobs that youth require, low cost housing and receive basic medical care at hospital emergency rooms (perhaps the most expensive way to get basic care and choking the facilities in many communities). Children from immigrants from Mexico and Central America youth have high dropout rates and only start to match native-born Americans in the second and third generation in school attendance and success. Schools bear a costly and critical burden.

A popular educational approach of teaching the immigrant child in the language of the home, "English as a second language" is a dubious solution. It rests on sketchy science that declares that one learns another language by first becoming fluent in the first one. It risks creating linguistic ghettoes of students that drop out of school early and do not acquire the language skills to become more capable in the new country.

The drug trade driven by American consumption provides one source of income as does property crime for persons increasingly difficult to integrate into an economy providing relatively few entry level jobs that lead to higher wages, more permanent employment and benefits. Jobs at McDonalds, Wal-Mart and lawn and garden care cannot meet the demand for work of older Americans that find retirement funds and savings inadequate, people with only high school or less education, entry level opportunities for teenagers and youth, and other Americans at the bottom of the employment skills ladder. Compared to Mexico, Central America and much of Asia and Africa face for more critical circumstances and even these conditions in the United States will not going to stem the flow. Conditions in these countries are so much more desperate that immigrants come in spite of risking arrest, physical assault, discrimination and loss of family and community. Control of the borders especially in Texas poses huge challenges.

Any decision if one comes with regard to immigration is exceedingly complex. Millions come to the United States in the hope of having a better, safer future and that has been true for decades. But that hope must include achieving citizenship not remaining in the shadows avoiding roles in civic culture. That is a critical issue for all here and for all that come.

Limits To Growth

Forty years ago The Club of Rome, a think tank in Italy, (Bardi & SpringerLink (Online service), 2011; Meadows & Club of Rome., 1972; Meadows, Randers, & Meadows, 2004) issued a report entitled, The Limits to Growth, that argued that the world was reaching limits in terms of global population and the natural resources that sustain life. Access to resources and population growth is a theme of economists and social policy theorists appearing in scholarship since 1500 and the discovery of the New World. That discovery and the ending of the Middle Ages also involved the development of science and technology that permitted rapid population growth associated with improved agriculture and nutrition.

First was the application of animal labor, horses, mules and oxen, with improved plows to till soils. New notions of the arrangement of labor came and factories displaced individual craftsmen. Villages consolidated households and grew into cities. The population of western societies burgeoned from 1800 to 1900 several fold.

But the growth saw the depletion of the forests of England and Europe used for buildings and fuel. Commonly held forests and meadows used by all villagers became overly exploited and governments developed to curtail access to these "commons". Legislation in England was called "enclosures" and thousands of "enclosure acts were written into law from 1750 to 1860 as England's population grew, became more urban and resource depletion became more evident. Fisheries, like forests and grazing meadows, were stressed by overfishing with catches and breeding stocks diminished. Robert Malthus, cleric and early economist (1766-1834), described this process and saw population growth reversing technological and economic progress and leading to poverty.

The popular writer and social critic, Charles Dickens, in A Christmas Carol examines the negative tone of the Malthusian perspective and argues for the progressive perspective that science and technology can overcome the apparent poverty rooted inherently in population growth. The population growth in Mexico and Central America in the 20th century requires we examine these perspectives as first developed in England and Europe in the 18th and 19th centuries.

When the report of the Club of Rome is read, one can see the findings and influences of L. King Hubbard relative to oil. The Club using similar bell curves of oil production that Hubbard presents to examine the growth, peaking and decline of other variables. Limits to Growth was a modern statement of the concerns of Thomas Malthus and utilized global assessments of population size and growth, available arable land, lumber, mines, oil deposits, fisheries, etc. Calculating statistical trends the think tank in that and subsequent reports argued for among other things population and consumption controls. (Meadows, Randers et al., 2004; Bardi and SpringerLink Online service, 2011)

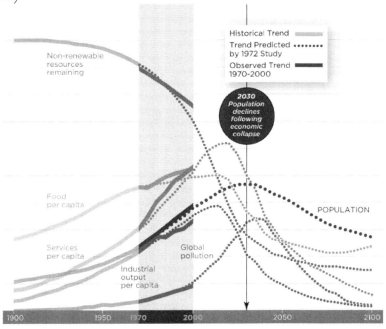

As we examine the populations of the United States, Mexico and then those states south of Mexico, these ideas demand consideration. The last three hundred years have been ones of remarkable growth of the world's population. Improved nutrition, expanded farming, the use of commerical fertilizers, increased technology and most important the availabilty of cheap energy sources has made this growth possible (Deffeyes, 2008; Engdah, 2013, March 13; Engdahl, 2004; Hefner, 2009; Rubin, 2009; Simmons, 2005). Larger nations that could field larger, better equpped armies prevailed in combat (Bobbitt,

2003) and globalization was driven by the most powerful nations. Today one must look at these populations with the question of how indviduals will support themselves and families in a world of rapid technological change and fewer jobs, or at least fewer jobs at the unskilled level. The following table shows the population and median ages of the United States and nations to its south. It shows large population numbers and young ages

Country	Population	Median Age
Belize	330,000.00	21
Costa Rica	4,500,000.00	29
El Salvador	6,000,000.00	24
Guatemala	13,000,000.00	20
Honduras	8,000,000.00	21
Nicaragua	5,600,000.00	23
Panama	3,400,000.00	28
TOTALS	40,830,000.00	23
Mexico	114,000,000.00	27
United States	314,000,000.00	37

Mexico with a small population of 15 millon in 1910 came to have a large urban population of over 100 million in the 20th century by political choice and subsidizing family size. That now, large urban population, is among her greatest problems.

Mexico and the United States have strong economies but with clear limits. The United States has acquired heavy public debts and lost much of its manufacturing capabilities. It no longer leads the world in average educational attainment. It still has abundant natural resources but limits on arable land, forests, energy, minerals, and fisheries are finite. It does not create adequate numbers of entry-level jobs for young people and that is particularly true with those with no post secondary education or technical training.

Mexico has created a nation with a young population that has in the last two decades seen a sharp reduction in family size but still reels with how you employ and educate a young population. How Mexico and the United States face these challenges in the next decade will configure the duration of the century as much as the 1910 Revolution and World War I and II did for the two countries in the past century.

A Failing State

The reality of Mexico of the 20th century is a culture that has failed to develop many of the civic mechanisms such as public education, honest, transparent government, health care, employment and civic participation that its population deserves. It remains a beautiful country with a people generous and hard working. But at its soul it is extremely authoritarian and continues colonial traditions. There was the potential of a genuine competitive democracy beginning with the election in 2000 of Vicente Fox and the PAN Party. However the PRI resumed control in the elections of 2012 and the efforts of the new President, Pena Nieto may be to restrict information and reporting on violence and corruption in Mexico. While he appears to have taken strong steps to break the grip to the two most powerful unions that control the state-owned energy monopoly, Pemex, and the teachers' union, his success may not match his avowed intentions.

Beginning in 2010, I collaborated with Professor Bob Inman and the Greater Austin Crime Commission on a program that year and repeated in the fall of 2012 to look at potential threats coming from the border (Inman, 2011; Lauderdale, Landuyt, Kelly, 2011). In these day-long seminars we have assessed where current threats exist and new ones lie. By that fall our concerns had been picked up by both the State of Texas and the U.S. Congress (Texas, 2013; United States House Committee on Homeland Security, 2012, November). In the November 2012 session I chaired a panel that included Alejandro Junco de la Vega, a graduate of the Journalism School at my University and one of the largest publishers in Mexico with papers in Monterrey, Guadalajara and Mexico City. In 2010 he moved his family to Austin for safety reasons and commutes weekly to Mexico. He showed a video clip from one of his reporters of two cartel gunmen intimidating the mayor of a city in Michoacán Mexico and telling him who would be the police chief and the police officers. Mr. Junco explained that the mayor in most cities hires the police chief and this cartel control was becoming common. In concluding he said this was the hometown of Felipe Calderon, the outgoing Mexican President. He said he was most dismayed not just that it was happening but that it was not news of interest in the United States.

Mexico failed to accomplish critical civic improvements in the 20th century. It has entered the 21st no better prepared. The United States has indeed been a distant neighbor and one that during the decades after World War II extending its reach globally far beyond its grasp, spent scarce resources carelessly and acquired massive debts. The next two decades will be one of reconciling goals in both countries with the realities of today.

There are several macro perspectives that provide alternative viewpoints on how change will occur. One is that we are depleting natural resources and that depletion will drive all change. (Engdahl, 2004; Kunstler, 2005; Rubin, 2009; Rubin, 2012; Ritholtz and Task, 2009; Tertzakian, 2007) Another is that banking and money provide the means of global trade and growth and those corrections can maintain prosperity. (Friedman, 2008) Another is that fundamental cultural beliefs and institutions direct the path of the society and can alter existing limits. (Boserup, 1968; Kotkin, 2010; Mandelbaum, 2010; Pfaff, 2010; Rose, 2010; Stiglitz, 2010; Ferguson, 2011; Acemoglu and Robinson, 2012) And another is that cultural change creates generational differences that drive social outcomes (Strauss and Howe, 1997). In all cases we conclude that continuing dislocations are the rule.

Failed states exist when the control of the central government collapses and smaller units such as tribes, regions and families become the paramount institutions. Current illustrations are Somalia on the Horn of Africa and Yemen near the oil fiefdoms. History is filled with examples as in time all states failed and among the prominent in our intellectual history is France in the late 1770's, the Chinese under Chaing Kai-shek when faced with the Maoist Revolution and the Soviet Union in 1991. The spillover of violence from Mexico into the United States is a consequence of a failing state.

America is faced with the prospects of a *dying elephant* on the southern border. In 2013, as has been the case since 2008, these are the four alternative scenarios that exist and in my estimate of the likely occurrence from most likely to least likely as the probabilities appear today. But these probabilities, as arranged, are not some invariant Newtonian process like planets in orbit. Rather they provide alternative signposts for the path ahead.

As I close this writing, I look at the members of one of my undergraduate classes at my university. One third of the class have Hispanic backgrounds with three having come during their secondary school years from Mexico and the others being born in the United States with parents or grandparents being born in Mexico. Such increasing percentages of Hispanics in higher education is heartening as it suggests cultural change and civic participation not seen at relative levels 20 years ago. Such small straws in the wind offer hope that Steve Murdock's negative alternative for Texas will not come to pass. Two of the students come from an Austin neighborhood where I am working with the Austin Police and my academic colleagues to increase civic participation in areas where there are several thousand people having come in the last decade from Mexico and Central

America to Austin. This is one neighborhood of many across much of the United States of an invisible population, living in the United States, but not part of the larger community. If our efforts are successful, those students will follow the path of increased participation in civic life and higher education. They and others will influence friends and family in Mexico and the path to a failed state will be a distant memory. That is the goal and that is the hope of our efforts and others across the Southwest.

Four Alternative Scenarios For Mexico

A. Collapse in progress

World recession deepens. Oil plays out in Mexico's top producing fields, Mexico cedes control to private actors over the south and north of the country with 10 million refugees in Mexico from the countries to its south, and 20 million refugees from within Mexico head to the northern cities of Mexico and the United States. Millions will come to Texas alone. Mexico is beset with guerilla bands controlling much of the countryside and several of the larger low-income neighborhoods in Mexico City. Staged attacks on American border cities occur with regular frequency and local police in Mexico are overwhelmed facing cartels that are better organized, funded and equipped and abandon their posts. American border cities are overwhelmed with refugees and violent gangs. American military units are required to defend against armed intrusions from Mexico.

B. American Protectorate

Cartels use hit squads to attack American law enforcement in border cities on both sides. The United States intervenes with military forces as it has done in other countries and creates a protectorate for the Mexican Federal government south to Monterrey, Saltillo and Durango. Wealthy and educated

Mexicans move to Texas for safety and call for more American military and police action to defeat cartel armies. The traditional northern Mexican antipathy toward the "chilangos" of Mexico City grows and a process of tying the northern Mexican states closely to the American Southwest accelerates. Leftist and nationalistic mobs burn and sack the American Embassy in Mexico City. The ancient fear of another American invasion of Mexico becomes real and kindles long simmering antipathy toward the north. Norteños from bases in Texas plan to re-take northern cities fallen into chaos and urge U.S. support.

C. Revival of Pax Americana

American economy revives and joint American and Mexican efforts suppress cartel activity with attendant boosts in tourism, maquila employment and domestic growth. America sharply reduces illegal drug consumption. Mexico increases its historical ties with Central America and opens the region to the south to economic growth and channels American technological knowhow through all of Latin America. Mexico curtails the power of its unions and its most wealthy and extends public education to 14 years for all citizens. America provides support for joint educational ventures with American and Mexican universities. The North American continent becomes the model for integrating raw material, labor resources and intellectual creativity in a bursting of prosperity and hemispheric free trade.

D. Reprieve

World economy rebounds. Oil prices rise to $200 a barrel. Mexico permits foreign investments and spins off Pemex, which modernizes engineering, refining and exploration. The rising price of oil removes the labor cost advantage of nations in Asia for manufactured items imported to the United States and Europe. Maquila partnerships and fully domestic manufacturing activity soars in Mexico. Corruption is curtailed and profits soar. Situation stabilizes to a significant degree as the wealth generation exceeds what is loss to corruption. Mexico continues to make progress in developing manufacturing relationships with various foreign companies. Tourism rebounds as the PRI controls press reports of crime.

Acknowledgements

This book comes from many friendships, research efforts and teaching experiences over 40 plus years. My dissertation research was based upon how small informal groups form, the development of norms and the role of leadership. My subjects were adolescents in natural field settings. I conducted the research in Oklahoma, Texas, Pennsylvania and New York City. When I completed my doctorate I worked in the mid-1960s for the Executive Offices of the President and several projects funded by the Office of Economic Opportunity. Among those efforts were field visits and technical assistance to communities in Louisiana, Arkansas, Oklahoma and New Mexico to establish citizen boards and legal charters for Community Action Agencies and Headstart Programs. My work was fundamental community organization where I would assess the needs and characteristics of a community, identify formal and informal leadership and advise the community in developing organizations to address local needs and problems. These experiences provided hundreds of lessons on how ethnicity, local laws and customs, the economy, and political power affected civic participation and the efforts of persons to improve their lives.

In 1967 I took a teaching position in the psychology department at New Mexico State University in Las Cruces, New Mexico and taught statistics as well at the University of Texas at El Paso. I continued to do research and consultation for the OEO, formed and ran a business to support my efforts and came to know a number of persons in business and civic life in El Paso, New Mexico, southern Mexico and Ciudad Juarez. Among those persons were Richard Hendrickson and Wendell Chino of the Mescalero Apache Reservation, Tom Walker of Pharr, Texas and George Rodriguez of El Paso, Jaime and Olivia Burmudez of Juarez, who explained to me much of the history of the two communities and the hopes of a growing Juarez.

I moved to Austin in 1969 and joined the faculty of the School of Social Work in 1970 and in the late 1970's initiated organizational research that continues today to improve the quality of services provided by Texas State Government. Julie Cunniff and Michael Kelly were the first two of many others that joined me in that effort. I was contacted early on by Don Rettberg to provide assistance to a new agency he headed funded by Ross Perot to address school drug abuse. Austin was beginning a rapid development of high technology companies as well as important development in the provision of health care. Norman Chenven, Bob Black and Ted Pickens were central to much of my work then with Prudential, the Austin Regional Clinic and 3M. The effort for the State of Texas came from a request from Governor William Clements to apply some of the research I was doing with large companies including Prudential, 3M and IBM for the State. That opportunity provided an empirical basis of how one can measure and improve employee commitment and creativity in an organization and also civic activities. Using Texas and its agencies and its counties as fundamental data sets, I was active in developing software and statistical protocols that could be manipulated on computers. The advent of personal computers accelerated my research, its visibility in Texas and nationally and led to a Federal grant to provide technical assistance to two central Mexican institutions, Desarrollo Integral de La Familia-DIF and Salud (Health and Human Services).

Mexico in the 1980s was transforming rapidly into large urban centers and was interested in developing the kind of centralized data bases we had created in Texas that permitted analyses over time to detect population patterns and forecast needs and resources. Two Cabinet Leaders of the Administration of Miguel de la Madrid were significant in assisting me to understand Mexico and the national efforts of Mexico in those years. Leobardo Ruiz, the Executive Director of DIF and the Deputy Director of Salud, Jose Laguna, spent many hours with me explaining the culture, history and governmental programs of Mexico and comparing them to those in the United States and the State of Texas. I am indebted to them and their colleagues in many ways. The complex relationships between especially Texas and Mexico were illuminated for me with conversations with Graciela Rodriguez, Ira Iscoe and Wayne Holtzman.

In 1984 as my research developed with national programs in Mexico and state programs in Texas, Governor Mark White appointed me as the Chair of the Board of the State's Good Neighbor Commission. That Commission and my research took me to Mexico City and border towns including Juarez, Nuevo Laredo, and Matamoros monthly. Among our achievements was the development of formal agreements between Texas and Mexico to share data on social factors and collaborate on civil proceedings that involved families with members in both Texas and Mexico. I also began to work with Hector Ayala, a professor of psychology at UNAM and Kathryn Selber, who had taught at UNAM and then became a student in our doctoral program. They enhanced my understanding of training issues in Mexican social services as well as assessments of the Mexican public school system and higher education. By the mid 1980s my School established a masters in social work program in El Paso using classrooms at UTEP and I assisted by developing internship training opportunities in El Paso, Las Cruces and Juarez. My teaching and research in those years after then took me away from Mexico and my last trip to Juarez was in 2003. By then I was spending available time working with Texas State agencies and the Austin Police. Increasingly we were seeing growing Mexican immigration into Austin and working to create police, school and community programs to address problems that came with aspects of the immigration.

Beginning in 2007, I participated in a series of programs initiated by the Greater Austin Area Crime Commission examining challenges to law enforcement. Jack Schumacher and I had two spirited days of presentation in 2007 and 2008 including the then current Mexican Counsel, Jorge Guajardo about the changing security of Mexico and the border. In many discussions with City and State leaders including Roy Butler and his wife Ann, Fred Ligarde, Ralph Wayne, Cary Roberts, Jim Pitts, Pete Laney, Steve McCraw, Albert Hawkins, John Barton, Jack Schumacher, Stanley Knee, Joe Holt, Richard Hill, Bob Inman, Pam Willeford, Patricia Ohlendorf, Adam Hamilton, Noel Landuyt, Brian Davis, Mack Brown, Robert Pitman, Fred Burton, Charles Rasner, Rick Muniz, Michelle Burman, Robert Dahlstrom, Robert Harkins, Terry McMahan, Pat Clubb and Gregory Thrash, I begin to assemble writing and thoughts that led to this volume. Ralph Wayne and Fred Ligarde discussed with me many times their experiences in Mexico and how ready Texas state and city government and citizens may be to understand what we are starting to see in Mexico and in Texas. I worked with Cary Roberts several times on presentations with the Greater Austin Crime Commission to increase civic awareness including city, state and federal entities of some of the challenges I list in this writing. I was support in this broad effort by my academic deans Barbara White and then since 2012, Luis Zayas. Luis has encouraged the clear ties of the work to Latin America as well as with the broad law enforcement and public safety community.

Aspects of those conversations and efforts as they developed included regular examinations with Art Acevedo, David Carter, Donald Baker, Kathryn Fitzgerald, Brian Manley, Allen McClure, Rick Bradstreet of the Austin Police and Robert Mendoza, Dee Gonzalez and Juan Villa of the Austin Schools. These conversations soon included Mike Levy, Sam Holt and Kim Rossmo of the City's Public Safety Commission as well as Sheryl Cole, Mike Martinez and Lee Leffingwell of the Austin City Council and Greg Anderson of Ms. Cole's offices. These discussions helped me develop my conclusions that the United States and particularly Texas will be a proving ground for effectiveness of American institutions to transform millions of immigrants into the independent thinking, progressiveness, civic participation and optimism that has been a fundamental belief during the history of the United States.

The primary institutions that will first and most fully address this challenge are the municipal police and the public schools. These are as large a set of challenges that these institutions have ever met. The schools must respond to many children with only a single parent at home and in other instances with both parents holding 2 or more jobs. In the case of immigrant children, the child will develop English fluency in most cases prior to the parent and that may marginalize the parent as the school and teachers seek family involvement. Residential patterns will continue to have some neighborhoods with low incomes and limits on family resources and other schools, many will be private, will have higher rates of school success. If the continuing American pattern since 1970 is toward the destruction of the middle class, the schools will have an improbable task of educating, preparing for citizenship and providing knowledge and skills for a fluid job market.

Police departments are the other fundamental institution that has high levels of contact with citizens. The American pattern of policing is three fold: service, auto and pedestrian order and crime control. The traditions from England of the neighborhood watch, through the sheriff's posses of the 19th Century and community policing of the last 40 years require trust and reciprocity between the citizen and the police. The same is true for the civil and criminal courts where fundamental decisions rest with the jury, the citizen control of the system. America's civic culture is at ebb. New persons from Latin America do not come with the attitudes and skills to be active in civic process.

If schools, police and the broader society meet the challenge, the 21st Century can perhaps be like the 20th Century and will be an American Century.

The jury is out. My bet is that the challenge will be met. As it is met in the United States, these similar beliefs of individual freedom, self-determination and progressive improvement will appear in Mexico and its transformation to its promise will succeed this time.

About The Author

Michael Lauderdale is a professor in the School of Social Work at the University of Texas at Austin. His doctoral work was done at the University of Oklahoma and the Pennsylvania State University. He studied with Muzafer Sherif and directed for him the "natural group studies" of how small youth groups form and function and the relation to the immediate social setting. The research was important in understanding juvenile delinquency but also how small group interaction is a critical socialization process throughout life and an insight into functioning in formal organizations. He conducted small group research directing as well as directing studies of other investigators of groups in Oklahoma City, San Antonio, Texas, Philadelphia and Altoona, Pennsylvania and Bronx, New York City, New York.

He has taught at the University of Oklahoma, New Mexico State University and the University of Texas at El Paso. He was a consultant for the Executive Offices of the President and then the Office of Economic Opportunity in the 1960s and assisted communities in Arkansas, Louisiana, Oklahoma, New Mexico and Texas to create and charter Community Action Agencies and Head Start programs. He served during the 1960s and 1970s as the consulting psychologist for the Mescalero Apache Tribe in New Mexico. He has conducted research in Mexico and the Mexican border since 1966, having been involved with Federal efforts to promote community development with El Paso being one major focal point. In the 1980s he chaired for the State of Texas The Good Neighbor Commission with offices in Austin and Mexico City, and conducted a multiyear collaborative research effort funded by the Federal Government and endorsed by the Mexican President, Miguel de la Madrid with University of Texas at Austin faculty, several Universidad Nacional Autónoma de México faculty, and the Mexican and Texas governments to apply geographical information systems (GIS) and desktop computing to forecast social needs and trends

He began in 1979 a continuing research effort for the State of Texas to improve functioning of its state agencies as well as customer relations with Texas citizens. In 1992 at the request of the Austin Police Department he joined with Professor Howard Prince of the LBJ School of the University to create a leadership program for the Police and other public safety agencies. Since 1999 he has served as Chair of the City's Public Safety Commission.

He is married to the former Camille Teresa Contreras and has two children, Gregory and Marisa, who reside in Austin as well.

References

Acemoglu, D., Robinson, James A. (2012). *Why nations fail: the origins of power, prosperity and poverty* (1st ed.). New York: Crown Publishers.

Agency, C. I. (2013). Factbook. https://www.cia.gov/library/publications/the-world-factbook/rankorder/2119rank.html

Alden, E. H. (2008). *The closing of the American border: terrorism, immigration, and security since 9/11* (1st ed.). New York, NY: Harper.

Anderson, C. (2013, January 26,). Mexico: The New China, *NY Times*.

Andrew, C. M. (1995). *For the president's eyes only: secret intelligence and the American presidency from Washington to Bush* (1st ed.). New York: HarperCollinsPublishers.

Appleby, J. O. (2010). *The relentless revolution: a history of capitalism* (1st ed.). New York, NY: W.W. Norton & Co.

Archibold, R. C. and Malkin., Elizabeth. (2013, February 28, 2013). Powerful Mexican Teachers' Leader Acused of Embezzlement, *NY Times*, p. 4.

Ashby, J. C. (1967). *Organized labor and the Mexican Revolution under Lázaro Cárdenas*. Chapel Hill, NC.: University of North Carolina Press.

Ayer, D. (Writer) & D. Ayer (Director). (2012). End of Watch. In D. Ayer (Producer). Hollywood, CA.: Open Road Films.

Bacevich, A. J. (2008). *The limits of power: the end of American exceptionalism* (1st ed.). New York: Metropolitan Books.

Bajarin, T. (2011, March 7). Technology's Role in Government Change. *PC Magazine*.

Banker, A. (2013, February 6). HSBC Reputation 'Crushed' by Mexican Money Laundering: CEO. *American Banker*.

Banks, H. W., & Prescott, W. H. (1916). *The boys' Prescott; the conquest of Mexico*. New York,: Frederick A. Stokes company.

Bardi, U., & SpringerLink (Online service). (2011). *The Limits to Growth Revisited SpringerBriefs in Energy*, (pp. 1 online resource.). Retrieved from http://dx.doi.org/10.1007/978-1-4419-9416-5

Berler, B., & Prescott, W. H. (1988). *The conquest of Mexico: a modern rendering of William H. Prescott's history*. San Antonio [Austin, Tex.: Corona Pub. Co. Distributed by Texas Monthly Press].

Bobbitt, P. (2003). *The Shield of Achilles-War, Peace and the Course of History*. New York: Alfred A. Knopf.

Bonfil Batalla, G., & Dennis, P. A. (1996). *Mâexico profundo: reclaiming a civilization* (1st ed.). Austin: University of Texas Press.

Bonne, J. (2001). Scourge of the heartland:
Meth takes root in surprising places Retrieved from http://www.nbcnews.com/id/3071773/ns/us_news-only/t/scourge-heartland/#.UQgZnfnhdjw website:

Boserup, E. 1965. The Conditions of Agricultural Growth: The Economics of Agrarian Change under Population Pressure. Chicago: Aldine. London: Allen & Unwin.

Bowden, C. (2002). *Down by the river: drugs, money, murder, and family*. New York: Simon & Schuster.

Bowden, M. (2001). *Killing Pablo: the hunt for the world's greatest outlaw* (1st ed.). New York: Atlantic Monthly Press.

Brands, H., & Army War College (U.S.). Strategic Studies Institute. (2009). Mexico's narco-insurgency and U.S.

counterdrug policy. from
http://purl.access.gpo.gov/GPO/LPS112370

Brooks, D. (July 29, 2008). "The Biggest Issue", *New York Times.*

Burman, M. (2012). *TDCJ's Handling of Members of Prison Threat Groups.* (Ph.D.), University of Texas at Austin, Austin, Texas.

Burton, F. (2008). *Ghost: confessions of a counterterrorism agent* (1st ed.). New York: Random House.

Campbell, H. (2009). *Drug war zone: frontline dispatches from the streets of El Paso and Juâarez* (1st ed.). Austin: University of Texas Press.

Castaneda, J. G. (2011). *Manana Forever: Mexico and the Mexicans.* New York: Random House.

Cave, D. (2013). Long Border Endless Struggle *Watching The Line* (pp. A1-A4). NY, NY.

Cha, A. E. (2012, September 3,). Young and without a future, *Organization for Economic Cooperation and Development. The Washington Post.* Retrieved from
http://www.washingtonpost.com/business/economy/young-and-without-a-future/2012/09/03/09eed50a-f211-11e1-adc6-87dfa8eff430_story.html

Clarke, R. A., & Knake, R. K. (2010). *Cyber war: the next threat to national security and what to do about it* (1st ed.). New York: Ecco.

Cockburn, A., & St. Clair, J. (1998). *Whiteout : the CIA, drugs, and the press.* London ; New York: Verso.

Coe, M. D., and Richard A. Diehl. (1980). *In the Land of the Olmec* (Vol. 2 vols). Austin, Texas: Univ. of Texas Press.

Contreras, J. (2009). *In the shadow of the giant: the Americanization of modern Mexico.* New Brunswick, N.J.: Rutgers University Press.

Cortés, H. (1986). *Letters from Mexico.* New Haven: Yale Univ. Press.

Dale, E. E. (1960). *The range cattle industry: ranching on the great plains from 1865 to 1925* (New ed.). Norman: University of Oklahoma press.

Danelo, D. J. (2008). *The border: exploring the U.S.-Mexican divide* (1st ed.). Mechanicsburg, PA: Stackpole Books.

de Sahagœn, F. B. (1950-1981). *The Florentine Codex: A General History of the Things of New Spain, Books 1-12* (A. J. O. A. a. C. E. Dibbie, Trans.). Salt Lake City: Univ. of Utah Press.

DEA. (2011, July 21). *Project Delirium.* DOJ Website: DOJ Retrieved from http://www.fbi.gov/news/pressrel/press-releases/project-delirium-results-in-nearly-2-000-arrests-during-20-month-operation-seizures-of-more-than-12-tons-of-drugs-and-62-million-in-u.s.-currency.

DEA. (2012 June 12). *Federal Grand Jury in Texas Indicts Los Zetas Leader in Money Laundering Scheme* Retrieved from http://www.fbi.gov/sanantonio/press-releases/2012/federal-grand-jury-in-texas-indicts-los-zetas-leader-in-money-laundering-scheme.

Defaults, M. (2011). Retrieved from (http://www.governing.com/gov-data/other/municipal-cities-counties-bankruptcies-and-defaults.html).

Deffeyes, K. S. S., & Ebooks Corporation Limited. (2008). *Hubbert's Peak The Impending World Oil Shortage (New Edition)* (pp. 1 online resource (229 p.)). Retrieved from http://www.UTXA.eblib.com/patron/FullRecord.aspx?p=537662

Deming, W. E. (1986). *Out of the crisis : quality, productivity, and competitive position.* Cambridge, Mass.: Massachusetts Institute of Technology Center for Advanced Engineering Study.

Diaz-Guerrero, R. (1986). *El ecosistema sociocultural y la calidad de la vida* (1a ed.). Mâexico, D.F.: Trillas.

Diaz-Guerrero, R., & Szalay, L. B. (1991). *Understanding Mexicans and Americans: cultural perspectives in conflict.* New York: Plenum Press.

Diaz, B. (2001). *The Conquest of New Spain.* New York: Penguin Classics.

Díaz del Castillo, B. (1986). *The Discovery and Conquest of Mexico1517-1521*. Laguna Beach, CA: Buccaneer Books.

Díaz del Castillo, B., & Cohen, J. M. (1963). *The conquest of New Spain*. Baltimore: Penguin Books.

Downey, M. (2009). *Oil 101* (1st ed.). S.l.: Wooden Table Press.

Ellingwood, K. (2008, November 22, 2008). Mexico traffickers bribed former anti-drug chief, officials say, *Los Angeles Times*.

Engdah, F. W. (2013, March 13). The Fracked-up USA Shale Gas Bubble. *Global Research*.

Engdahl, W. (2004). *A century of war : Anglo-American oil politics and the new world order* (Revised ed.). London: Ann Arbor, MI: Pluto Press.

Farb, P. (1968). *Man's rise to civilization as shown by the Indians of North America from primeval times to the coming of the industrial state* (1st ed.). New York, NY: Dutton.

Fehrenbach, T. R. (1973). *Fire and blood: a history of Mexico*. New York,: Macmillan.

Fehrenbach, T. R. (1979). *Fire and blood: a history of Mexico* (1st Collier Books ed.). New York: Collier Books.

Fehrenbach, T. R. (2003). *Comanches: the history of a people* (1st Anchor Books ed.). New York: Anchor Books.

Ferguson, N. (2011). *Civilization: the west and the rest*. London ; New York: Allen Lane.

Fergusson, A. (1975). *When money dies: the nightmare of the Weimar collapse*. London: Kimber.

Fischer, D. H. (1999). *The great wave: price revolutions and the rhythm of history* (1st pbk. ed.). New York: Oxford University Press.

Fisher, L. E. (1988). *Pyramid of the Sun, Pyramid of the Moon*. New York: Macmillan.

Fontenay, C. L. (1980). *Estes Kefauver, a biography*. Knoxville: University of Tennessee Press.

Ford, D. H. (2005). *Contrabando: confessions of a drug-smuggling Texas cowboy* (1st ed.). El Paso, TX: Cinco Puntos Press.

Friedman, G. (2009). *The next 100 years: a forecast for the 21st century* (1st ed.). New York: Doubleday.

Friedman, T. L. (2008). *Hot, flat, and crowded: why we need a green revolution, and how it can renew America* (1st ed.). New York: Farrar, Straus and Giroux.

Frye, D. L. (1996). *Indians into Mexicans: history and identity in a Mexican town* (1st ed.). Austin, Tx: University of Texas Press.

Frye, D. L. (1996). <u>*Indians into Mexicans : history and identity in a Mexican town*</u>. *,*. Austin, TX: University of Texas Press.

Fuentes, C. (1996). *A Time for Mexico*. Berekely,Calif.: University of California Press.

Fuentes, C. (1997). *A new time for Mexico*. Berkeley, Calif.: University of California Press.

Gitlow, H. S., & Gitlow, S. J. (1987). *The Deming Guide to Quality and Competitive Position*. Englewood Cliffs, NJ: Prentice Hall.

Goetzmann, W. H. (2009). *Beyond the Revolution : a history of American thought from Paine to pragmatism*. New York, NY: Basic Books.

Goldin, C. a. K., Lawrence. (2008). *"The Race Between Education and Technology"*. New York, NY: Oxford University Press.

Graham, D. (2003). *Kings of Texas : the 150-year saga of an American ranching empire*. Hoboken, N.J.: Wiley.

Grayson, G. W. (2008. May). *Los Zetos: The Ruthless Army Spawned By A Drug Cartel*. In http://www.fpri.org/enotes/200805.grayson.loszetas.html

Grayson, G. W. (2010). *Mexico: Narco-Violence and a Faled Statee?* New Brunswick, N.J.: Transaction.

Grayson, G. W., & Logan, S. (2012). *The executioner's men : Los Zetas, rogue soldiers, criminal entrepreneurs, and the shadow state they created*. New Brunswick: Transaction Publishers.

Grigoriadis, V., Mary Cuddehe. (2011). An American Druglord in Acapulco. *Rolling Stone* (August 25, 2011).

Grillo, I. (2011). *El Narco: inside Mexico's criminal insurgency* (1st U.S. ed.). New York, N.Y.: Bloomsbury Press.

Gwynne, S. C. (2012) *Empire of the summer moon : Quanah Parker and the rise and fall of the Comanches, the most powerful Indian tribe in American history* (1st Scribner hardcover ed.). New York, N.Y.: Scribner.

Hagan, W. T. (1993). *Quanah Parker, Comanche Chief.* Norman: Universihy of Oklahoma Press.

Hamalainen, P. (2009). *The Comanche Empire (The Lamar Series in Western History) [Paperback].* New Haven, Conn.: Yale University Press.

Heckman, J. (2008). "Schools, Skills and Synapses". *Economic Inquiry, 46(3),* 289-324.

Hefner, R. A. (2009). *The grand energy transition: the rise of energy gases, sustainable life and growth, and the next great economic expansion.* Hoboken, N.J.: Wiley.

Hendricks, D. (February 11, 2012). New bank rule may lead to Mexican withdrawals. Houston Chronicle.

Hill, S. (2010). The War for Drugs-How Juárez became the world's deadliest city. *Boston Review, July-August.*

Hoffmann, S. J. (2009). *Planet water: investing in the world's most valuable resource.* Hoboken, N.J.: Wiley.

Holtzman, W. H., Dâiaz-Guerrero, R., & Swartz, J. D. (1975). *Personality development in two cultures: a cross-cultural longitudinal study of school children in Mexico and the United States.* Austin: University of Texas Press.

Inman, B. (2011). Get Ready Now. *International Journal of Continuing Education in Social Work, Vol. 14, No. 2, Fall 2011.*

Jackson, J. (1986). *Los mesteños: Spanish ranching in Texas, 1721-1821* (1st ed.). College Station: Texas A&M University Press.

Jenkins, H. W. J. (2012, April 24). Wal-Mart Innocents Abroad. *Wall Street Journal.*

Johansen, B. E. (2006-11). *The Native Peoples of North America.* Rutgers, NJ.: Rutgers University Press. .

Johnson, C. (2010). *Dismantling the empire : America's last best hope* (1st ed.). New York: Metropolitan Books.

Joseph, G. M., & Henderson, T. J. (2002). *The Mexico reader: history, culture, politics.* Durham: Duke University Press.

Joseph, G. M., & Spenser, D. (2008). *In from the cold : Latin America's new encounter with the Cold War.* Durham: Duke University Press.

Kaiser, D. E. (2008). *The road to Dallas: the assassination of John F. Kennedy.* Cambridge, Mass.: Belknap Press of Harvard University Press.

Karl, K. J., & United States. Minerals Management Service. Gulf of Mexico OCS Region. (2007). *Gulf of Mexico oil and gas production forecast, 2007-2016 MMS report MMS 2007-020* (pp. 1 online resource (iv, 19 p.)). Retrieved from http://purl.fdlp.gov/GPO/gpo8268

Katz, C. G. a. L. (2008). *"The Race Between Education and Technology".* New York, NY: Oxford University Press.

Katz, F. (1981). *The secret war in Mexico: Europe, the United States, and the Mexican Revolution.* Chicago: University of Chicago Press.

Kelly, M., Landuyt, Noel and Lauderdale, Michael. (2008). Building Social Capital and Creating Innovation in Organizations. *Professional Development: The International Journal of Continuing Social Work Education, 11(3)*, 8-16.

Kelly, M. J., and Michael Lauderdale. (2003). Meeting Transformational Challenges: Continuing Education and Leadership." Professional Development. *The International Journal of Continuing Social Work Education, 6(2)*, 32-39.

Kemper, R. V. (1982). The Compadrazgo in Urban Mexico. *Anthropological Quarterly, 55*(1), 17-30.

Kemper, R. V. (2002). Mexico City. In M. E. a. C. R. Ember (Ed.), *Encyclopedia of Urban Cultures* (Vol. 3, pp. 184-197). Danbury, CT: Grolier Publishing Co.

Kiddle, A. M., & Muñoz, M. L. O. (2010). *Populism in twentieth century Mexico: the presidencies of Lázaro Cárdenas and Luis Echeverría.* Tucson: University of Arizona Press.

Kling, A. S., & Schulz, N. (2009). *From poverty to prosperity: intangible assets, hidden liabilities and the lasting triumph over scarcity* (1st American ed.). New York: Encounter Books.

Knee, S. (2012). [Building a Successful Leadership Philosophy] conversations with Stanley Knee. Austin, Tx.

Kotkin, J. (2010). *The next hundred million : America in 2050.* New York: Penguin Press.

Krauze, E. (1990). *Mexico: Biography of Power.* New York: Harper.

Krepinevich, A. F. (2009). *7 deadly scenarios: a military futurist explores war in the 21st century.* New York: Bantam Dell.

Kunstler, J. H. (2005). *The long emergency: surviving the converging catastrophes of the twenty-first century* (1st ed.). New York: Atlantic Monthly Press.

Landuyt, N. (1999). Employee Perceptions of Organizational Quality and Learned Helplessness in Higher Education. *Dissertation Abstracts.*

Lopez-Stafford, G. (1996). *A place in El Paso: a Mexican-American childhood* (1st ed.). Albuquerque: University of New Mexico Press.

Lauderdale, M. (1986). Applications of GIS to Mexican Social Data. *Third Robert Sutherland Seminar, 3.*

Lauderdale, M. (1999). *Reinventing Texas Government.* Austin, Tx: University of Texas Press.

Lauderdale, M. and. Prince, H. (2007). Austin, Tx: [University of Texas at Austin Leadership Academy].

Lauderdale, M., Landuyt, N.; Hawkins, A.; Barton, J. (1999). *1999 Governor's Organizational Excellence Conference*, State Capitol Auditorium, Austin, Tx.

Lauderdale, M., Landuyt, N.; Kelly, M. (2011). Proceedings of the Global Security Summit with Admiral Bob Inman. *International Journal of Continuing Education in Social Work, Vol. 14, No. 2, Fall 2011.*

Lewis, O. (1959). *Five families; Mexican case studies in the culture of poverty.* New York, NY: Basic Books.

Lewis, O. (1963). *The children of Sáanchez: autobiography of a Mexican family.* New York: Vintage Books.

Logan, S. (2009 March 11,). Los Zetas: Evolution of a Criminal Organization. *http://www.isn.ethz.ch/isn/Current-Affairs/Security-Watch/Detail/?lng=en&id=97554*.

Longmire, S. (2011). *Cartel: the coming invasion of Mexico's drug wars* (1st ed.). New York: Palgrave Macmillan.

Madsen, W. (1964). *The Mexican-Americans of South Texas*. New York, NY: Holt, Rinehart and Winston.

Mailer, N. (1970). *A fire on the moon*. London: Weidenfeld & Nicolson.

Malkin, C. K. (2010, March 8). Mexico Oil Politics Keeps Riches Just Out of Reach, *NY Times,* p. 1. Retrieved from http://www.nytimes.com/2010/03/09/business/global/09pemex.html

Mandelbaum, M. (2010). *The Frugal Superpower America's Global Leadership in a Cash-Strapped Era* (pp. 1 online resource (225 p.)). Retrieved from http://www.UTXA.eblib.com/EBLWeb/patron?target=patron&extendedid=P_584886_0&

Manyika, J., Jeff Sinclair, et al. (2012 November). Manufacturing the future: The next era of global growth and innovation. Retrieved from http://www.mckinsey.com/insights/mgi/research/productivity_competitiveness_and_growth/the_future_of_manufacturing

Markillie, P. (2012, April 21). A third industrial revolution. *The Economist.*

Marks, J. (1979). *The search for the "Manchurian candidate" : the CIA and mind control*. New York: Times Books.

Martinez, L. (2013, February 11). County sheriff's deputy pleads guilty to smuggling, *Brownsville Herald.*

Massey, D. S., Durand, J., & Malone, N. J. (2002). *Beyond smoke and mirrors: Mexican immigration in an era of economic integration*. New York: Russell Sage Foundation.

McPherson, J. (1990). *Abraham Lincoln and the Second American Revolution*. New York: Oxford.

Meadows, D. H., & Club of Rome. (1972). *The Limits to growth; a report for the Club of Rome's project on the predicament of mankind.* New York: Universe Books.

Meadows, D. H., Randers, J., & Meadows, D. L. (2004). *The limits to growth : the 30-year update.* White River Junction, Vt: Chelsea Green Pub.

Meyer, M. C., Sherman, W. L., & Deeds, S. M. (2003). *The course of Mexican history* (7th ed.). New York: Oxford University Press.

Meyer, M. C., Sherman, W. L., & Deeds, S. M. (2010). *The course of Mexican history* (9th ed.). New York: Oxford University Press.

Michel, V. H. a. R., Dora Irene (2004 February 23). *Mileno.*

Middleton, R. a. L., Anne. (2011). *Colonial America: A History to 1763 (4th ed. 2011).* New York: John Wiley and Sons.

Miles, R. E. (1976). *Awakening from the American dream: the social and political limits to growth.* New York: Universe Books.

Miller, M. (1937). *Mexico around me.* New York, N.Y.: Reynall & Hitchcock.

Miller, M. (1943). *Land where time stands still.* New York, N.Y.: Dodd, Mead & Company.

Montana Macias, S. (2008). *Social Capital in Human Service/Child Welfare Organizations: Implications for Work Motivation, Job Satisfaction, Innovation, and Quality.* (Ph.D.), University of Texas at Austin.

Montana, S. P. D. (2008). Social Capial: Implications for Human Service Organizations and Child Welfare. *The International Journal of Continuing Social Work Education, 11.3*, 17-29.

Moynihan, D. P. (2009). How do Public Organizations Learn? Bridging Structural and Cultural Divides.". *Public Administration Review, 69(6)*, 1097-1105.

Murdock, S. (1996). *Texas Challenged: The Implications of Population Change for Public Service Demand in Texas.* Austin, TX: Texas Legislative Council.

National Gang Intelligence Center (U.S.), & National Drug Intelligence Center (U.S.). (2009). National gang threat

assessment 2009. from
http://purl.access.gpo.gov/GPO/LPS125365

Neeley, B. (1995). *The last Comanche chief: the life and times of Quanah Parker*. New York: J. Wiley.

New Cambridge Modern History, V. X. (1962). London: Cambridge University Press.

Noyes, S. (1999). *Comanches in the New West: 1895-1908*. Austin: University of Texas Press.

O'Boyle, M. (2013, March 12). Mexico's planned telecoms shake-up threatens Slim, Televisa, *Reuters*. Retrieved from http://www.reuters.com/article/2013/03/12/us-mexico-telecoms-idUSBRE92A11S20130312

Ortiz, I. (2013, March 11). 'Four trucks filled with bodies' after Reynosa firefight, *The Monitor*. Retrieved from http://www.themonitor.com/news/local/article_68fe53 40-8aaf-11e2-ae7d-001a4bcf6878.html

Paredes, A. (1958). *"With his pistol in his hand": a border ballad and its hero*. Austin: University of Texas Press.

Payan, T. (2006). *The three U.S.-Mexico border wars: drugs, immigration, and Homeland Security*. Westport, Conn.: Praeger Security International.

Paz, O. (1950; 1994). *Labyrinth of Solitude* (L. Kemp, Trans.). New York: Grove.

Paz, O. (1985). *The labyrinth of solitude ; The other Mexico ; Return to the labyrinth of solitude ; Mexico and the United States ; The philanthropic ogre*. New York: Grove Press.

Pfaff, W. (2010). *The irony of manifest destiny : the tragedy of America's foreign policy* (1st U.S. ed.). New York: Walker & Co.

Phippen, W. (2013, March 11). Corrupt Pima Sheriff's Deputy Sentenced for Aiding Smugglers, *Phoenix New Times*.

Pitman, R. (2012 June 18). *FORMER AUSTIN POLICE OFFICER SENTENCED TO PRISON ON FEDERAL TAX CHARGE*. San Antonio, Texas: DOJ Retrieved from http://www.justice.gov/usao/Txw/press_releases/2012 /Ballard_tax_Austin_sen.pdf.

Plohetski, T. (2012, January 4). Police are investigating private security work of some officers, *Austin American Statesman*. Retrieved from http://www.statesman.com/news/news/local/police-are-investigating-private-security-work-of-/nRjS9/

Poppa, T. E. (1990). *Druglord : the life and death of a Mexican kingpin : a true story*. New York: Pharos Books.

Poppa, T. E., & Bowden, C. (2010). *Drug lord the life & death of a Mexican kingpin: a true story* (pp. 1 online resource (xx, 346 p.)). Retrieved from http://www.UTXA.eblib.com/patron/FullRecord.aspx?p=665726

Prescott, W. H. (2000). *History of the conquest of Mexico ; & History of the conquest of Peru* (1st Cooper Square Press ed.). New York: Cooper Square Press.

Preston, J., & Dillon, S. (2004). *Opening Mexico : the making of a democracy* (1st ed.). New York: Farrar, Straus and Giroux.

Proctor, R. (2005, October 28). Parents Wonder: Is Briseño's Blood on Austin High's Hands?, *Austin Chronicle*. Retrieved from http://www.austinchronicle.com/news/2005-10-28/303818/

Proctor, R. (2006, April 4). Austin High Student's Teenaged Killer Found Guilty, *Austin Chronicle*. Retrieved from http://www.austinchronicle.com/news/2006-04-14/356701/

Putnam, R. (1996). The Strange Disappearance of Civic America,. *The American Prospect, no. 24*(Winter).

Putnam, R. (2000). *Bowling Alone: The Collapse and Revival of American Community*. New York: Simon and Schuster.

Putnam, R. D. (1996). The Strange Disappearance of Civic America. *The American Prospect, 7*(24).

Reding, N. (2009). *Methland: The Death and Life of an American Small Town*. New York: Bloomsbury.

Reeves, J. L., & Campbell, R. (1994). *Cracked coverage : television news, the anti-cocaine crusade, and the Reagan legacy*. Durham: Duke University Press.

Reinarman, C., & Levine, H. G. (1997). *Crack in America : demon drugs and social justice*. Berkeley: University of California Press.

Reinhart, C. M., & Rogoff, K. (2009). This Time Is Different Eight Centuries of Financial Folly. from http://www.WISC.eblib.com/patron/FullRecord.aspx?p=483517 Available through EBL

Reitz, J.; Heather G. Z; Hawkins, Naoko. (2011). Comparisons of the success of racial minority immigrant offspring in the United States, Canada and Australia. *Social Science Research, 40*, 1051-1066.

Riding, A. (1988). *Distant Neighbors: A Portrait of the Mexicans*.

Ritholtz, B., & Task, A. (2009). *Bailout nation: how greed and easy money corrupted Wall Street and shook the world economy*. Hoboken, N.J.: John Wiley & Sons.

Roach, J. G. (1996). *Collective heart: Texans in World War II* (1st ed.). Austin, Tx.: Eakin Press.

Rose, S. J. (2010). *Rebound : why America will emerge stronger from the financial crisis* (1st ed.). New York, N.Y.: St. Martin's Press.

Rubin, J. (2009). *Why your world is about to get a whole lot smaller: oil and the end of globalization* (1st U.S. ed.). New York, N.Y.: Random House.

Rubin, J. (2012). *The big flatline: oil and the no-growth economy* (1st Palgrave Macmillan ed.). New York, NY: Palgrave Macmillan.

Sampson, R. J. (1988). Local friendship ties and community attachment in mass society. *American Sociological Review, 53*, 774-802.

Scott, P. D. (1972). *Heroin traffic: some amazing coincidences linking the cia, the mafia, air america. earth, v.3, no.2, march, 1972*.

Scott, P. D. (2000). Washington and the politics of drugs. *Variant, 2(11)*.

Scott, P. D. (2010). *American war machine: deep politics, the CIA global drug connection, and the road to Afghanistan.* Lanham, Md.: Rowman & Littlefield Publishers.

Semple, K. (2011, November 24). In New York Mexicans Lag in Education, *NY Times,* p. 1.

Shiller, D. (2013, May 17). As feds announce a Gulf Cartel boss gets life in prison, the boss of bosses will be free well before retirement age, *Houston Chronicle.*

Simmons, M. (Producer). (2008). The Era of Cheap Oil Is Over. Retrieved from http://www.simmonsco-intl.com/research.aspx?Type=msspeeches

Simmons, M. R. (2005). *Twilight in the desert : the coming Saudi oil shock and the world economy.* Hoboken, N.J.: John Wiley & Sons.

Skocpol, T. (2003). *Diminished Democracy From Membership to Management in American Civic Life.* Norman, Ok.: University of Oklahoma Press.

Smith, F. T. (1996). *The Caddos, the Wichitas, and the United States, 1846-1901.* College Station: Texas A&M University Press.

Soderbergh, S., Gaghan, S., Zwick, E., Herskovitz, M., Bickford, L., Cheadle, D., USA Films (Firm). (2002). Traffic [2 videodiscs (147 min.)]. [U.S.A.]: Criterion Collection.

Statistics, B. of L. (2012, August 21). *EMPLOYMENT AND UNEMPLOYMENT AMONG YOUTH -- SUMMER 2012.* Washington, D.C.: U.S. Government.

Staudt, K. (2009.). *Violence and Activism at the Border: Gender, Fear, and Everyday Life in Ciudad Juarez.* Austin, Tx: University of Texas Press.

Stiglitz, J. E. (2010). *Freefall : America, free markets, and the sinking of the world economy* (Pbk. ed.). New York: W. W. Norton & Co.

Stratfor Global Intelligence (Firm). (2009). *Mexico in crisis : lost borders and the struggle for regional status.* Austin, Tx: Stratfor.

Strauss, W., & Howe, N. (1997). *The fourth turning : an American prophecy* (1st ed.). New York: Broadway Books.

Taleb, N. (2007). *The black swan : the impact of the highly improbable* (1st ed.). New York: Random House.

Tertzakian, P. (2007). *A thousand barrels a second : the coming oil break point and the challenges facing an energy dependent world.* New York: McGraw-Hill.

Tertzakian, P. a. H., Keith. (2009). *The end of energy obesity : breaking today's energy addiction for a prosperous and secure tomorrow.* Hoboken, N.J.: John Wiley & Sons.

Texas, S. o. (2013). *Texas Gang Threat Assessment for 2012.* Austin, Texas: Retrieved from http://www.Txdps.state.Tx.us/director_staff/media_an d_communications/TXGangThreatAssessment.pdf.

Thomas, H. (1995). *Conquest: Cortes, Montezuma, and the Fall of Old Mexico [Paperback].* New York: Simon and Schuster.

Thompson, G. (2005 September 30,). Mexico Fears Its Drug Traffickers Get Help From Guatemalans., *NY Times.*

Thornton, R. (1990). *American Indian Holocaust and Survival: A Population History since 1492.* Norman, Oklahoma: University of Oklahoma Press.

Thornton, R. (April 1997). Aboriginal North American Population and Rates of Decline, ca. A.D. 1500-1900. *Current Anthropology, 38*(2), 310-315.

Tocqueville, A. de. (1835 and 2000). *Democracy in Ameirca* (H. M. a. D. Winthrop, Trans.). Chicago: University of Chicago Press.

Trento, J. J. (2001). *The secret history of the CIA* (1st ed.). Roseville, Calif.: Forum.

Trevizo, D. (2011). *Rural protest and the making of democracy in Mexico, 1968-2000.* University Park, Pa.: Pennsylvania State University Press.

Trigger, B. G., & Washburn, W. E. (1996). *The Cambridge history of the native peoples of the Americas.* Cambridge, England ; New York, N.Y.: Cambridge University Press.

Tuchman, B. W. (1979). *The Zimmermann telegram* (First Ballantine books ed.). New York, N.Y.: Ballantine.

Turner, F. J. (1984). *The significance of the frontier in American history.* Madison, Wis.: Silver Buckle Press.

Uchitelle, L. (2009. July 21,). Obama's Strategy to Reverse Manufacturing's Fall., *Page B 1. NY Times.*

United States House Committee on Homeland Security, M., Michael T. Chair. (2012, November). *A LINE IN THE SAND: COUNTERING CRIME,VIOLENCE AND TERROR AT THESOUTHWEST BORDER.* U. S. Congress: Retrieved from http://homeland.house.gov/hearing/subcommittee-hearing-line-sand-assessing-dangerous-threats-our-nation%E2%80%99s-borders.

EB 5 Visa (2012).

Uslaner, E. M. (2002). *The moral foundations of trust.* Cambridge ; New York, N.Y.: Cambridge University Press.

Uslaner, E. M. (2012). *Segregation and mistrust : diversity, isolation, and social cohesion.* New York, N.Y.: Cambridge University Press.

Wallace, E., & Hoebel, E. A. (1952). *The Comanches: lords of the south plains* ([1st ed.). Norman, Ok.: University of Oklahoma Press.

William Beezley, a. M. M., eds., ch 12 (Ed.). (2010). *The Oxford History of Mexico (2nd ed.).*

William, F. (Writer). (1985). To Live and Die in L.A. Hollywood: MGM.

Williams, J. (2008). Shadow Statistics. from http://www.shadowstats.com/

Zúñiga, V., & Hernández-León, R. (2005). *New destinations : Mexican immigration in the United States.* New York: Russell Sage Foundation.

Internet Sites

http://www.mexicosolidarity.org/
http://www.trace-sc.com/
http://www.unam.mx/
http://lanic.utexas.edu/la/mexico/

http://www.presidencia.gob.mx/

http://www.mexconnect.com/

http://www.mexonline.com/

http:// www.inegi.gob.mx/

(http://www.lapoliticaeslapolitica.com/2013/02/after-arrest-of-teachers-union-leader.html). (2013a). *Feds Seeking Houses of Texas State University Professor:Sindy Chapa.*

(http://www.lapoliticaeslapolitica.com/2013/02/after-arrest-of-teachers-union-leader.html). (2013b). *Teachers' Union Leader Arrested: Ester Gordillo.*

(http://www.governing.com/gov-data/other/municipal-cities-counties-bankruptcies-and-defaults.html)

http://www.fairus.org/issue/how-many-illegal-immigrants ;

http://www.pewresearch.org/2013/05/16/immigration-tip-sheet-on-u-s-public-opinion/ ;

http://www.pewhispanic.org/2013/05/01/a-demographic-portrait-of-mexican-origin-hispanics-in-the-united-states/

http://www.mexidata.info/id140.html;

http://www.lapoliticaeslapolitica.com/2012/01/who-was-miguel-nazar-haro.html;

---

i Map resources available and discussions of border trade in North America at several sites:

http://bordercross.tamu.edu/plans_docs/ ;

www.borderplanning.fhwa.dot.gov/TTIstudy/TTIAppA.doc;

http://etd.ohiolink.edu/view.cgi/Matisziw%20Timothy%20C.pdf?osu1118336803

http://www.mexconnect.com/articles/1305-francisco-pancho-villa; http://www.mexconnect.com/articles/1853-pancho-villa-as-a-german-agent

Made in the USA
San Bernardino, CA
13 January 2014